IBN SAUD

Also by Leslie McLoughlin

ARABIAN SANDS (*translation into Arabic from the English of Wilfred Thesiger*)
DEATH IN BEIRUT (*translation from the Arabic of T. Y. Awwad*)
LEVANTINE ARABIC
TEN HOURS TO ARABIC

Ibn Saud

Founder of a Kingdom

Leslie McLoughlin

St. Martin's Press   New York

First published in the United States of America in 1993

Printed in Hong Kong

ISBN 0–312–07988–5

Library of Congress Cataloging-in-Publication Data
McLoughlin, Leslie J., 1935–
Ibn Saud : founder of a kingdom / Leslie McLoughlin.
    p.   cm.
Includes bibliographical references and index.
ISBN 0–312–07988–5
1. Ibn Sa'ud, King of Saudi Arabia. 1880–1953.   2. Saudi Arabia–
–Kings and rulers —Biography.   3. Saudi Arabia—History.   I. Title.
DS244.5.I2M35   1993
953.805—dc20   92–3491
                                                                            CIP

To my family

Contents

List of Plates

The earliest known photograph of Ibn Saud, 1910 (*Royal Geographical Society*)

Map 1 Arabia, 1900: a map from a typical world atlas (*Royal Geographical Society*)

Map 2 Arabia, 1916: a British military map (*Royal Geographical Society*)

Map 3 The Kingdom of Saudi Arabia, 1953 (*Bartholomew, Edinburgh*)

King Abdul-Aziz ('Ibn Saud'): one of the last photographs taken (*Saudi Research and Marketing (UK) Ltd*)

Preface

This biography is being written as the world follows on television and radio and in the press the consequences of the war between Iraq and the forces of the United Nations in the very area in which so much of the story of Ibn Saud unfolds.

The rulers of Kuwait, Bahrain and Qatar all gave refuge to Ibn Saud and his family when they fled from Riyadh, after defeat in battle, just 100 years ago. Basra was where Ibn Saud, in 1916, first saw for himself British armed might preparing to advance on Bagdad and where he saw his first aeroplane. The very borders of Saudi Arabia with both Kuwait and Iraq were drawn by a British government representative in 1922 at Ujayr, which was the heart of Allied military preparations in 1991.

Readers will form their own conclusions about the relevance of the story of Ibn Saud to events in the Gulf region.

It is customary in books dealing with the Arabian Peninsula, Ibn Saud, Arabian tribes and similar subjects to insert at this point a number of preliminary remarks or disclaimers on recondite subjects such as the rendering of Arabic names into English. The author can see no way of avoiding treading this path but will attempt to be brief.

Transliteration
The general reader who does not know Arabic will be confused or irritated by attempts to render with novel symbols sounds not existing in English, such as the voiceless bilabial plosive. At the same time the specialist who knows Arabic will not stand in need of such aids and will be distracted in all probability by trying to spot inconsistencies in such painful attempts.

The author proposes to be cheerfully inconsistent and commonsense. The name of Ibn Saud's brother will be written 'Saad' as an acceptable convention, lacking in phonetic authenticity. The name of his grandfather, his son and the Hashimite King of Iraq will all be rendered 'Feisal', even though some authors have distinguished between Saudis and Hashimites by different spellings.

Place-names will use, as far as possible, spellings based on Bartholomew's maps.

Some Arabic words have become by 1991 usable without explanation or translation, such as Koran, Muslim and so on, and these will be spelled in ways which reflect common usage in books and newspapers if not the original Arabic spelling.

A glossary of Arabic words is at page 211.

The Saudis and Ibn Saud

Unfortunately, even before we can get into our stride, the matter of key names has to be cleared up, taking into account concepts from phonetics and tribal anthropology. Appendices B, C and D should be referred to in order to place Ibn Saud in context.

1. 'Saud' will be the standard spelling used for the eponymous ancestor of the royal family of the Kingdom. The family as a whole is called Al Saud.
2. 'Al', with no following hyphen, is used for the Arabic word meaning 'extended family of . . . '.
3. 'Al-', with a hyphen, is used for the Arabic definite article ('the') in all occurrences: for example, Al-Rahman and Abdul-Rahman. Here the author follows Philby's usage.
4. Ibn Saud is the style of reference adopted for the subject of this biography, whose full name is Abdul-Aziz Bin Abdul-Rahman Bin Feisal Bin Turki Al Saud.
5. 'Bin' or 'Ibn' is a rendering of the variable way of pronouncing the word for 'son of . . . '.
6. 'Ibn Saud' was actually a style of address or reference which the subject did not like.
7. Some tribes, such as the Ruwalla, still use 'Ibn Saud' to refer to the current Saudi monarch.

Acknowledgements

It is a great pleasure to record thanks to all who have stimulated the author's interest in matters Arabic and Arabian since his first visit to the Kingdom in 1963. He has always found the greatest encouragement from Saudis high and low to get to know their country (and indeed to embrace Islam!). He readily acknowledges also his debt to the many writers who have dealt with aspects of the life of Ibn Saud and trusts that his readers will feel encouraged to proceed to find the same pleasure in them, even in the author whose books were memorably dismissed once as 'All those damned Wadis!'

Thanks are due to the staff of many libraries and record offices, but in particular to Mr B. R. Pridham and his staff at the Centre for Arab Gulf Studies at the University of Exeter, to the staff of Exeter University Library, to Dr D. Hopwood and his staff at the Middle East Centre, St Antony's College, Oxford, and to the staff of the libraries of photographs and maps at the Royal Geographical Society, London.

The author is happy also to record his appreciation to St Antony's College, Oxford, and to Macmillan for their joint invitation to undertake the writing of this brief biography of Ibn Saud for their series.

The author is solely responsible for the views expressed in this book.

* * *

The study of general contacts and relations and of general resemblances and differences is the only avenue to a general perspective without which neither profit nor pleasure can be extracted from historical research.

Polybius, Book I, Chapter 4

LESLIE MCLOUGHLIN
Whimple, 1991

Introduction

Read no history: nothing but biography, for that is life without theory.

Benjamin Disraeli, *Contarini Fleming*, 1844.

All biography is lies.

Aneurin Bevan, *ob. dict.*

Of all liars the most arrogant are biographers, those who would have us believe, having surveyed a few boxes full of letters, diaries, bank statements and photographs, that they can play at the recording angel and tell the whole truth about another human life.

A. N. Wilson, *Incline Our Hearts*, quoted in the *Sunday Times Magazine*, 5 May 1991

Ibn Saud and Joseph Stalin were almost exact contemporaries.

Unlikely as it may seem, it is possible to mention in the same breath Ibn Saud and one whom he regarded as the Devil incarnate. Both were individuals who made decisive contributions to the history of the twentieth century. Both were, for some 30 years, the rulers, though not unquestioned, of vast countries possessed of great wealth, potential and actual, and with enormous strategic importance. In 1945 both sat down in conference with President Roosevelt and Prime Minister Winston Churchill. Stalin and Ibn Saud both died in 1953 and both were followed by leaders who, by general consent, were found to be inadequate and had to be removed.

Other features of similarity would possibly be viewed as far-fetched. The point of mentioning the two figures together is to emphasise how little we know of Ibn Saud. We can follow almost every step in Stalin's life, even in the most secret and conspiratorial phase, through official documents, memoirs, press reports, photographs, film and sound records and mountains of unpublished material.

In the case of Ibn Saud we do not know his date of birth, even to the year: authorities on the subject place it between 1867 and 1887.[1] Furthermore, his death took place in the full glare of publicity and yet his interpreter who wrote his biography misstates the date.[2] In the details of his life there are great discrepancies between the authorities on crucial facts. One example of many is Ibn Saud's *coup-de-main* in recapturing Riyadh in 1902 from the Rashidis. Philby, the most prolific writer on Ibn Saud, frequently gives the date as 1901, as did Amin Rihani, the American of Lebanese origin who spent long periods in the 1920s with Ibn Saud and wrote much about him in English and Arabic. As will be seen often in this story, such mistakes are very common.[3]

More serious is a total neglect of Ibn Saud in major reference books. Perhaps one example will be telling enough. *The New Cambridge Modern History*, Vol. XII, deals with the period 1898–1945 and has a chapter dealing with the Middle East in which the Peninsula and the Gulf are discussed. Not only is Ibn Saud not once mentioned but Saudi Arabia also escapes the author's notice.[4]

A compelling reason for our lack of knowledge of Ibn Saud is the poverty of reliable documentary evidence, especially in Arabic.[5] We can follow the story of his life from about 1910 in British official documents although this record has to be treated with considerable caution at some points. British files can be supplemented by the often highly entertaining memoirs of British officials in close contact with Ibn Saud, especially from about 1930. From 1945 the American official record is substantial in giving a picture of Ibn Saud while records, official and otherwise, in other European languages give other perspectives on the subject. But the volume is insignificant compared to what would be needed to present a full portrait.[6]

Ibn Saud was the determining figure in the history of the Arabian Peninsula for over 50 years. For over 40 years he was a figure to be reckoned with in calculations of international developments. He had a vast family: at his death 34 sons were alive, along with uncounted daughters. Many scores of grandchildren were alive in 1953, not to mention collateral relatives and at the time of writing the fourth generation flourishes.

From family sources we have practically no information in comparison with what might have been accumulated, in either documentary or sound recordings. From the official and published record going back over 40 years we can count on only a relatively slight quantity of original, reliable information.

This book is a modest attempt to present a factual account of the ascertainable truth of the life of Ibn Saud, based on sources in English, German, French, Italian and Arabic. The author has accepted the view that the available documents in Persian and Turkish, although important for the diplomatic background, have little to offer which would change the strictly biographical picture.

The book aims mainly to inform the general reader about the personal and political life of Ibn Saud. It may also have interest for the specialist by indicating discrepancies in various received accounts and in suggesting areas worthy of further research. A graded Bibliography is at page 228 and a Chronology of Ibn Saud's life is at page 196.

A modern writer[7] has recently made a plea for the biographer to make more use of the techniques of the novelist and to have a care for composition, structure, dramatic effect and sub-plot.

The present writer must confess that, in the absence of reliable documentation, it is a sufficiently arduous task to get into chronological order the events of a long life, for over 50 years of which Ibn Saud was involved in international power politics.

Ibn Saud fought as a warrior with sword and rifle from his earliest manhood and lived to discuss the wisdom of using the atomic bomb in the Korean War in 1950. In 1902 his dominions were the walled town of Riyadh which then measured some 700 yards by 700 yards.[8] By 1952 the extent of the Kingdom of Saudi Arabia was about 865 000 square miles. His revenue[9] at the time of his recapturing Riyadh in 1902 was around £50 000 a year while in the year of his death the income of Saudi Arabia annually from oil was over £100 000 000. In the first ten years after he re-established Saudi rule in Riyadh he was engaged in battle not only with the House of Rashid, based on Hail, but also with dissidents from the Ajman tribe in the east of the Peninsula and with members of his own family who claimed precedence over him. As late as 1932 Ibn Saud had to put down a rebellion in the west of the country fomented from abroad, while the last war Saudi forces fought to establish the country's frontiers was in 1934 against the Yemen.

There alone is sufficient material for plot and several sub-plots but the author hopes that he may be allowed to content himself with von Ranke's ambition, to narrate 'wie es eigentlich gewesen ist', that is, to relate how things actually happened.

It is, however, only honest to mention at the outset what must be some of the sub-plots and what are some of the author's reservations.

A bold literary critic has recently suggested that what the reader really wants in biography in addition to facts on grandparents is full knowledge of the subject's love life.

This last theme has engaged the avid attention of many writers on

Ibn Saud since Philby quoted him in 1918 as saying, 'By God, in my lifetime I have married five and seventy wives and if God wills I have not done with wiving yet. I am yet young and strong.'[10] That his last son was born in 1947 is sufficient indication that he was philoprogenitive.[11]

This biography will take a chronological approach to the subject, by summarising family developments from Chapter 3 onwards in order to outline the sequence of his family-building but, at this stage, it is essential to state the context of Ibn Saud's approach to marriage.

As has been pointed out by a Biblical scholar[12] there is a very close resemblance between the policy of David, King of Israel, and that of the founder of the Saudi Kingdom in the twentieth century. Ibn Saud was always keenly aware of the need to bind the tribes to the Al Saud by marriage ties and it is instructive to note that the Arabic word *musahara* means just that. This is the word used quite unselfconsciously about his marriages in Arabic histories of Al Saud.

Two other sub-plots may be mentioned at this point.

The first is Ibn Saud's relations with the British. The Al Saud tried from as early as 1902 to make official contact with the British, having noted during their sojourn in Kuwait the total dominance of Britain in the Gulf region. In Ibn Saud's last year he regretted that his friend Winston Churchill had now displayed enmity towards him over the Buraimi oasis. During the intervening 50 years[13] there were many fluctuations in the degree of warmth between the two countries, to be described in due course.

The second major sub-plot will be that of Ibn Saud's relations with his rivals for power within the Peninsula. Some of these have been mentioned already and others will appear in the course of this story. One of the most remarkable features of the life of Ibn Saud was his extraordinary skill in weighing up complex situations and taking or not taking decisive action. It was this skill which made Sir Percy Cox, who had over 30 years' experience of Gulf politics, say that he had never known Ibn Saud make a wrong move.

That opinion is possibly overstating matters[14] somewhat but Ibn Saud was certainly the most remarkable Arab leader of the twentieth century. Through his deep faith in God and by his quite extraordinary force of will, his energy, shrewdness, charm and farsightedness he founded a kingdom where previously there had been a power-vacuum and incipient chaos.

Si monumentum requiris, circumspice.

1
The Setting

In the dreary waste of Arabia a boundless level of sand is inter-
sected by sharp and naked mountains and the face of the desert
without shade or shelter is scorched by the direct and intense rays
of a tropical sun. Instead of refreshing breezes the winds, particularly from the south-west, diffuse a noxious and even deadly
vapour . . . whole caravans, whole armies have been lost and
buried in the whirlwind.

> Edward Gibbon, *Decline and Fall of the Roman Empire*,
> single-volume edn, London 1830, p. 903

In no part of the world, of Asia at least, does a stranger meet with
a kinder, more liberal or even a politer reception than in Upper
Nejd.

> W. G. Palgrave, *Journal of the Royal Geographical Society*,
> no. 34, p. 135

The story of Ibn Saud's life cannot be properly understood without
knowledge of the environment in which he operated. The alarming
picture painted by Gibbon is an example of the idea of the Arabian
Peninsula in the outside world until almost exactly the year of Ibn
Saud's birth in 1876. Just before that date a bestselling travel book in
London was a two-volume account of a journey through Nejd to the
Gulf coast by William Palgrave,[1] an English Jew, temporarily become a Jesuit priest. The Suez Canal, which was conceived by the
French and for long opposed by the British, was opened six years
later and it may be that Palgrave was acting for the Emperor Napo-
leon III in exploring for strategic purposes what was still a vast *terra
incognita* between Africa and India.

In 1879, just after Ibn Saud's birth, the Englishman Wilfrid Scawen
Blunt[2] and his wife Lady Anne continued their search for Arab
thoroughbred horses among the Bedu tribes by making their way to
Hail in Northern Nejd. It is one of the more bizarre coincidences of
Arabian desert travel that there should have been no less than three

1

English travellers in the Nefud desert at one time, the other one being Charles Doughty. His *Arabia Deserta* was published only in 1888 but the Blunts published in 1881 another two-volume bestseller about their travels. This revealed to a startled public, among other things, that a telephone was to be found at Hail. Although there was no connection to the instrument we have here evidence of a remarkable fact.

An area viewed as inconceivably remote was being brought into contact with the Western world in its widest sense since the first telephone exchange to operate commercially was opened in New Haven, Connecticut only in January 1878. The Rashidi rulers of Hail, through their contact with Damascus and Constantinople and their possession of considerable wealth, were able to pick up fragments of knowledge of modern technology such as this. Among the themes of Ibn Saud's life will be his much greater success in adopting Western technology, both civilian and military.

Before embarking on the story of Ibn Saud it is essential to understand the geographical and genealogical factors which affected his actions. Distances and methods of transport must first be taken into account.

The present Kingdom of Saudi Arabia extends through 16 degrees of latitude and 20 degrees of longitude. To put matters another way the east–west extent of the country is of the range of the distance from Budapest to Le Havre or from New York City to Des Moines, Iowa. The distance from north to south is similar to that from Berlin to Naples or from Madison, Wisconsin to New Orleans. A notable feature of the country is that the east–west maximum distance is very close to the north–south maximum, over one thousand miles.

The first car made its appearance in Nejd, according to Philby, in about 1919, while the first cars to operate in the Hejaz date from some ten years earlier, from about the time that a British official made his way overland by car from Kuwait to London. But it was only in 1935 that Ibn Saud changed from camel transport to motor transport for his retinue on its travels around the country. Until the late 1920s the conveying of people, goods and news was virtually entirely on camel-back, an average day's travel being about 25 miles, depending on the going. In the period of his early campaigns to extend his dominions Ibn Saud took this factor into account in striking manner. Before setting out from Riyadh to raid some town or region he would round up everyone from the target area and detain them until he had reached the object of his campaign.

As for topography and climate, the area of the Kingdom can be divided broadly into three regions: the Western Highlands from Aqaba in the north to the border with Yemen in the south; the Eastern Coastlands; and the Desert Interior.

In the west is a sub-area for climatic purposes, that of the immediate coastlands. The coastal plain is very narrow in the north but widens to the south and within it the conditions of Jedda[3] may be taken as typical. There the winter temperature, from December to February inclusive, is acceptable at 23°C. but for much of the rest of the year there is very severe humidity and a prevailing temperature of 40°C. Away from the coast the mountains rise steeply and rest can be found from the heat of the coast. Taif, at 5100 feet, has traditionally been a place of refuge from the heat of Jedda and Mecca. From north to south peaks can be found between 2000 and 10 000 feet, with the highest peaks in the Asir region. This area, just north of the Yemen border, has many peaks of between 8000 and 10 000 feet[4] and a climate of mild temperatures and humidity with long summers.

In the Eastern Coastlands no location is at an altitude of more than 600 feet and the predominant features are undulating plains with very occasional low hills. The region of Hasa[5] differs from elsewhere on the east coast in that it has extensive oases around Hofuf. These have seven gigantic natural springs, the most productive of which in Ibn Saud's day put out 22 500 gallons a minute. Furthermore, as can be seen by the air-traveller between Bahrain and Dhahran today, there are even springs of fresh water in the open sea. North of Qatif, however, towards Kuwait the coastal plain is barren and before the exploitation of oil it was almost totally uninhabited. During the lifetime of Ibn Saud there was for most of the time only one poor harbour, that of Ujair.

Most of the interior of the Kingdom consists of desert, or rather of deserts, since the interior is very varied in character. The easiest to comprehend is possibly the most famous, the Empty Quarter, or Rub' Al-Khali, with an area of some 250 000 square miles, more than a quarter of the area of the Kingdom. It occupies the land[6] enclosed by Oman, the United Arab Emirates, the Hadramaut, Yemen and Asir, and is probably the third biggest hot desert in the world. In 1918 Philby, on meeting Hogarth, the Oxford scholar regarded as the world's greatest authority on Arabian travel, was so stimulated by his talk of this, the largest blank space on the world map, that he decided to become the first person properly to explore the Empty Quarter.[7]

Despite the occurrence of one of the world's largest oilfields within its area the Empty Quarter remains almost totally uninhabited and largely unexplored because of its inhospitable nature. The greater part of its surface is covered by sand dunes and there is a negligible number of wells. In addition, as Thesiger[8] has so vividly described, the land rises in parts to 2000 feet in the west while in the east there are lower elevations, up to 600 feet. Ibn Saud took refuge in the Empty Quarter just before the final phase of his raid to recapture Riyadh for the Al Saud in 1902.

The other two great desert areas of the Kingdom are the Syrian desert (Badiat Al-Shaam) and the Nefud, or Great Nefud.[9]

The Syrian desert extends north from a line drawn from Aqaba to Jawf to Kuwait and has a character totally different from the Empty Quarter. It is, by and large, a treeless rocky plain, or steppe, at an altitude of 2000–3000 feet. However, it can support pastoralists since it has a more or less predictable rainfall of between 2 and 6 inches per annum. Hence there has always been a tendency for the nomadic tribes to move considerable distances throughout the region in search of pasture, with scant regard for national boundaries. This new phenomenon of frontiers, introduced in the lifetime of Ibn Saud, was to present grave problems for him, for the tribes and for the British, as we shall see.

The Great Nefud is the desert area of northern Arabia which links the Empty Quarter to the Syrian Desert. Starting in the Jawf area it puts out two arms which go to east and west of Riyadh. The one to the west stops short of joining up with the Empty Quarter and thus presents the main access route from Riyadh to the Hejaz. The eastern arm runs into the Empty Quarter and has over large areas a striking reddish-brown colour. Climatic conditions throughout the Nefud can be extremely forbidding, with temperatures of up to 48°C. but with a night-time drop of 27°C. Frost is also common in winter and snow at Hail is not unknown. In addition the desert is subject to sudden violent windstorms, while rainfall is rare and can sometimes fail for years. On the other hand there is access to water in wells found in scattered oases. These make it possible to cultivate dates and barley and to support comparatively large populations: thus, in the lifetime of Ibn Saud, individual oases could sustain up to 15 000 people. Such oases were vital points in the military planning of Ibn Saud which enabled him to extend his dominions from Nejd, the heartland.

Nejd, the homeland of the Al Saud, straddles the two arms of the Nefud. The name Nejd signifies 'elevated stony table-land' but there is considerable variety in the region as anyone knows who has driven out in any direction from Riyadh. There are uplands, small plateaus, escarpments, broad valleys and dry river-gaps with considerable oases at Riyadh itself: the name means 'orchards' or 'gardens'. There are very large oases also at Buraida, Hail, Jabrin and Anaiza. These have traditionally been able to produce dates, barley, wheat, millet and lucerne grass with a considerable variety of fruits such as walnuts, figs and apricots.

The nature of the terrain and the climate of Nejd have been decisive in establishing a pattern of social life over the centuries. There was true pastoral nomadism but the nomads had far shorter distances to travel than in the Syrian desert. Moreover, settlement in oases was possible, with the result that each nomadic group was associated with some permanent stronghold such as Hail or Buraida which had a number of tributary agricultural villages. It was in this geographical and social environment that the Al Saud established themselves and it was because of this fact of their origins among the nomads and the settled Arabs (the 'Bedu' and the 'Hadar') that Ibn Saud continued until almost the end of his life the tradition of moving with his retinue among the settlements every year.

Let us now look at the origins of the Al Saud and examine some of the factors in their rise to prominence and eventual supremacy.

Pride in descent from famous ancestors was and still is a distinguishing feature of the Arab and in particular of the Arab of the Peninsula. For a family to quote from memory the names of ancestors going back over 300 years is not uncommon.

In the case of the Al Saud the earliest recorded ascertainable ancestor dates from the early fifteenth century, while pious belief takes their origins, as with some other famous families, back to the original ancestors of the northern Arabs, Adnan, through the tribal confederation of the Anaza. These beliefs are of great importance in the process of establishing the primacy of the Al Saud.

The first known ancestor of Ibn Saud was Mani' Al-Muraidi. About AD 1446 he was invited by a cousin to move from the Qatif area in the east of the Peninsula to the Wadi Hanifa area, near Riyadh. Mani' traced his ancestry to the tribe of the Duru' and his cousin in the Riyadh area was the head of the settlers from the Duru' and was styled 'Ibn Dar'. It was from this origin that the principal settlement

of the Al Saud came to be called Dar'iya. This town was to be their
capital until its destruction by Egyptian artillery in 1819. Its significance in the history of Al Saud is indicated by the fact that the road
from Riyadh leading out to Dar'iya is today lined with the palaces
and homes of former kings and senior princes, the sons of Ibn Saud
and their close relatives.

The traveller on this road leaves the area of the palaces before
coming to the vast campus of King Saud University on the outskirts
of Dar'iya. Making his way across the Wadi Hanifa into the oasis
of Dar'iya the traveller comes up one of the saddest sights in the
whole country. Here are the ruins of the former capital of the Al
Saud.

In any light at any season of the year the visitor cannot but be
moved to imagine the process of destruction of an entire capital city,
of mosques, homes, palaces and markets by Egyptian field guns.
Four years after the battle of Waterloo the artillery of Ibrahim Pasha
pounded Dar'iya to symbolise the destruction of the power of the Al
Saud. Thereafter Riyadh, a nearby settlement which for long had
opposed Dar'iya, became the Saudi capital.

The first Saudi/Wahhabi state had threatened the prestige of the
Sultan-Caliph in Constantinople by its expansion beyond the borders of Nejd and even beyond the Peninsula. An eight-year campaign by the sons of the Sultan's Egyptian viceroy was needed to
destroy the Saudi state but at the end of it Dar'iya was left in ruins
and was never again to be inhabited. The Al Saud have preserved
the ruins to this day. Ibn Saud was always particularly mindful that
the history of his family had been one of great triumphs and overwhelming defeats.

It is now time to review the events leading up to the final disaster
of the nineteenth century, when in 1891 the father of Ibn Saud, the
Amir Abdul-Rahman bin Feisal, was forced to flee with his family
from the Saudi capital Riyadh, to wander for two years between
Bahrain, Qatar and Hasa before finding refuge in Kuwait.

The Nejd homeland of the Al Saud was assured for centuries of a
high degree of isolation through the difficult topography, forbidding
climate and lack of resources of large areas of the Peninsula. Before
the eighteenth century it would be fair to describe Nejd as an almost
totally closed society which had only minimal contact with the outside world.

There was some little trading contact for subsistence purposes and
camel-trading with the Gulf Coast and with Damascus and there

was religious contact with the Hejaz for the purposes of performing the Hajj, as well as with some of the major Islamic teaching centres such as Cairo and Bagdad. But, by and large, the society in which the Al Saud lived had only the slightest contact with developments beyond the borders of Nejd.

The family of Al Saud was able to establish a clear enough identity and status to create what Philby, eccentrically, calls the Barony of Dar'iya but not without considerable internal dissension in the three hundred years between the arrival there of Mani' Al-Muraidi and the establishment of the first Saudi state.

Almost exactly three centuries after Mani's arrival there occurred a unique coincidence of circumstances which has determined the course of history in the Peninsula and will continue to condition the life of the Kingdom of Saudi Arabia.

In 1744 the ruler of Dar'iya Muhammad bin Saud welcomed and gave refuge to Sheikh Muhammad bin Abdul-Wahhab, from whose name the world has wrongly derived the term Wahhabis to indicate those who adhered to his school of religious thought. The Sheikh – as he is known to this day, his descendants being called Al Al-Sheikh – had been forced to flee from his native town of Al-Uyaina, north of Riyadh, since his revivalist doctrines had been found too strong for some prominent members of the community. Among his principles was one which called for the strict implementation of the *Hudood*, that is to say, Islamic punishment according to the word of God. The immediate cause for alarm was his insisting on the stoning to death of an adulteress.

At Dar'iya he found a more welcome atmosphere for his beliefs and in some accounts it was Mudhi, the wife of the Amir Muhammad bin Saud, who persuaded her husband to accept his preaching a revival of pure Islam and to give protection to the new religious direction. That the matter was not a foregone conclusion, however, is indicated by two things affecting the parties to the new arrangement. The Sheikh's own brother published a refutation of the new school of thought and on the Saudi side Thunayan, the brother of Muhammad bin Saud, opposed the adoption of the new relationship between the Al Saud and the Sheikh. Nonetheless the Amir Muhammad bin Saud undertook to give his protection to the Sheikh in a compact which has been compared, not unjustly, to the compact between the Prophet Muhammad and the people of Medina when Muhammad left Mecca, marking the beginning of the Islamic calendar.

Philby describes the exchange which took place, possibly with a little poetic licence.

> 'Welcome!' said the prince. 'Welcome to a country better than your own country: You shall have all honour and support from us!'
> Then did the Prince take the Sheikh's hand in his own, swearing loyalty to the region of God and His Prophet, and promising to wage war in God's cause.[10]

In the modern secular world it requires some effort of the imagination to comprehend the force of a religious idea which can induce whole communities to abandon a previous way of life. Comparisons which may spring to mind for a British observer are the Puritan and Methodist movements which had far-reaching effects on religious feeling and practice and led to great changes in thinking about the ordering of society. What is distinctive about the ideas of the Sheikh, however, is that, after they had been given the protection of Al Saud, they led to the establishment of a theocratic state whose successor still exists today, namely the Kingdom of Saudi Arabia, and they gave rise soon to the military expansion of that state far beyond the borders of Nejd. Within a period of 60 years from the arrival of the Sheikh in Dar'iya the Saudi armies had disturbed the balance of power in the Peninsula and far beyond. Their warriors occupied Mecca and Medina. Destroying shrines which they regarded as non-Islamic, they attacked the Shia holy places of Nejf and Kerbela in Iraq, and were powerful enough to be able to demand taxes in the area of Aleppo in Northern Syria. As we have seen, the retribution of the Sultan was terrible; the first Saudi state was destroyed, its capital was left in ruins and the Amir Abdullah bin Saud was beheaded in Constantinople.

Before we look at the sequence of events which led to the destruction of the second Saudi state a word must be said about the nature of the religious ideas of the Sheikh. These ideas were given the backing of military force not once, in the events just outlined, but a second time when the Ikhwan movement in the first two decades of the twentieth century enabled Ibn Saud to complete the conquest of the Hejaz and the Asir region and even in the third decade to fight a victorious war against the Yemen.

The power of the ideas lay in their simplicity. The Sheikh had studied the religious sciences in Bagdad, in Basra and in Persia and

had returned to his homeland appalled at the
believed the purity of Islam had been polluted
sanctioned by the Koran and the Sunna. He called
strict application of those principles and only thos
were sanctioned in God's Holy Book and in the sa
of the Prophet.

The Saudi flag today bears the words

laa ilaaha illa allaah wa muhammad rasool allaah
(There is no god but God and Muhammad is His Prophet)

and it is these words which sum up the rigour and simplicity of the
teachings of Muhammad bin Abdul-Wahhab. To understand the full
force of their impact it is essential to realise that underlying them is
the unquestioning belief that the unit of organisation is the ideal
Islamic community. There is not in Islam the clear distinction between Church and State, as can be seen in the Saudi context from the
fact that the ruler was called the Imam even down to Ibn Saud's day,
that is, the man who leads the community in prayer. Nor is there
a clear division between the secular and the religious in law, for
example. God's law, the Shari'a, has been given for the correct
ordering of the Islamic community in all aspects of its activities. The
Koran and the Sunna contain all that is needed for the regulation of
the community.

The Sheikh restated these ideas and by his agreement with
Muhammad bin Saud achieved the means to enforce them in a
closed community and then in a rapidly expanding society. It was
implicit, also, that it was the duty of the believers to bring about the
enlightenment of other Muslims who had not received the benefit of
the teachings of the Sheikh.

These ideas had impact both positive and negative. The outside
world has perhaps tended to emphasise what it has learned of the
more striking examples of prohibition. Not only were shrines forbidden for the Wahhabis, but also tobacco, dancing, alcohol, the
wearing of robes which touched the ground, silk garments, gold
ornaments, luxuriant moustaches, laughing and music. It is prohibitions such as some of these which still characterise Saudi
Arabia today. The outside world has given emphasis also to those
prohibitions which were imposed on some of the habits and prac-
tices of the Nejd community of the eighteenth century such as belief
in demons and *jinns*, protection of crops from the evil eye, camel

crifices over revered graves and circumcision male and female
when not performed according to Islamic prescription.[11]

Emphasis has also been given to those aspects of the Sheikh's
doctrines which licence the use of force against those who are
mushrikoon – that is, polytheists, which can mean both Christians and
those Muslims who do not revere the One-ness of God, by praying at
shrines for local 'saints'. Another distinguishing feature of the doctrines of the Wahhabis in their starkest form was the belief that other
Muslims could be attacked if they did not accept the doctrines of the
Sheikh.

However, the picture must be completed by mentioning positive
aspects of the new doctrines. In the context of the society of Nejd,
which was strongly tribal and Beduin, the new emphasis on the
Islamic community had the enormous benefit of cancelling out tribal
allegiances which had been maintained at the expense of the unity of
the community. This aspect was to be of the greatest significance in
the lifetime of Ibn Saud, as Wilfred Thesiger was to testify as late as
1947. Tribe was no longer to be against tribe, raiding and counter-
raiding, in an atmosphere of general lawlessness and insecurity.
Instead, the community, made into *Ikhwan* (Brethren) by adopting
the rule of God's Law, could concentrate on productive activities
such as religion and agriculture. It could have perfect security with
the ultimate sanction of the imposition of the punishments provided
for in the Shari'a. In Ibn Saud's time possibly the clearest example of
the creation of security and peace through the imposition of sanctions was the rule of his cousin and deputy for the east of the
country, as will become apparent later in the account of the establishment of the third Saudi state.

The destruction of the Saudi capital of Dar'iya did not mark the
end of foreign interventions. The Egyptian commander, Ibrahim,
had reached the Gulf coast after defeating the Saudis and so the
British in India felt obliged to establish what were the implications of
this foreign presence on the route to India. A Captain Sadlier was
accordingly dispatched by Delhi to carry a message conveying to
Ibrahim British congratulations on having put an end to the Wahhabi
menace. He failed to make contact with the Egyptian headquarters
when he arrived at Qatif but set off to rendezvous with him inland.
Once more he failed to find him and in the course of the next 11
weeks contrived to cross the peninsula as far as Medina in vain
search for Ibrahim. There at last he was able to convey British good
wishes to the Egyptian commander and he then continued on his

way to Jedda, having inadvertently completed the first documented east–west crossing of the Peninsula. The significance of this episode is not so much in Sadlier's crossing but in the evidence of Egyptian presence.

The Egyptians were to have great influence on the second Saudi state until well into the 1840s. Two examples of their relationship and that of their Turkish overlords with the Saudi state may indicate the fragility of the Saudi power structure.

In 1838 the Egyptians installed as ruler the Amir Khalid bin Saud, one of the Saudi princes they had taken as hostage to Egypt in 1819. In 1843 the Amir Feisal bin Turki was able to escape from his exile in Egypt, where he had been taken with his sons and nephew after his defeat in battle. The return of Feisal to Riyadh inaugurated the longest period of independent existence of the Saudi state in the nineteenth century, from 1843 to 1865.

The death of Feisal in 1865 led to a long period of internal strife for the Al Saud. This was anticipated by a British visitor to Feisal in Riyadh in 1865, Colonel Lewis R. Pelly, the Political Resident in the Gulf. As he expected, two sons of Feisal, Abdullah and Saud, disputed the succession and each later became the ruler after temporarily supplanting the other. Abdullah ruled during 1865–9 and 1874–84, while Saud was ruler in the years 1869–74. (It was the descendants of Saud who were to dispute the succession with Ibn Saud, the son of the youngest son, Abdul-Rahman.)

The power-struggles between brothers were the direct cause of the defeat and exile of the Al Saud in 1891 since the power-vacuum was filled by the Al Rashid from Jebel Shammar in Northern Nejd. This extended family ruled from 1835 to 1921 from Hail, where they had been installed by the Al Saud for services rendered. In the troubled period of the 1830s, in particular, they assisted the Saudis by avenging the assassination of one of them. Thereafter they extended their influence over the tribes continuously and it was to Hail that intrepid travellers, such as Palgrave, the Blunts and Doughty, made their way in order to pay their respects to the most powerful figure between Damascus and Riyadh and to report on the bizarre nature of the Rashidi regime and its convoluted rivalries and jealousies. Despite these problems they were able eventually to challenge the Al Saud openly.

The period of open conflict was the 1880s when the Saudis had to accept a Rashidi governor at Riyadh. In 1891 the allies of the Saudis were defeated in pitched battle at Mulaida and although Ibn Saud's father was not present at the battle he read correctly the implications of the defeat. He made the decision to abandon Riyadh with his family and it was thus that in 1891 Ibn Saud came to leave Riyadh for exile on camel-back, travelling in one saddlebag while in some accounts his beloved sister Nura travelled in the other.[12]

Ibn Saud was probably 15 years of age[13] at this time but we have only the sketchiest knowledge of the course of his life up to then. It is reasonably certain, however, that he had been present at two crucial events in the period before the exile of the Al Saud.

In 1889 a party of the Al Saud met the Rashidis to negotiate once again for a *modus vivendi* and it seems that Ibn Saud was taken along to watch and learn.

He also seems to have had his introduction to murder for political ends in a particularly ghastly manner. On the occasion of Eed Al-Adha 1889 Ibn Saud's father anticipated treachery on the part of the Rashidi governor of Riyadh who had arranged to call on him to congratulate him on the Eed. Abdul-Rahman arranged for measures to be taken to forestall treachery. As the Rashidis entered the reception hall a signal was given and they were massacred, although the Rashidi governor himself managed to slip away.

By the age of 15 therefore Ibn Saud was no stranger to the ways of negotiation, of conspiracy and swift and violent action to resolve a situation. But, above all, he was conscious of the position of the Al Saud, of how his forefathers had ruled vast territories and had now fallen low. He was aware that two of the main reasons for the destruction of the first Saudi state were the invading Egyptians' buying the support of the Bedu against the Al Saud and the value of superior technology, in this case modern field artillery.

He was aware also of the involvement of the Al Saud with foreign powers. Had not the British themselves sent their envoy, Pelly, to Riyadh to negotiate with his grandfather the Amir Feisal bin Turki in 1865? And had not his own father been in Bagdad in 1872, a hostage of the Turks, until he was able to persuade them of the value of allowing him to return to Riyadh?

When Ibn Saud arrived in Kuwait he was to continue his political education in the most dramatic way possible.

2

The Challenge: Arabia in the Late 1890s

Ibn Rashid kicked off with a gentle pass out to his left wing where Saadun Pasha was forced to concede a corner before play reverted to mid-field.

Philby, *Arabian Jubilee*, p. 9

The political world into which the Al Saud found themselves exiled was sufficiently complicated as not to stand in need of the extra difficulties imposed by Philby's resorting to metaphors from the soccer-field. His remarks may serve, however, as a means of introducing some of the elements in the problem of the disposition of power in the Gulf region in the late nineteenth century.

Ibn Rashid we have already met in the context of Nejd. The Rashidis' influence reached the Gulf precisely at Kuwait which was the port of most direct entry for goods destined for Nejd, whether for Riyadh or for Hail and then on to Damascus. A feature of the last decade of the nineteenth century and the first decade of the twentieth century was to be the threat of Kuwait being overwhelmed by armed tribesmen under the direction of the Rashidis from Hail. A further complication was that for Kuwait to fall to the Rashidis would have meant it falling to the Turks. The Sultan in Constantinople had established a client relationship with the Rashidis which was to last until the end of the First World War.

By the year 1891 Turkey effectively dominated Mesopotamia, with strong garrisons at Bagdad and Basra and a mature, if firmly oriental, system of administration covering the country. Basra, for example, was a Vilayet or administrative province.

Kuwait, however, had established a separate personality and had become a distinct entity under the rule of the Al Sabah family, who had emerged as rulers in the late eighteenth century. They had developed the role of Kuwait as regional port, so that Kuwait merchants by the late nineteenth century were dealing with all parts of the world. The Al Saud, when eventually they found themselves living in Kuwait, mingled with traders and sailors from the entire Gulf region, from the Arab side and the Persian side. They met merchants from the Indian sub-continent and the Far East, from Zanzibar and other parts of Africa, and encountered Damascus entrepreneurs and Jewish middlemen from Bagdad.

Turkey's position in relation to Kuwait was not entirely clearcut. The Turks had garrisons in Basra as well as along the coast in Hasa and Qatar but not in Kuwait. There the Turks had great influence but not suzerainty. It was because of Turkish influence, however, that the Al Saud were able to settle in Kuwait. This happened only when, after much delay, the Turks gave their approval to the residence of the new guests of the Al Sabah and arranged monthly subsistence payments to them.

After leaving Riyadh in 1891 the Al Saud had been obliged to take refuge with the Al-Murra tribe in the sands in the east of the Peninsula while seeking permission to live in greater security in Bahrain and Qatar, out of reach of the Rashidis. This period of living with the Al-Murra gave Ibn Saud, then in his teens, a valuable apprenticeship in the background and mentality of the Bedu, of the truly nomadic tribes, and taught him many skills of desert existence, of camping, tracking, knowledge of wildlife, horsemanship and the use of the sword, rifle and dagger, not to mention his immersion in Al-Murra terminology. This dialect was to cause endless problems for the interpreters of his visitors to the end of his days.

It was Bahrain which first gave shelter to the women and children of the Al Saud and one result of this was that Ibn Saud always had a warm regard for the island's ruler, Sheikh Eisa bin Ali, and was to visit Bahrain on many occasions throughout his life.

Bahrain has special significance for Ibn Saud in another respect. Ibn Saud was sent by his father to Bahrain for medical treatment for rheumatism in the period of exile with the Al-Murra, when he was about 16 years of age. It is a curiosity of Ibn Saud that although he became very tall by his twenties, of powerful physique and possessed of great energy and endurance, he had phases of delicate health in his early teens. This may explain why he had great interest in matters medical throughout his life and had special regard for physicians. Bahrain was the best centre on the Gulf coast for medical help, largely because of the presence of foreign missionaries, some of whom became valuable eye-witnesses of the development of Nejd and later of the Kingdom of Saudi Arabia.

The Al Saud could not remain in Bahrain, however, and were given asylum in Qatar, but again on a temporary basis and on sufferance from the Turks. The Qatar period seems to have been from August to November 1892, during which time the women and children joined the menfolk from Bahrain. We have little direct evidence of the events of the period before the Turks finally approved of the family settling in Kuwait but a period of two years clearly cannot be ignored in the story of the youthful development of Ibn Saud.

We know of his training in Bedu lore by the Al-Murra if only because of the observable results in his skills as horseman, warrior and leader. For his personal development we have indirect evidence of the influence of his parents.

His mother, Sarah Sudairi, was of the Dawasir tribe from south of Riyadh. She died in 1910 when Ibn Saud was about 34 and is said to have given Ibn Saud his love of poetry. However, given the reclusive nature of Nejdi society we must be content with a picture traditionally lacking in any detail. What is clear is that it was from his mother that he inherited his strong, big-boned physique since his father Abdul-Rahman was a man of slight build.

Abdul-Rahman died in 1928 and the story of his influence on and relationship with Ibn Saud is one that will run through his story until the moment of his death which, we know from an eye-witness, caused a traumatic shock to his son.

There is good evidence of the care which Abdul-Rahman took with the religious education of Ibn Saud.[1] He appears to have assigned a strict religious teacher to take the young boy in hand before the family left Riyadh in 1891. This was Qadi Abdullah Al-Kharaji, who taught Ibn Saud basic reading and the Koran and schooled him in the discipline of rising two hours before dawn for prayer. Although Ibn Saud himself told of how restless and impatient he was at his lessons and how he much preferred shooting instruction, which he received at the age of seven years, the strict routine which he endured with the Qadi evidently had a lasting effect, since Ibn Saud always had a deep love of the Koran and employed retainers, often blind, to intone its verses constantly in his palaces in later years.

In the 1890s it was Abdul-Rahman who, as head of the family in exile, made the contacts necessary for obtaining asylum for the family. At some stage in 1893 the Turks gave permission for the women and children to settle in Kuwait while the men remained with the Al-Murra in the area between Jabrin and Hasa. Permission for all the family to settle probably came around the turn of the year 1893–4.

The delay in giving permission arose from the anxiety of the ruler of Kuwait about arousing the hostility of the Rashidis should he extend a welcome to the Al Saud. The Turks' attitude played its part also, since it was always part of their political management of the area to keep a tension between the strongest tribes so that no one group should be of overwhelming strength. The Al Saud were given permission by the Turks to settle in Kuwait only when Constantinople came to the conclusion that it was in Turkey's interest to give support to the Al Saud, a group which might occupy the attentions of their own client, the Al Rashid.

None of these manoeuvrings and calculations could have escaped the notice of Ibn Saud as the family made its home in Kuwait. We know from many sources that thoughts of return to Riyadh were always in the minds of Ibn Saud and his father, but for the moment they were fully occupied with the indignity of their situation.

The family lived in insalubrious surroundings in a three-bedroomed flat-roofed house constructed of baked mud. The modern observer can only marvel at how Ibn Saud and his family survived exposure to contagious diseases in a port city which had no sanitary facilities whatsoever[2] but such appears to have been the case, except for the first wife of Ibn Saud.

Ibn Saud was of marriageable age on arrival in Kuwait, indeed in terms of Bedu society he was some way past the normal start-line, being about eighteen years of age. It is probable that he took his first wife in 1894 but little is known of her since she died within six months. Indeed one writer says that her name and tribe are not known.[3] What seems to be beyond doubt is that the Al Saud were so poor that the wedding could take place only through the financial support of a merchant called Yusuf Ibrahim.

Ibn Saud did not marry again, so far as we can ascertain, until 1899, but in the intervening five years he was to have much to occupy his attention as he observed the play of international power-politics involving Kuwait. The port of Kuwait was of interest not only to the Turks but to Germany, France, Russia and above all to Britain.

For Britain the Gulf was of great strategic importance because of communications with India, her greatest imperial possession. Although for maritime communications the Suez Canal route had won since 1869 the long debate over the 'Red Sea versus Gulf' question, the electric telegraph ran through Mesopotamia and Persia, and the question of which countries dominated the flanks of the Gulf route was crucial. The issue of domination of the Gulf had now suddenly acquired urgency with the interest of both Germany and Russia in building railways which could conceivably debouch on to the Gulf at Kuwait.

The Germany of Kaiser Wilhelm II had since 1890 developed an active foreign policy, particularly in the East since abandoning its Reinsurance treaty with Russia. The most dramatic element of the new *Drang nach Osten* was the concept of the Berlin-to-Bagdad railway. Negotiations by German banks and industrialists had led to Constantinople granting generous facilities for the construction of the permanent way through Asia Minor with accompanying concessions for exploitation of mineral resources along the route. When the Kaiser visited Damascus and Jerusalem in 1898 he was giving the most obvious proof of Germany's desire for a place in the sun. A close relationship with Turkey[4] now developed, with German military teams being sent as training advisers and German-medium schools opening in the Levant which survive to this day.

The Russian presence in the Arab world was of less recent origin: it was, after all, Russian concern for its historical role in relation to the Orthodox Church and the Holy Places in Palestine which was a contributory factor in the outbreak of the Crimean War. Russia had fought the latest in a long series of wars against the Turks as recently as 1877–8. But active Russian interest in the Gulf area was to have an impact on the position of Kuwait, which was in turn to affect the position of Ibn Saud.

In 1895 the Tsarist government sent a survey ship to the Strait of Hormuz. At about the same time a Russian aristocrat in business on his own account was actively promoting the idea of a rail link between the Gulf and the Mediterranean, with the proposed railhead at Tripoli. Kuwait was to be the other terminus and the British took alarm when in 1897 the Russian government adopted the project.

When the British surveyed not only these threats to their position but also French moves to engage in trade with Muscat in the 1890s, they could be excused for thinking that they must move swiftly and decisively to protect their own exclusive position. This they were to do in 1899 in a way which was to have a direct bearing on Ibn Saud's eventually making his momentous decision in 1901 to leave Kuwait in order to recapture Riyadh for the Al Saud.

Before describing developments in the period to 1901 on the international scene it is important to note the turn of domestic events in Kuwait which were to play a vital role in the life of Ibn Saud.

In 1896 the ruler of Kuwait, Sheikh Muhammad, who had initially fought shy of having the Al Saud in Kuwait, was assassinated by his half-brother Mubarak, known as Mubarak the Great in Kuwait's history. Mubarak was to have a close relationship with Ibn Saud until his death in 1915, as we can see from their correspondence, in which Mubarak would address Ibn Saud as 'walad-na al-aziz': 'our dear son'.

From the time of his accession Mubarak was to welcome Ibn Saud constantly in his *majlis* in which Mubarak received not only his own subjects and petitioners, as would any Arab ruler in the area, but also the representatives of the foreign powers with interests in the Gulf region. For Ibn Saud to observe the proceedings was a valuable political education for him, especially given the experience which he had already had in tribal and dynastic politics before the age of 15.

Mubarak, it seems clear, regarded the Al Saud as a valuable card to play at some time in the game of balancing forces and playing-off one side against the other. Bearing in mind the threat to Kuwait from the Rashidis it was essential for Mubarak to have a potential means of striking back at Hail or of getting in a pre-emptive strike.

Such calculations became all the more relevant from 1897 when Muhammad bin Rashid died in Hail after 25 years of strong and successful rule. He had consolidated Hail's wealth and influence and expelled the Rashidis' main rival for power in Nejd, the Al Saud. The news of his death was immediately seen to be of significance for two reasons. Firstly, his successor Abdul-Aziz was known to be young, inexperienced and weak by comparison with his late uncle. Secondly, the history of murders, intrigue, fratricide and revenge killings in the Rashidi family was such as to encourage hope that the death of Muhammad would lead to the disintegration of the house of Rashid. This was indeed to be the case for, in its remaining 25 years, there were to be no less than seven rulers of Hail, most of whom died violent deaths.

The position of Sheikh Mubarak of Kuwait in 1897, therefore, was one of being ready to do everything possible to maximise the advantages of Kuwait's position. He was the object of the most pressing attentions of France, Russia, Turkey, Germany and Britain and could exploit the advantages of a seller's market. The Al Saud represented another advantage to him.

Mubarak therefore lavished attention on Ibn Saud which was not entirely to the liking of his father, Abdul-Rahman. The head of the Al Saud distrusted what he regarded as Mubarak's loose morals, for religion sat lightly upon him by comparison with a Wahhabi from Nejd. In Abdul-Rahman's view, Mubarak was far too addicted to the company of dancing girls and to forbidden pleasures such as tobacco. While there is no clear evidence that Ibn Saud was in any way seduced by the sensual delights available in an eastern port or at the court of a comparatively wealthy ruler it is clear that Ibn Saud spent as much time as possible in Mubarak's company, both privately and in his *majlis*. It is even believed that Mubarak arranged for Ibn Saud to be given lessons in history, geography, mathematics and English.[5] The education of Ibn Saud proceeded apace in Kuwait in relation to formal knowledge and to great affairs of state and international relations. One of the characteristics of Ibn Saud throughout his life and commented on by all who knew him was his eager interest in international affairs. This was given its initial impetus in Kuwait in the late 1890s.

His father, Abdul-Rahman, ensured, however, that his religious education did not suffer: he arranged for a devout religious teacher to be brought for him to Kuwait from Qassim. This goodly man supervised his more advanced religious education and ensured that he would cleave to the pure Islamic teaching of the Sheikh.

By the year 1899, when he was 23, Ibn Saud had reached a significant degree of maturity in his personal development. He had considerable experience at first hand of the reality of the exercise of power and of international relations. He had received what amounted to above-average basic education, judged by the standard of those times. His religious education had been thoroughly supervised and in 1899 he had married his second wife, and the first of whom we have reasonably detailed knowledge, Wadhba, who was of the bani Khalid tribe and bore him his first son, Turki, and his successor as King of Saudi Arabia, Saud.

It was in 1899 also that Ibn Saud derived some of his most valuable lessons in international power politics for it was in this year that Mubarak concluded his secret dealings with Britain and emerged with a treaty of protection. Kuwait agreed (i) to have no dealings with any foreign power before obtaining the agreement of Britain and (ii) not to cede any of its territory without British agreement. In return Mubarak obtained his final guarantee of defence against the Turks and others. Such matters were so sensitive that the treaty was kept secret from the Turks. What was striking for Ibn Saud was that the British were clearly men of their word and were determined to stand by Kuwait because it was in their imperial interest to do so.

Sheikh Mubarak, having received his guarantee, was now ready to adopt a more forward policy and from this time on there is a growing interaction between events on the Gulf coast and developments in the interior of the Peninsula, especially in Riyadh and Hail. From 1900 onwards the manoeuvres described in Philby's soccer metaphors began to take place, which were to lead to Ibn Saud's commando raid on Riyadh in 1902.

In early 1901 Sheikh Mubarak led a large-scale raid on Rashidi territory in which the Al Saud took part. The main body became involved in fighting in the Hail area while a smaller group made for Riyadh. Ibn Saud was the leader of this group and succeeded in breaking into and holding Riyadh for up to three months.[6]

This episode is one of the most remarkable in Ibn Saud's life but there is little direct evidence of its details. We have tantalising indications of Ibn Saud's personal motivation in remarks which he made 20 years later to Amin Rihani.[7] He told Rihani that his first wife's death after two very happy years had so distressed him that 'I left Kuwait . . . and came to Nejd seeking oblivion'. It is possible also that the death of his uncle in Riyadh in 1899 had spurred him to the idea of revenge. Muhammad, the brother of his father, had, by some accounts, been murdered by the Rashidis after being retained by them in Riyadh as nominal ruler.

There are even accounts of Ibn Saud having made more than one unsuccessful attempt on Riyadh before 1902 but these cannot be confirmed. The attempt on Riyadh in 1901, however, was not successful since the main body of the forces of Mubarak and his Saudi allies was decisively defeated in a bloody battle fought in a salt-pan area at Sarif, sometimes called Tarafiya.

In this engagement, which was probably fought in mid-March 1901, the casualty rate was so high that 'the rain mingling with the blood of the fallen flowed in a broad red stream into the snow-white basin of salt'.[8] The Kuwaiti–Saudi force suffered the heaviest casualties and the force retired to Kuwait to await the inevitable counter-attack.

This came in September 1901 when Rashidi raiding parties approached Kuwait from Hail. The tribesmen of Kuwait were mobilised and the Saudi forces joined them under the green banner with the motto 'There is no god but God and Muhammad is His Prophet'.

The commander of the British naval force off Kuwait was present to guarantee Kuwait and was able to report that some 10 000 tribesmen were mobilised and ready to resist. The size of this force and the guns and ammunition landed by the British were sufficient to deter the Rashidis, who withdrew with only moderate booty of livestock.

Ibn Saud now made the most important decision of his life. He asked permission of his father and of Sheikh Mubarak to take a force to raid Riyadh, taking advantage of the preoccupation of the main Rashidi force far away from the capital of Nejd. Only a small garrison was installed there and the walls of the town were not properly fortified, as Ibn Saud knew from his own recent observation. His father and the ruler of Kuwait readily gave permission and so at some time in October 1901 Ibn Saud rode out of Kuwait south-westwards towards Riyadh.

He was accompanied by between 40 and 60 relatives and retainers, all prepared for combat. The plan appears to have been to gather support from the tribes through whose areas they would pass, so as to have a substantial force for the final assault. The initial party, therefore, in addition to nine of his relatives, who included his brother Muhammad, had members of the main eastern tribes.[9] Raids were carried out in the Hasa region but the prospects were not sufficiently attractive to hold the Bedu, who joined the successive raiding parties. By the beginning of Ramadan in December 1901 when the group reached Haradh the party was back to its original size. Ibn Saud now adopted the strategem of going deep into the sands, so as to be out of contact with all neighbouring tribes and to give the impression to those who had known of their presence that they had abandoned the enterprise. They spent part of the month of Ramadan in strict observance of the fast in the remote oasis of Jabrin before making an approach by stealth towards the outskirts of Riyadh as Ramadan came to an end.[10]

During the night of 15–16 January 1902 Ibn Saud led his raiding party forward through the palm groves, protected by the moonless night, and on finding a point at which they could get over the walls, by using palm trunks which they found nearby, Ibn Saud gave his final instructions. He took forward a group of men, including his cousin Abdullah bin Jiluwi, and told the remainder to wait 24 hours: if they did not announce victory within that time the members of the reserve party could return to Kuwait to announce their deaths.

Of the success of the *coup de main* which followed there can be no doubt, since by the following morning the Rashidi governor had been killed and Ibn Saud had been proclaimed ruler of Riyadh. The details are now impossible to establish of how a fierce hand-to-hand engagement led to the fall of the Mismak fortress to the Al Saud.

It seems reasonably certain that Ibn Saud himself led the assault from the house facing the fortress-gate where they had waited for the dawn and the moment of action. Shortly before dawn Ibn Saud had summoned the rest of the 40-strong party to reinforce his small group as they lay in wait, dozing, watching and praying. At the moment of the assault when the Rashidi governor rode out from the gate it seems likely that Ibn Saud was wounded slightly. Bin Jiluwi displayed blind courage in forcing the gate of the fortress and enabling the rest of the party to rush in. Surprise of the Rashidi garrison was total and they soon laid down their arms. By noon Ibn Saud was leading the people of Riyadh in prayer and he afterwards received their allegiance. Riyadh had been reconquered for the Al Saud by Ibn Saud but the continued survival of the family as masters of the capital was by no means certain.

3

Return to Nejd, 1902–13

Nejd is verily one of the two horns of the Devil for out of it all deceit is born and every rascality evolved.

The Prophet Muhammad (attrib.)

(Ibn Saud) built up his power throughout the Emirate with diplomatic help and unconcealed brutality.

Lexikon zur Geschichte und Politik im 20. Jahrhundert,
Kiepenheuer u. Witsch, 1971

Riyadh in 1902 was, in the immortal words of Lorimer,[1] 'not in the slightest degree picturesque' but its capture by Ibn Saud was an event of the highest importance. This small walled town now once again had within it the two elements of the Saudi state, namely a Saudi prince capable of directing armed force and the descendants of the Sheikh, for the Abdul-Wahhab family had not left Riyadh in 1891 with the Al Saud. Furthermore, but unbeknown to Ibn Saud for some weeks yet, a second son had been born in Kuwait. Saud bin Abdul-Aziz was probably born on the night of the raid on Riyadh but for the moment Ibn Saud was totally absorbed not with the unknown but with a range of practical problems. He could have fully understood the force of Ibn Rashid's remark on the Saudi position had he known of it, 'The rabbit is in the hole and the caravan is waiting around it.'[2]

His most urgent task was to fortify the town and so the task of repairing the walls was put urgently in hand. Ibn Saud knew only too well from his two personal experiences that an assault party could breach the walls of Riyadh. He knew that another essential element in the security of the Saudi position was to have the allegiance of both the Bedu and the settled people of Nejd. He therefore began a programme of visits to the inhabited area of Nejd south of Riyadh in the first few months after the recapture of Riyadh. Throughout Al-Kharj and Aflaj, Hauta and Hariq he engaged in a campaign of hospitality and persuasion, visiting the tribal chiefs in a manner far removed from the harsh description at the head of this chapter. He was better able to do without a policy of *Schrecklichkeit* since the tribal areas had been harshly treated and heavily taxed by the Rashidis. As an example of this the tribesmen of Wadi Dawasir[3] sent a delegation to pledge loyalty to the Al Saud.

Ibn Saud next arranged for his family to join him from Riyadh. The arrival of his father was an essential step, since he was styled, and was regarded as being, the Imam of the Wahhabis. Ibn Saud received him with all deference and submission – as, indeed, he was to do all his life. From this time on, he established the custom of formally visiting his father every day and receiving a formal visit from him after Friday prayers.

The relative positions of father and son were established by consultation with the Ulema, the Wahhabi scholars learned in religious law: Prince Abdul-Rahman would remain Imam but Ibn Saud would be the effective ruler. Other adult relatives who arrived had roles to play, principally his elder brother Muhammad and the bin Jiluwis, of whom we have already met the most striking, Ibn Saud's cousin Abdullah bin Jiluwi. They joined Ibn Saud in his visits to the tribal areas, emphasising, for all to see, the element of family solidarity and demonstrating the status of the Al Saud as a fighting group, able to defend and propagate the message of the Sheikh.

In the first six months after the recapture of Riyadh the only recorded recourse to force was when the Qahtani tribe was attacked and subdued. By the autumn of 1902 the Al Saud had won valuable support and established firm bases south of Riyadh to withstand the expected Rashidi assault.

The ruler of Hail, Abdul-Aziz, Ibn Rashid, was curiously slow in making his first move. The summer had gone before he reached the Riyadh area, which he bypassed, making for the southern Nejd provinces. In the area of Dilam in November 1902 the inevitable armed clash took place but this battle, or rather skirmish, had a distinctive character.

Armed clashes between tribal parties traditionally had more about them of sound and fury than of the application of the principles of war. Ibn Saud, however, had an instinctive understanding of the overwhelming value in war of economy of effort and the concentration of force. He realised fully, also, the value of modern technology in the sense of the heightened power of concentrated rifle-fire. He had ensured the purchase of comparatively large quantities of ammunition from Kuwait as well as hiring the services of Kuwaiti marksmen. These men he instructed personally in the tactics needed to confront the Rashidi force.

As the Rashidis advanced towards the palm groves the Saudis and Kuwaitis lay concealed, waiting behind their camel saddles. They did not open fire until the Rashidis were almost upon them, achieving total surprise and killing and wounding numbers far in excess of the usual numbers of casualties in tribal raids.[4] The Saudis then launched their cavalry against the Rashidis and a fierce battle raged from midday until the sun went down. By the end of the day the Rashidis had retreated and escaped from the pursuing Saudi cavalry[5] and Ibn Saud had achieved his first victory in open conflict with Ibn Rashid.

He had learned, in addition to the lessons mentioned above, the value of the economical use of ammunition. Had the Rashidis known how close Ibn Saud had been to exhaustion of his stocks of ammunition they might have persevered in their attacks and there might have been a totally different outcome to this and the succeeding battles. Ibn Saud was never to forget this lesson in battle management and because of this in later years he was to be seen personally counting out rounds of ammunition.[6]

Months of desert skirmishings and manoeuvring followed the battle of Dilam with the Rashidis at the disadvantage of operating hundreds of miles from their base at Hail. By the time that campaigning ended in the summer of 1903 Ibn Saud had established the position of the Al Saud in the major settlements both north and south of Riyadh and was poised to make an advance into the Qassim region with its major towns of Buraida and Anaiza.

Through the winter of 1903–4 Ibn Saud pursued his aim of spreading wider the authority of the Al Saud by a mixture of means, military and political.

In military terms we have vivid pictures of numbers of engagements in which Ibn Saud personally fought, from letters in which he described such fights and because modern writers have transcribed Ibn Saud's own accounts. In a letter to Sheikh Mubarak of Kuwait he describes the taking of Anaiza in the spring of 1904.

> After we had said the morning prayer we sent against them Abdullah bin Jiluwi, with him 100 men of the people of Riyadh to assist. . . . We broke them and slaughtered of them 370 men. . . . And by Almighty God, but two beduin on our side were slain.[7]

Years later Amin Rihani recorded an example of Ibn Saud's role as a fighting man in the capture of Anaiza in 1904, related by Ibn Saud himself.

> I struck him first on the leg and disabled him; quickly after that I struck at the neck; the head fell to one side, the blood spurted up like a fountain, the third blow at the heart I saw the heart which was cut in two palpitate like that. . . . It was a joyous moment. I kissed the sword.[8]

Crossed swords below a palm tree are with reason the emblem of the Kingdom of Saudi Arabia, commemorating the essential role of military action in establishing stability and unity. We have only slight information, however, of the role of what in modern parlance would be termed espionage, counter-espionage, subversion, deception, psychological warfare and other non-military means for prevailing over the enemy. Throughout the period up to and including the fall of Hail in November 1921 it is possible to make deductions about such methods from comments made by Ibn Saud himself.[9] One could also deduce theoretically that intelligence and counter-intelligence methods must have played a part, simply from the nature of the environment and the lack of telecommunications. Information could be obtained and transmitted only at the speed of the fastest camel and therefore the obtaining of battle intelligence must have had the highest priority. As to subversion there is ample evidence for this from the number of occasions on which towns such as Buraida and Anaiza would be lost and retaken without there always having to be the tiresome necessity of launching direct assault.[10] To the north of Riyadh at this day there is a small town inhabited for hundreds of years where rule passed down in the same family for many generations. The town is now no longer inhabited but its most prominent feature, a corner watch-tower, is still called 'Burj al-kha'in': 'Traitor's Gate'. This, like so many other defensive positions was on some unrecorded occasion surrendered to persuasion and not to an assaulting force.

The events of the period 1902 to 1905 took place largely beyond the field of vision of the major foreign power in the Gulf region, Britain, but were followed closely by the Turks. The British position in the making of treaties with the Trucial Coast, Oman and Bahrain had been based on a wish to preserve the maritime routes without being drawn into the problems of the hinterland. It was the treaty with Kuwait in 1899 which was to involve the British more and more deeply in the affairs of Central Arabia and it was Ibn Saud who was the catalyst in this.

The Al Saud believed that the visit of Colonel Pelly to Feisal bin Turki in 1865 had resulted in a treaty between Britain and the Saudis, and Ibn Saud was frequently to refer in his discussions with British representatives to this 'treaty' as a prelude to discussion of new relationships with Britain.[11] From as early as 1902 we know of an official Saudi approach to the British. In May 1902 Ibn Saud's father wrote to the Political Representative.

I have no wish to look to anyone but yourself because of the favours and protection you extend to all those who place themselves under your eyes. May the eyes of the British Government be fixed upon us. . . . I request of your benevolent Government to consider me as one of their proteges.[12]

The British reaction to this approach was studiously to ignore it out of a wish to avoid unnecessary complications in general and in particular to avoid compromising British relations with Constantinople.

The Turks had claims to sovereignty over Nejd, and the British position was based on a wish to avoid action displeasing to them because of the delicate balance of power in Europe. As a result of unease about Germany's ambitions, the British and French in 1904 were to conclude the Entente Cordiale and in the context of the Near and Middle East Britain wished to avoid giving Germany scope for benefiting from any Turkish displeasure with Britain. Ibn Saud was perfectly well aware of these refinements of the situation and had a totally different perspective on the matter. His great concern was to ensure protection against the Turks.

That he was wise to fear Turkish direct action against the Al Saud was shown in late summer 1904, when the Turks ordered a force of no less than 2400 men, in six to eight battalions with field-artillery, to move from Mesopotamia and march on Central Arabia.

Ibn Saud's forces clashed with the Turkish–Rashidi force between July and September 1904 in an extended series of battles, often referred to as the battle of Bukairiya. In this engagement we have yet another account of Ibn Saud being wounded in battle, probably on this occasion through shrapnel from Turkish artillery. Although wounded in hand and leg Ibn Saud remained as the vigorous commander of the Saudi forces throughout weeks of confused blow and counter-blow amid the palm-groves. What seems to have been decisive in giving victory to Ibn Saud was the combination of three factors: (a) the inability of Turkish regular forces to sustain a guerrilla war; (b) the inability of the Rashidis to hold the loyalty of the Bedu and (c) the drive and determination of Ibn Saud himself. He was able to exploit the weakness of the two parties in the coalition and at the decisive moment launch his cavalry, commanded by his brother Muhammad, against the demoralised Rashidis, who fled in panic.

The result was, according to one Arab chronicler:

> Some of them followed the Badawin and escaped; others made for the desert and perished; and the rest surrendered to the Imam who gave them shelter and treated them honourably.[13]

It is worth noting this reference to a feature of Ibn Saud's policy of magnanimity in victory which he was to display throughout his long career of fighting battles, the last of which he joined personally in 1930. Ibn Saud was to suffer some occasions of disenchantment when those enemies whom he treated with generosity later turned on him but, in many instances, his abstaining from a vengeful policy in victory was to bind his former enemies to him for ever.

Central Arabia was not the only scene of Ibn Saud's operations in the period immediately following his retaking Riyadh. He returned to the Gulf coast on a number of occasions and two are highly significant as they brought him directly and personally to the attention of the British government.

In March 1903 great alarm was caused to British representatives in the Gulf region from Muscat to Kuwait by the arrival of warships belonging to both France and Russia.[14] Britain was not yet in the Entente Cordiale mode with France and the arrival of a French warship was a most unwelcome development. Yet more sinister from the British point of view was the new phenomenon of Russian naval presence in the Gulf.

The Russian warship carried out a programme of port calls and purposeful socialising in Muscat and Kuwait which led to British fears for the worst. There was even anguished speculation that the Russians had plans to purchase the Strait of Hormuz.

The Russian account of meetings with Ibn Saud and Sheikh

Mubarak makes clear the range of choices open to Ibn Saud at this, as at many other stages in his life. He was invited aboard with his brothers Muhammad and Saad and with Sheikh Mubarak and regaled his hosts with detailed accounts of his retaking Riyadh and of the politics of Central Arabia, mentioning his fears of Turkish intervention. We learn, too, from the Russian account, how emotional Sheikh Mubarak became about the success of his protégé. At one point the ruler of Kuwait flung down his head-dress and swore that he wished to become the servant of Ibn Saud.

Ibn Saud was able, however, to separate a warm social atmosphere from any kind of political commitment. He did not accept the Russian aid offered on this occasion, nor does he seem ever to have wavered in his belief that the key to his success was a good understanding with Britain in order to guarantee his own state's protection and independence.

The episode of the Russian warship's visit was to show the wisdom of Ibn Saud's policy of restraint, for it made the British decide to make unmistakably clear their claim to hegemony in the Gulf.

They took two steps whose meaning was crystal-clear. The first was that the Foreign Secretary Lord Lansdowne rose in the Lords on 5 May 1903 to make plain Britain's position in regard to the Gulf area.

> I say it without hesitation, that we should regard the establishment of a naval base or a fortified port in the Persian Gulf by any other power a very grave menace to British interest and we should certainly resist it with all means at our disposal.

The second British response was a *coup de théâtre* in that it despatched to the Gulf the Viceroy of India, George Nathaniel Viscount Curzon.[15] The first Viceroy ever to visit the Gulf, Curzon made a series of triumphal visitations in the Gulf Sheikhdoms before arriving at Kuwait. Here, after landing, occurred one of the great moments in imperial history when his companion, the British Minister to Tehran, Hardinge, took a fall from his horse 'but courageously resumed his seat and amid a hail of bullets continued the uneven tenor of his way'.[16]

The serious business of the visit was contained in the ringing speeches which Curzon made throughout his tour as, on 21 November, he told his Arab audience:

'The peace of these waters must still be maintained; your independence will continue to be upheld; and the British government
must remain supreme.[17]

In 1904 the British followed up by opening a political representation at Kuwait and the first Political Agent took up his post in that
year. That officer's successor was to be Captain William Shakespear
who was to serve there from 1909 to his death in 1915. He was the
British representative who was to have the closest relationship of
any with Ibn Saud before the First World War and was to bring the
world the first pictures of Ibn Saud and the Saudi forces.

Against this background of British concern for their position of
dominance in the Gulf it can be seen why the second major contact
between Ibn Saud and the British, in 1905–6, caused further alarm.
Ibn Saud proceeded to make a formal visit to the Gulf with his
armed escort in the direction of the Trucial Coast. He reached as far
as the base of the Qatar Peninsula in the early summer of 1905 and
thereby revived memories, not happy to all concerned, of how the
Wahhabis in the nineteenth century had raided as far as Central
Oman and had been so far able to impose themselves as to collect
taxes.

The British response was made by a man who was now to play a
large part in Ibn Saud's life. Percy Zacharia Cox, recently appointed
Political Representative by Curzon's personal choice, wrote to Ibn
Saud after consulting with the rulers of Abu Dhabi and Muscat. Cox
firmly but politely warned Ibn Saud off preceding further, and received an emollient reply indicating that he had no harmful intentions. By the summer of 1905 Ibn Saud had returned to Nejd and
could take stock of an increasingly favourable situation.[18]

After defeating the Turks and Rashidis and capturing Turkish
artillery pieces in late 1904, Ibn Saud had, in concert with Abdul-
Rahman, made approaches to the Turks to assure them that he
accepted Turkish sovereignty. This approach may have taken account of the fact that the Turks were in no position to take stern
counter-measures following their defeat. An uprising had been fomented against them in Yemen and they naturally feared over-
extending themselves. Whatever were the considerations in Ibn Saud's
mind this disarming approach was almost the final step in ensuring
that Turkish troops were never again stationed in Central Arabia.
Negotiations took place in Kuwait between Abdul-Rahman and
Turkish representatives when the Turks attempted to ensure a con-

tinuing Turkish military presence. They were clearly aiming to set up some sort of buffer-zone in the Qassim area, but they had no means of imposing their will, following their defeat, and Turkish troops duly departed Nejd, this time for good.

The Saudi position in Central Arabia was further strengthened in the spring of 1906 when the ruler of the Rashidis was himself killed in battle. He died in battle at Rawdat Al-Muhanna against Saudi forces led by Ibn Saud. The effect of the death of Ibn Rashid was to usher in a period of the most remarkable series of bloody coups and family killings at Hail. The complexities at times defy the imagination and caused Ibn Saud to comment wonderingly on one occasion: 'They are a melancholy people . . . they do strange things . . . '.[19]

An example of the uniqueness of the Rashidis' methods in arranging the succession is quoted by Philby[20] from the period immediately after the death of Ibn Rashid in 1906. The Regent at Hail, ruling until the new infant ruler should achieve manhood, chose to strengthen his position by marrying Ibn Rashid's widow and the mother of the heir. This lady had previously been the wife of the great Muhammad who died in 1897 after ruling for 25 years. On his death she married her husband's nephew and successor, Abdul-Aziz, and on his death she married the man who had murdered her step-son.

The British could be forgiven for saying of Central Arabian affairs: 'Reports as to the actual state of Arabia have been somewhat complicating but according to the latest information the Saud party are apparently in the ascendant.'[21]

While it would be going too far to say with the *Encyclopedia Britannica* that by 1906 Ibn Saud was the unchallenged master of Arabia,[22] he had in four years established Al Saud as a major party in the struggle for supremacy. The Rashidis had been pushed back to Hail, but there were still problems to be resolved in handling the tribes. From around 1907 the name of Feisal bin Duwish, leader of the Mutair tribe, frequently appears in Arabic accounts of the period. His ancestor of the same name had rallied to the Egyptians against the Al Saud in the early nineteenth century and now he was frequently to oppose Ibn Saud before making his peace with him and becoming one of the most prominent leaders of the Ikhwan movement which was to have its genesis in the years before the First World War.

Feisal bin Duwish changed sides a number of times in the period 1907–8 when Ibn Saud won, lost and won again towns such as

Buraida and Anaiza. It was the fickleness of the behaviour of the Bedu such as Duwish which gave Ibn Saud pause to ponder the best means for achieving stability and unity in the domains which he was now acquiring. Ibn Saud's reflections are nowhere documented but we can to some extent judge of them by the events of the period 1910–12 when the Bedu came to be settled in growing numbers in agricultural–military–religious colonies called '*hijar*'.

In the period before the establishment of these colonies Ibn Saud had to face two severe new problems: dissent from within the Al Saud and the threat from the new Emir of Mecca, Hussain bin Ali, of the House of Hashim.

Ibn Saud's cousins on his father's side had not become automatically reconciled with each other or with Ibn Saud by his recapturing Riyadh in 1902. Numbers of them had taken refuge with Ibn Rashid at Hail and in 1904 some of these had been discovered among Rashidi captives taken when Anaiza fell. Ibn Saud had welcomed them back into the fold and is said to have laughingly applied to them the nickname Ara'if, meaning camels lost to another tribe's raid and subsequently recovered. Three of these cousins came into the immediate family circle of Ibn Saud by marrying his sisters, while the head of the main dissident group, Saud Al-Kabir, was given special distinction by receiving the hand of his favourite sister, Nura. By 1910, for reasons which remain unclear, disputes arose and a number of the cousins left Riyadh while Ibn Saud was in camp near Riyadh. They joined the Ajman, a tribe which had been and was long to remain reluctant to accept the rule of Ibn Saud.[23] The split within the Al Saud was to last to 1916, when Saud Al-Kabir made his submission to Ibn Saud, and it was to lead almost to the death and defeat of Ibn Saud.

The problems of Ibn Saud with the Ara'if merged with his other major new difficulty, which was the growth in power and ambition of the Emir or Grand Sherif of Mecca, Hussain bin Ali, following his appointment by Constantinople in 1908. Hussain showed great energy in support of his suzerain the Sultan in putting down a rebellion by the Idrisi chieftain Muhammad who had taken control of Abha and the Asir highlands. Following his triumphant return to Mecca, Hussain bin Ali was urged by the Turks to undertake an expedition to impose their influence on the desert areas inland.

The forces of Hussain bin Ali had the great good fortune on their first expedition into the Utaiba country on the Nejd border in 1910 to run into a smaller Saudi force. This force was led by Ibn Saud's full brother, Saad, who was recruiting among the Utaiba for soldiers to fight the Ara'if and their allies in the districts of Hauta and Hariq. Saad was taken hostage and word was sent to Ibn Saud with a ransom demand.[24]

Ibn Saud made attempts at negotiation but there was clearly little room for manoeuvre and eventually he had to agree to pay Hussain bin Ali a ransom, and to recognise Turkish sovereignty in order to obtain Saad's release. Once Saad was free Ibn Saud refused to honour the agreement, saying that it was not binding as it had been extracted under duress.

Ibn Saud and Saad, now reunited, proceeded to deal with another concurrent problem, that of a rebellion of the Hazzani chiefs in the Aflaj province in support of the Araif. While a relative on his mother's side, Ahmad Al-Sudairi, held one part of the province firmly, Ibn Saud besieged the rebel chiefs at a town called Laila where they had been joined by one of the Araif, Saud bin Abdullah. The other Araif fled to take refuge with the Hashimites. Eventually Ibn Saud was able to capture the town after threatening to mine it and blow it up and he took the surrender of the Hazzanis.

He now displayed his understanding of the roles of judge and ruler. The Hazzani chiefs were all sentenced to death and promptly executed while Saud was offered a remarkably generous choice. He could either leave and join his cousins or he could pledge his allegiance to Ibn Saud and remain with him. The rebel close to remain with Ibn Saud and became a devoted supporter of his throughout his life.

In his last years Ibn Saud was to look back on the ten years following the recapture of Riyadh as the best years of his life.[25] He would recall the need for constant vigilance and instant readiness to move on receipt of news of danger or of an opportunity to be seized. It is significant that he arranged for his sons to be trained in skills vital for survival. As he said to Amin Rihani in 1922,

> We have to be always ready and fit. I train my own children to walk barefoot, to rise two hours before dawn, to eat but little, to ride horses bareback – sometimes we have not a moment to saddle a horse, leap to his back and go.[26]

Amidst all the military activity, political planning and strategic thinking, Ibn Saud was raising a family or rather creating an extended family by his policy for marrying within the limits prescribed in the Koran. Some time around 1907 Ibn Saud had married Jawhara, the mother of the future King Khalid and of Muhammad, both of whom were to play important military roles in the 1920s and 1930s.

Jawhara was already from the inner family circle, being the sister of Musaid bin Jiluwi and was to acquire much fame from the eloquence of Ibn Saud's laments for her death, which occurred in the terrible epidemic of influenza in 1919. She remained so vivid a memory with him that, in talking of her with Muhammad Asad in the 1930s he would almost break down. She was evidently a great comfort to him in the days when he was fighting to establish his rule against dangers of which we have seen only some so far.

> Whenever the world was dark around me and I could not see my way out of dangers and difficulties that beset me I would sit down and compose an ode to Jawhara; and when it was finished the world was suddenly lighted, and I knew what I had to do.[27]

Some writers[28] have also attributed to Jawhara a considerable role in commending to Ibn Saud's attention the idea of establishing the Ikhwan colonies, when he was on the brink of giving up the struggle.

Jawhara is also said to have been the object of an ode written by Ibn Saud which he sent to her before embarking on a military plan which was to be his greatest exploit, the capture of Hasa from the Turks in the spring of 1913. The Turks had had garrisons in Hasa since 1871, from the time of troubles, of the period of interfamily quarrels in the Al Saud. Ibn Saud had long been reviewing his overall strategic situation, whereby, for all his efforts, he was in effect confined to the desert regions of Central Arabia, a confinement made all the more painful as a severe drought had for years been afflicting Nejd. To the west he was beset by the Hashimites, to his north the Rashidis could still muster military forces of some strength, to the south lay the Empty Quarter and on the east, based on Hofuf, lay the armed forces of the Ottoman Empire.

The Empire had been for decades, in the hackneyed phrase, 'the sick man of Europe', having lost many of its European provinces to Austria and Russia. In the Arab world, since before the turn of the century, Turkey had also lost territories which recognised its suzerainty: Tunisia in 1881 to France, and Egypt in 1882 to the British; while in 1911 Tripolitania was lost to Italy. Of all these events and their context Ibn Saud was aware, since he had by now a variety of means for acquiring information.

He had his purchasing agents in Kuwait and Damascus who kept him supplied with not only goods but with the local press and items of information and, as time went by, with recruits to act as his advisers. He followed the Arabic press in Cairo, Beirut and Damascus and he had his new British friend, Shakespear, the Political Agent in Kuwait, whom he met for the first time in Kuwait in 1910. We know from Shakespear's reports that he discussed with him possible British reaction to his moving against the Turks in Hasa and the implications of the Balkan wars of 1912–13.

The Turks themselves were also useful sources of information. At some time before 1913, according to Philby,[29] Ibn Saud was sought out by the Turkish Wali of Basra for his views on the proper role for Arab nationalist feelings in the Ottoman Empire. Such contacts were of the greatest value for someone as shrewd as Ibn Saud: his wide background knowledge and native political sense enabled him to acquire and evaluate information rapidly. He is said to have deduced, for example, from talking with a Turkish army officer captured in his attack on Hasa that war was inevitable in Europe.[30]

A further source of information for Ibn Saud in the years immediately before the First World War, affording him a window on the world, was the growing number of travellers, some being thinly-disguised intelligence officers, such as Leachman, the gung-ho officer of the Royal Sussex Regiment, who made an adventurous trip from Bagdad through the desert and Nejd to Riyadh and the coast; and the Dane, Barclay Raunkaier, who before his tragically early death, wrote an account of his journey through Nejd, published in English as *On Camelback through Wahhabiland*.

The decision to seize Hasa was not a wild gamble but a bold stroke, based on a shrewd calculation that the Turks were unlikely to be able to respond adequately.

Recalling the feelings he experienced just before he launched the raid on Hofuf, Ibn Saud told one writer in later years,

We were already in view of Hofuf. From the sand dune on which I was sitting I could clearly see the walls of the powerful citadel overlooking the town. My heart was heavy with indecision as I weighed the advantages and dangers of this undertaking. I felt

tired; I longed for peace and home; and with the thought of home
the face of my wife Jawhara came before my eyes. I began to think
of verses which I might tell her if she were by my side – and before
I realised it I was busy composing a poem to her, completely
forgetting where I was and how grave a decision I had to make. As
soon as the poem was ready in my mind I wrote it down, sealed it,
called one of my couriers and commanded him, 'Take the two
fastest dromedaries, ride to Riyadh without stopping and hand
this over to Muhammad's mother.' And as the courier was disappearing in a cloud of sand dust I suddenly found that my mind
had made a decision regarding the war: I would attack Hofuf and
God would lead me to victory.[31]

In May 1913 he gathered a force of around 300 men from the
settled areas not from the Bedu and made a rapid march on Hofuf.
Although acting on this occasion against a regular army – indeed,
against a garrison of some 1200 men – he was able to exploit, as in
1902, the element of surprise and to some extent the lack of vigilance
of the guards to make a lightning raid on the command post of the
garrison. By the morning of 9 May 1913 the Saudi forces had dis-
armed the Turkish garrison and the Saudi state had reached the
Gulf. For the long term the Al Saud were now conveniently placed in
possession of the greatest concentration of oil reserves on the face of
the earth. In the short term Ibn Saud had forced the issue and
brought himself and the Saudi state in the most obvious way possible to the attention of Britain.

Almost exactly ten years after Lord Lansdowne had declared British supremacy in the Gulf, Ibn Saud had brought off a coup which
forced the British to reconsider all their previous political calculations for the Gulf region. Eleven years after the British had thought
it wisest not to reply to the letter from the Al Saud requesting
protection against the Turks, Ibn Saud had ensured that the name of
Ibn Saud would be constantly on the minds of British representatives in their ever more tense dealings with Constantinople in the
final year before the outbreak of the First World War.[32]

As we have seen so far, the British had to tread a very delicate path
in their dealings with Ibn Saud. Ever since he had come to the
personal attention of Cox, the Political Resident, a body of opinion in
the Indian government apparatus to which Cox reported, as well as
in the India Office in London, had urged His Majesty's Government
to give greater support to Ibn Saud in order that at the very least the

British should have some control over his ambitions.

The Foreign Office gave greater weight to the overall world strategic situation and the need at all costs to keep Turkey out of the German camp. During the debate between London and Delhi a crucial question became how far one individual, Captain Shakespear, could be allowed to go in his dealings with Ibn Saud. Each request by Shakespear to be allowed to meet Ibn Saud produced an anguished debate, but one side-effect of the non-official meetings which the two men had before the war was that we have not only photographs of Ibn Saud but word-pictures as well.

In 1911 Shakespear reported to Cox his impressions of Ibn Saud, stating that he

> gave the impression of being endowed with a particularly straightforward, frank and generous nature. He treated me most hospitably and in the most genuinely friendly manner. He and his brothers did not show a trace of the fanatical spirit which might have been expected from the ruling Wahhabi family and his advisers and the leaders of his forces also treated me and my men with the most cordial friendship. I feel convinced of the correctness of this impression for I frequently discussed matters of doctrine, custom and religion which are held to be anathema by the Wahhabi sect and I was always answered with calm and intelligent reasoning.[33]

By 1914 Shakespear's knowledge not only of Ibn Saud but of Arabian Peninsula politics and of Ibn Saud's contacts with other Arab leaders had developed to the point where he could report to the Political Department of the India Office that

> the Arabs have now found a leader who stands head and shoulders above any other chief and in whose star all have implicit faith. The other Sheikhs of the Arab alliance refer all kinds of matters to Bin Sa'ud for his advice, more especially those affecting their relations with the Porte.[34]

FAMILY LIFE

We have noted up to now two wives of Ibn Saud, the first one totally unknown and the second who gave birth to Ibn Saud's first-born, Turki, and the future King Saud, being of the Bani Khalid tribe, Wadhba bint Muhammad.

The third wife, Tarfa, was of the family of the Sheikh;[35] that is, a descendant of the founder of the Wahhabi doctrine, Muhammad bin Abdul-Wahhab. She gave birth in 1904 to the future King Feisal and to a daughter Anud.

Ibn Saud fully respected the right of the Muslim to have four wives on the conditions laid down in the Koran:

> Marry women of your choice, two or three or four but if ye fear that ye will not be able to deal justly with them then only one.
>
> Sura IV, verse 3

He also exercised his right to divorce his wives, but we have little information on the sequence of these transactions. It is revealing that not only do we not know the name of his first wife but that the major reference work on the Al Saud in English[36] gives the name of his last wife to produce children as 'unknown'.

These notes will concentrate on those wives who bore him children and on his brothers.

In the period to 1913 he married Jawhara bint Musaid bin Jiluwi, whose mother was of the Sudairi family. She bore him two sons, Muhammad and the future King Khalid, who were to have important military roles in the 1920s and 1930s. She died in the influenza epidemic of 1919.

Ibn Saud's father also had a number of wives throughout his long life and a number of his sons played a role in the life of Ibn Saud, as did one daughter, Nura, whom we have already met as his travelling companion on the road to exile from Riyadh in 1891.

In the period to 1913 the following brothers may be noted:

– Muhammad, a half-brother, who may have been a little younger than Ibn Saud but if Ibn Saud was actually born in 1876 is probably four years younger. He took an active role in many military operations even before the First World War;

– Abdullah, a half-brother, born about 1900 who also played important military roles and lived to become one of Ibn Saud's closest advisers;

– Saad, a full brother of Ibn Saud, who was very close to him. Ibn Saud had to ransom him in this period when he fell into the hands of the Emir of Mecca, Hussain bin Ali. Saad was killed in battle in 1915 and Ibn Saud was to marry his widow, by whom he had several children.

There are two other brothers who may be mentioned but of whom we have practically no information: Feisal, born about 1870 and probably died about 1890, and Fahd who was born about 1875.

4

Expanding Horizons, 1913–24

(Ibn Saud) must be dealt with as a Turkish official or not at all.
> Sir Edward Grey, British Foreign Secretary,
> 18 May 1914

When the English want something they get it. When we want something we have to fight for it.
> Ibn Saud, 1918

After 1922 Ibn Saud was ready for further adventures.
> United Kingdom Memorial on the Buraimi dispute

In May 1913 Ibn Saud entered Hofuf as a conqueror, and in October 1924 he entered Mecca, again as a result of conquest but this time in the humble garb of a pilgrim. In between these two dates Ibn Saud fought personally in many battles and was severely wounded. His wife and three of his sons died in the appalling influenza epidemic of 1919. His second surviving son made the first official visit of the Al Saud to a foreign country when Feisal visited London where he was received by King George V. Ibn Saud left Nejd for the first of the three occasions on which he left the Peninsula in his lifetime when the British in 1916 invited him to Basra, where he saw his first aircraft, had his hand X-rayed and met Gertrude Bell, who was probably the first unveiled woman outside his family that he ever met. In these years Ibn Saud granted his first oil concession, and conquered Asir and most of the Hejaz. He destroyed the power of the Hashimites in the Peninsula, put an end to the Rashidis as a competing dynasty and welcomed them to Riyadh in a spirit of reconciliation which has lasted to this day. He was frequently reported to have died in these years. He gained a subsidy from the British which enabled him to maintain his rule and when he lost it embarked on actions which were to establish the Kingdom of Saudi

Arabia. In this time he encountered many foreigners who were to write about him, principally Amin Rihani and Philby but, above all, it was in this period that he involved the Al Saud with the British Government in a network of relationships and negotiations over frontier problems which were not to be resolved before his death. It is these years which are the most full of incident, personal and political, the most full of the beginnings of great questions, the most turbulent and dramatic of all periods of Ibn Saud's life. The period including the Second World War was far less disturbed than that of the First World War and at any time in this period Ibn Saud could have made the wrong choice and destroyed his own future and that of the Al Saud.

Three distinct issues were involved in the choices which Ibn Saud faced, three issues which emerged before the period under consideration and which were not to be settled before the end of the period. These were (i) income, (ii) the British and (iii) the Ikhwan.

The three questions ran into each other in the most complex manner throughout the period since, to give two examples, Ibn Saud was for most of this period dependent on the British for his income, by which he kept the Ikhwan and other parties contented and, when the British ended their subsidy in 1924, Ibn Saud prepared to use the Ikhwan to conquer the Hejaz.

The subject of the Ikhwan involved considerations religious, tribal, political, military, agricultural and financial and all of these Ibn Saud kept constantly in mind.

He could not have been unaware of the view of the Koran on the Bedu (IX, 98): 'The Arabs of the desert are the worst in unbelief' is a verse which is often quoted in this context. As a pious Muslim and one devoted to the Koran Ibn Saud was perfectly familiar with the rest of that section of the Word of God.

> The Arabs of the desert are the worst in unbelief and hypocrisy and most fitted to be in ignorance of the command which God hath sent down to His Apostle. . . . Some of the desert Arabs look upon their payments as a fine and watch for disasters for you. . . . But some of the desert Arabs believe in God and the last day and look upon their payments as pious gifts bringing them nearer to God. . . .

These verses of the Koran could almost be taken as a text to explain the problems which Ibn Saud was to have with the Ikhwan for many years, covering as they do both financial and religious matters. There can be no doubt, however, of the seriousness of Ibn Saud's view of his religious duty to end the state of loose religious observance common among numbers of the tribes. As we have seen, he had intimate knowledge at first hand of the mentality and every-day life of the Bedu of Nejd and Hasa and we know of his own strict religious upbringing, of his love of the Koran and of his concern for the role of the leader of the Al Saud as the Imam of his people. The father of Ibn Saud was formally the Imam but, increasingly from this time, we find that it is Ibn Saud himself who is referred to as the Imam.

It was, in any event, Ibn Saud who arranged for preachers to be sent to the tribes to ensure the spread of the principles of the Sheikh and right observance of strict religious practice: some Bedu did not even pray five times a day or observe properly the fast of Ramadan.

We do not know for sure when the movement for bringing the Bedu back into the religious fold began. Dates as early as 1906 have been mentioned and as late as 1913. There have also been a number of imaginative suggestions as to the genesis of the idea in Ibn Saud's mind: a writer in German who met Ibn Saud in the 1930s suggested that, firstly, Ibn Saud had a blinding revelation at the oasis of Jabrin of the power of faith when he saw divers working deep down the wells without drawing breath; and that, secondly, it was his wife Jawhara, the mother of Muhammad and Khalid, who gave him the decisive support[1] for the idea of the Ikhwan as a movement. We can never know but it seems that around 1910 preachers were becoming more active[2] in Nejd and the date of 1912 seems to be accepted as that of the firm establishment of the agricultural colony of the Ikhwan (*hijra*) at Artawiya.

This settlement on the road from Kuwait to Riyadh harboured a body of tribesmen from both the Harb and Mutair tribes and may be taken as a type of the more successful settlements which were later to be numbered in hundreds. The basis of the settlement was indeed *hijra*; that is, a turning-away or new departure. To indicate in visual terms that they had abandoned the nomadic life, the settlers ceased to use the headrope for securing the head-dress since this had originally been an instrument for hobbling camels. They now wore head-dress without the headrope or *agal*, a feature by which their descendants can still be recognised in modern Saudi Arabia. The settlement gave itself to a new occupation, namely agriculture and tending their animals, in addition to their main preoccupation, the religious life. To guarantee the material side of life Ibn Saud arranged for them to be given land and paid for them to have seeds and the services of preachers. In this way encouragement was given to the movement of establishing colonies throughout Nejd which in the next few years were to become bases for mobilising military forces.

For this was the new element in the thinking of Ibn Saud. Not only were the colonies to be a means for converting the Bedu and a way of making them useful producers but they were to be a more highly-developed form of the means for mobilising the Bedu in the cause of both spreading the word of God and of expanding the influence of the Al Saud.

In the seventh century AD, following the death of the Prophet, the tribes had burst out of the Peninsula in an unprecedented surge which took them westwards within 100 years as far as Tours in France, northwards into Asia Minor and eastwards into Central Asia. Similarly less than 100 years before the birth of Ibn Saud the tribesmen under the leadership of the Al Saud and with the inspiration of the principles of the Wahhabi doctrines, had disturbed the stability of the Ottoman Empire and had extended the influence of the Al Saud into Oman, Mesopotamia and Syria and given them control of the Holy Cities of Mecca and Medina. Ibn Saud was acutely aware that the early Muslim Empire and the rule of his forebears had come to perdition, and was seeking for a military means of preventing this happening again.

Again we have no means of knowing for sure at what point the concept of religious settlements became in Ibn Saud's mind one of military settlements. We can only take note of the observable results. The Ikhwan in their colonies located at strategic points all over Nejd became a formidable fighting body, capable of being mobilised at great speed and acting, before the term was even known, as a Rapid Deployment Force. Even more importantly Ibn Saud was spared the expense of maintaining a standing army. He had to bear the expense of paying modest subsidies and giving presents to the tribal leaders, of providing land and seeds, of paying for the preachers and to some extent of providing arms and ammunition but he was spared the enormous overheads of accommodation, supply, administration, training and personnel problems. The Ikhwan were, in the period before 1919, to become Ibn Saud's most valuable fighting asset but, for the moment, he was able to let the concept of the colonies mature while he dealt with the other two problems mentioned, namely the British and his finances.

In staging the *coup de main* by which he conquered Hasa, Ibn Saud had probably doubled his annual income. Harry St John Philby may be formally introduced at this point as it is to him that we owe the most reliable figures for the income of Ibn Saud in his early days. For all his faults Philby was a specialist in financial and tax administration and his early books are full of shrewd observations on Ibn Saud's financial methods.[3] He estimates that before the conquest of Hasa Ibn Saud's annual income was £50 000 and that it was £100 000 for the period until he conquered the Hejaz: Hasa had many taxable activities such as trading, land-owning and agriculture and fruit-growing, the return from which enabled Ibn Saud to meet the expenses of government and maintaining his household.

From this time we begin to get clear indications of the policy of Ibn Saud in financial management. One of his moving ideas was 'al-jood laa yufqir', that is to say that 'Generosity never made anyone poor'. This must be understood in the context in which Ibn Saud was operating: a considerable part of his budget had to be allocated to keeping the tribal leaders happy and on this subject Ibn Saud commented quite frankly on numerous occasions. Of the many occasions on which he would feed 500 of the Bedu from his own table (for which Philby quotes the Bedu as saying, 'an'am allaah 'alayk, yaa Abu Turki!' ('May God requite you for it, O Abu Turki') he would explain, as he did to Amin Rihani, that even if he had very limited resources he had great faith in the future.

Furthermore there was the eminently practical consideration of favours being returned by the recipients of his generosity.

If I sow well in peace and prosperity I shall reap the fruit in war and adversity. In peace I give all, even this cloak to any who need it. In war I ask and my people give all they have to me.[4]

However, despite Ibn Saud's faith in God the Provider for the future, it was essential for him to establish a firm base of finance to meet his growing expenses as a ruler of expanding dominions, with commitments growing at a greater rate than his income was growing. It was imperative to obtain financial subsidy and in this connection the best hope must be the British Government.

We know from the record kept by Captain Shakespear how often Ibn Saud pressed the case for formal relations to be established with the British. Discussion covered a wide range of possibilities from a simple subsidy to formal protectorate status but all the time Shakespear had to bear in mind the instructions of London, in particular the Foreign Office, that nothing must be done to upset the Turks. The British were throughout 1913 engaged in intensive discussions with the Turks, aiming at a formal Convention to regulate all questions between the two governments in the Gulf area against the background of a Europe resolving itself into two mutually hostile alliances. Turkey must not be allowed to be drawn into the camp of the Central Powers, with Austria-Hungary and Germany. To this end the Foreign Office was prepared to take a line which was characterised by the senior official in the India Office as a policy 'of pretending that Saud (*sic*) does not exist'.[5]

So sharp was the disagreement between the heads of the India Office and the Foreign Office that the Foreign Secretary himself, Sir Edward Grey, was compelled to take a personal interest in a matter of dealing with a minor Arabian princeling when he was concerned night and day with the threat of Armageddon in Europe. On 18 May 1914, barely six weeks before the assassination of the Archduke Ferdinand in Sarajevo, Grey felt obliged to lay down the law. Ibn Saud was, by agreement between Britain and Turkey (in a Convention made, but never ratified and made out of date by the outbreak of the First World War), 'in Turkish territory and subject to Turkey and must be treated as such. He must be dealt with as a Turkish official or not at all.'

Ibn Saud understood clearly the drift of the message being conveyed to him indirectly by Shakespear. It was clear that although Shakespear was making friendly gestures he was cleaving to the official London line that direct British contact with Ibn Saud must be kept to a minimum and that no encouragement must be given to his wish to be independent of Turkey. The result was that on almost the same day as Grey's stern memorandum on the subject of Ibn Saud the Turks signed an agreement with Ibn Saud near Kuwait.

Although Philby and others denied[6] there was ever any such agreement, the copy found in Basra when the British drove the Turks out made clear that Ibn Saud, failing to reach an understanding with the British, had agreed terms with the Turks as follows:[7]

1. Ibn Saud was to be the 'Wali and Commandant of Nejd';
2. He should allow the stationing of Turkish troops and gendarmerie in specified numbers and locations;

3.   He should allow the flying of the Turkish flag on all public buildings and allow the use of the Turkish Post Offices and postal stamps;

4.   He should have relations with no other foreign powers and should be committed to join the Turkish forces in resisting any aggression.

Had this agreement come into force, Ibn Saud would indeed have been a Turkish official but events overtook the treaty. The outbreak of war and then the accession of the Turks to the German side cancelled all such arrangements. Ibn Saud had been driven to the step of making such a treaty with the Turks by the negative attitude of the British government, as Cox rightly observed when he discovered the treaty with the Turks.

Once bitten, twice shy: Ibn Saud was now determined to keep his position open and to negotiate the best possible deal with the British. Following the Turkish adhesion to the enemy, the British government was determined to engage all allies possible and approaches were made to Ibn Saud, the more urgently since it was known that Ibn Rashid at Hail was firmly on the Turkish side. However, when Shakespear met Ibn Saud on the last day of 1914, it was clear to him that Ibn Saud was determined to protect his neutrality until such time as he could get a firm, negotiated treaty with Britain.

Negotiations then proceeded for almost a year until the Anglo-Saudi treaty was signed on 26 December 1915 by Cox and Ibn Saud. By this treaty the British recognised Nejd and Hasa as 'the countries of Bin Saud and his fathers before him', and of his descendants, with the proviso that such heirs should not be persons antagonistic to Britain. The British committed themselves to coming to the aid of Ibn Saud in the event of aggression while Ibn Saud undertook not to enter into relations with foreign powers. Ibn Saud further undertook not to cede or lease any of his territories without British agreement and to follow British advice, provided it was not damaging to his interests. Ibn Saud's final commitment by this treaty was not to make any aggression against any of the Gulf principalities and sheikhdoms with which Britain had protective treaties, since this matter had given great concern to the rulers of Abu Dhabi, Qatar, Muscat, Kuwait and Dubai.

In return for signing this treaty[8] Ibn Saud received a loan of £20 000 and 1000 weapons and 200 000 rounds of ammunition, and later a monthly subsidy of £5000 was agreed.

Such benefits of money and weapons were a great reassurance to bn Saud, not in connection with waging war alongside the British, since the Saudi role in the war was of only slight importance, but in connection with confronting his domestic enemies.

Throughout 1915 and 1916 Ibn Saud was faced with the need for constant military vigilance and readiness to fight at a moment's notice. He faced problems from the Ajman tribe, which had for long taken sides with his opponents; with the Al-Murra tribe, which rebelled in 1915; from his dissident cousins; from the Rashidis of Hail; and, to a greater extent as time went on, from the Emir Hussain bin Ali of the Hejaz.

In the fighting with the Ajman, Ibn Saud came as close to disaster and indeed to the end of his life as in possibly any other engagement. His relations with the Ajman tribe had been for some time very bad because of their spirit of rejection of the rule of Ibn Saud, which had made them ready to ally with the *araif*, the dissident cousins of Ibn Saud. He had, however, managed to persuade the Ajman to join him in battle against the Rashidis in the early days of January 1915. The Rashidis had been resupplied by the Turks and had now made fresh moves against the Al Saud, so that by early 1915 both armies were manoeuvring for position in the area near Zilfi, north of Riyadh.

Captain Shakespear had joined Ibn Saud shortly before, as we have seen, now fully authorised by his masters to negotiate with Ibn Saud following the British declaration of war on Turkey on 5 November. He remained with Ibn Saud[9] as the forces marched and counter-marched while the cavalry sought for openings. The Saudis also had field-pieces captured in previous engagements and Shakespear placed himself near the guns in a not inconspicuous manner since he was wearing khaki uniform and a sun helmet as he helped in directing fire. In the confused fighting around Jarrab on 24 January 1915 the Ajman were supposed to hold a flank against the Rashidi cavalry but, whether from treachery, or incompetence or panic they allowed the Rashidi horsemen to break through. They charged and overran the guns and Shakespear was killed.

Ibn Saud was deeply moved at the death of Shakespear, the more so as he had several times urged him to leave the battlefield, coming to his tent in person to urge him to seek safety. He later wrote to Cox to express 'his great sorrow at the loss of his intimate and trusted friend and begs that his sorrow and condolence may be submitted to His Majesty's Government'.[10]

It may be worth lingering over this tragic incident to consider a factor other than Ibn Saud's distrust of the Ajman, for the death of an outstanding British representative, known to have a close relationship with Ibn Saud inevitably attracted much comment in the official documents. Gertrude Bell makes her first appearance in Ibn Saud's life at this stage since she was entrusted with the task of compiling a corpus of information on personalities and tribal matters. Knowing Arabic and having even visited Hail, where she was detained by the Rashidis, she had established a position of authority among the many able specialist officers gathering in Cairo and the Gulf region preparing to deal with the many problems of the Peninsula.

In her notes supplied to Hogarth, the founder of the Arab Bureau in Cairo which became the fount of all knowledge on matters Peninsular, she made a remark which probably became a major part of the received official wisdom:

> When Captain Shakespear was killed in a skirmish Ibn Saud behaved badly and created the impression that he was unreliable.[1]

This judgment came in the same paragraph as remarks on Ibn Saud's domestic arrangements which were equally wide of the mark:

> He says, seemingly with pride, that he has been married 65 times each wife lasts about 3 days; he divorces each one, giving them to his sheikhs or to his ordinary followers.

In facing the many problems which confronted him in 1915 Ibn Saud seems to have decided to cut his losses by reaching an understanding with the Rashidis. He came to an understanding with them in the middle of the year whereby the Rashidis recognised a division of spheres of influence between Riyadh and Hail. Under Ibn Saud's influence by this agreement were the tribes of Mutair, Utaiba, Al Murra, Manasir, Bani Hajir, Sebai, Sahul, Qahtan, Dawasir and Ajman.[12]

Despite their being allocated in this manner, however, the Ajman continued in their rebellious state and shortly after this agreement they fell upon Ibn Saud in a cleverly-staged ambush at Kinzan. Ibn Saud had made an approach by a night-march to their position where they left fires in their camp area to give the impression that they were in camp and unaware of Ibn Saud's presence. Ibn Saud was accompanied by his full brother, Saad, who had a reputation for impetuousness. Whether at his instigation or not Ibn Saud's force approached the Ajman camp and was fallen on from the rear. Saad was killed and Ibn Saud wounded, though how severely is difficult to say. A number of writers have linked the incident of his being wounded with stories of how Ibn Saud restored the faith of his wavering followers by demonstrating his conjugal strength. A picture has been given of his demanding to be found a bride though wounded and of his reinvigorating his dejected forces when cries from the tent indicated that Ibn Saud had lost none of his vigour. The story may be apocryphal, but is recorded in these terms by Zirikli who has the virtue of dating the battle in 1915 and not in 1916 as a number of non-Arab writers have done.

What is certain, however, is that Ibn Saud fought against the Ajman throughout the winter of 1915–16 and defeated them only in September 1916, having received from the British the loan mentioned previously, along with the invaluable weapons and ammunition. A complication of the fighting with the Ajman was that in the intervals of fighting the tribesmen took refuge in Kuwait, much to the fury of Ibn Saud. He had had a close relationship with Mubarak, as we have seen, but regarded the asylum extended to the Ajman rebels as a hostile act, indicating treachery based on jealousy of the growing influence of the Al Saud. Some writers have referred to correspondence intercepted by Ibn Saud between Mubarak and Salim, his son, indicating that Mubarak was ready to back whichever party would be of harm to Ibn Saud but, whatever is the truth, the matter of Mubarak's attitude was closed when he died suddenly in December 1915. His successor continued the policy of support for the Ajman, which Ibn Saud resented deeply: this and other matters such as Saudi attempts to use their own ports rather than import through Kuwait were to poison the atmosphere between the neighbours for many years.

Ibn Saud, having resolved one difficulty, that of the Ajman, with the expenditure of much blood and treasure, was able to turn to other domestic problems, such as the return to raiding amongst the tribes of Nejd. This had begun in his enforced absence in the east while he was dealing with the Ajman. On his return to Riyadh he managed to get a return to stability by a combination of force and persuasion, much different from his uncompromising methods with the Ajman. Those tribesmen who showed readiness to accept his offer of reconciliation if they abstained from raiding were welcomed back into the fold and before the end of 1916 Ibn Saud was ready to accept the risk of leaving his domains to visit Basra.

The British had thought it politic to invite Ibn Saud to attend an Imperial Durbar where there would be the opportunity to demonstrate to him the power of modern military technology, including aircraft, and to discuss with him the intricacies of Arab politics and the developing strategic situation, with a view to having the Al Saud taking a more active part in the war against the Turks. As can be seen from the British military handbook for 1916 on Arabia there was more than a hint of suspicion that Ibn Saud was not only not taking an active part on the Allied side but that he was turning a blind eye to the smuggling of camels and the supplies they bore to the Rashidis in Hail and thence to the Turks in Damascus.

And so it came about that Ibn Saud emerged from Nejd to go for the first time in his life to foreign parts other than Kuwait and Bahrain. The visit to Kuwait and Basra has many unique features, one of them being that Ibn Saud, like the late Sheikh Mubarak of Kuwait, became entitled to call himself 'Sir', since he was invested by the representative of the Viceroy in Delhi with an Indian Empire order, KCIE. He also travelled by car for the first time in his life, had his hand X-rayed and encountered Miss Gertrude Bell.

That she made an impression on him may be gathered from the way in which Ibn Saud in later years often presented his party-piece, being his imitation of Miss Bell bustling around and drawing his attention to various matters by calling out to him 'Yaa Abdul-Aziz, yaa Abdul-Aziz'.

That Ibn Saud comported himself with the greatest dignity may be gathered from Cox's comment, that

> Ibn Saud met Miss Bell with complete frankness and sang-froid as if he had been associated with European ladies all his life.[13]

We owe to Ibn Saud's visit to Basra a famous description written by Gertrude Bell and regarded as so important that it became an official document. In a letter separate from the document she gave her impression of the way in which Ibn Saud reacted to the novel scene unfolded for him at Basra:

> We had an extraordinarily interesting day with Ibn Saud who is one of the most striking personalities I have encountered. He is

splendid to look at, well over 6'3", with an immense amount of dignity and self-possession. We took him in trains and motors, showed him aeroplanes, high-explosives, anti-aircraft guns, hospitals, base depots, everything. He was full of wonder but never agape. He asked innumerable questions and made intelligent comments. He's a big man. . . .'[14]

Having spent so much time with this man whom she had previously tried to evaluate on the basis of other people's reports, Gertrude Bell now gave her own measured judgement:

Ibn Saud is now barely forty though he looks some years older. He is a man of splendid physique, standing well over six feet and carrying himself with the air of one accustomed to command. Though he is more massively built than the typical nomad sheikh he has the qualities of the well-bred Arab, the strongly-marked aquiline profile, full-flesh nostrils, prominent lips and a long narrow chin accentuated by a pointed beard. His hands are fine with slender fingers . . . and in spite of his great height and breadth of shoulder he conveys the impression, common enough in the desert of an indefinable lassitude . . . the secular weariness of an ancient and self-contained people which has made heavy drafts on its vital forces and borrowed little from beyond its forbidding frontiers. His deliberate movements, his slow sweet smile and the contemplative glance of his heavy-lidded eyes, though they add to his dignity and charm do not accord with the Western conception of a vigorous personality . . .. Nevertheless report credits him with powers of physical endurance rare even in hard-bitten Arabia. Among men bred in the camel saddle he is said to have few rivals as a tireless rider. As a leader of irregular forces he is of proved daring and he combines with his qualities as a soldier that grasp of state-craft which is yet more highly prized by the tribesmen. Such men as he are the exception in any community but they are thrown up persistently by the Arab race. . . .

In this same document Gertrude Bell describes how Ibn Saud, the ruler of Kuwait, and the ruler of Muhammerah 'stood side by side in amity and proclaimed their adherence to the British cause'.[15]

Ibn Saud even went on to speak kindly in an extempore speech of the role being played by the Emir Hussain bin Ali, who had in June 1916 proclaimed the Arab Revolt against the Turks and had had himself proclaimed King of the Arabs. In speaking in this way Ibn Saud could only have been wishing to be polite to his hosts since his relations with Hussain bin Ali were by now poisonous.

The Emir of Mecca had made contact with the British, through his son, Abdullah, as early as 1914 when Kitchener in Egypt had secret contacts with him with a view to establishing the possibility of organising a movement hostile to the Turks. Although no immediate action resulted from these contacts the British had undoubtedly learned of the existence of secret cells of Arab nationalists, civilian and military, in such bodies as the 'Ahd or 'Convenant' secret society. The stimulus to more urgent and direct action came with the Allies' failure in the disastrous campaign at Gallipoli (April 1915 to January 1916). The best hope for paralysing the Central Powers on the Eastern Front had gone at a time when it was clearly impossible to achieve a breakthrough on the Western Front. Any action on the Eastern Front must clearly take into account now the possibility of using subversion and guerrilla tactics in addition to the regular military push which was being prepared through the Gulf and Basra in an attempt to take Bagdad.

The fact that many of the Ottoman troops who defeated the Allies at Gallipoli were in fact Arabs observing their obligations as subjects of the Ottoman Empire, and Muslims, made it essential to follow through with the concept of winning away the loyalty of Arab officers and men. Attention began to be concentrated in Cairo on renewing contact with Hussain bin Ali and lining up firmly on the Allied side a leader with impeccable Arab and Muslim qualifications as a descendant of the Prophet. To have the Hashimites in the Allied camp would also be of the greatest reassurance in connection with the loyalty of the Muslim troops in the Indian Army: from the beginning of the First World War the British authorities had been rightly concerned with the possibility of a successful campaign of subversion by the agents of the Turkish Sultan who was also the Caliph of Islam and therefore able, to a degree difficult to establish, to claim the loyalty of Muslims everywhere. Should the Caliph be able to convince Muslim troops in India – who only 60 years before had mutinied against British rule – that they were being used as cannon-fodder fighting on behalf of Christians against Muslims, the nightmare existed that not only would the Allies be deprived of valuable fighting men for the Mesopotamian and Western Fronts but British forces would be tied down in India in trying to prevent further mutinies.

The British High Commissioner in Egypt, Sir Henry McMahon, was given urgent instructions to negotiate with Hussain bin Ali so as to bring him in on the Allied side. The correspondence which ensued has been the subject of much learned debate as to how much was promised by the British, in particular in relation to the status of Palestine, but what is relevant here is that the promises held out were sufficient to guarantee the intervention of Hussain bin Ali on the Allied side. From June 1916 the Arab Revolt was proclaimed and the Hashimites received supplies of gold, weapons, ammunition, advisers and military assistance. Hussain bin Ali promptly proclaimed himself 'King of the Arabs' and destroyed any hope there might be that it was possible to bring about any cooperation between bn Saud and the Hashimites.

In January 1915 there had been correspondence between Ibn Saud and Abdullah bin Hussain in which Abdullah had urged Ibn Saud to make clear his attitude to the British and the Turks. As has been seen, Ibn Saud was at this precise moment fighting for his life and negotiating for a treaty with the British, and therefore made reply urging Abdullah to put off declaring a clear attitude. Abdullah followed up by what was in Ibn Saud's view[16] clearly a hostile act when he led a force into western Nejd: this was clearly a repetition of the action of 1910 when the Hashimite forces had humiliated and angered him by capturing his beloved brother, Saad. By September 1916 Ibn Saud was writing to Cox that he had no wish to align himself with Hussain and had only considered doing so because of British desires and his own wish to expel the Turks.

The true nature of relations between Ibn Saud and Hussain bin Ali is best judged from an exchange of letters between them in 1916 before Ibn Saud travelled to Basra at the invitation of the British. Ibn Saud had written cautiously to Hussain bin Ali asking for guarantees of his sovereignty before aligning himself with the Hashimites and had received an insulting reply in which Hussain delivered himself of the judgement that such a letter as Ibn Saud's could only have been written by one 'bereft of his reason'. Not content with this Hussain even returned Ibn Saud's letter with its enclosures 'so that you may reflect on what you wrote to us in them'.

Ibn Saud exemplified at many times in his life the principle 'Don't get mad: get even.' He recognised at all times the limit of his possibilities and in this situation he kept firmly to the forefront of his mind that it was useless to rage against Hussain and take some rash action: Ibn Saud's overriding need was to maintain good relations with the British in order to ensure his survival. He had gained treaty with them and a subsidy. He had suppressed the revolts of th Ajman and the Al-Murra and had received the submission of th most senior of the 'Araif, Saud Al-Kabir. A pause was needed t ensure continued stability and therefore in relation to the militar needs of the British, benevolent neutrality must suffice.

The inactivity of the Saudi front did not go unnoticed in Delh London and Cairo and there was vigorous debate as to what any action was needed to ensure Ibn Saud's taking a more activ role.

Agreement was eventually reached that the most useful role fc Ibn Saud would be as a means of reducing the threat from th Rashidis, the allies of the Turks, who were still in a position t menace the flank of the British advance from Basra to Bagdad. H should be encouraged to move on Hail and eliminate the threat fror Ibn Rashid and to bring this about it was agreed that Storrs (later t be the first British Military Governor of Jerusalem and, as he notec a successor therefore to Pontius Pilate) should proceed to Riyadl Another great moment in imperial history now occurred when o his first day on camelback heading across the sands he succumbed t heat-stroke and the mission was called off.

A consequence of incalculable effect on Ibn Saud's life of thi extraordinary accident was that Ibn Saud came to know H. St Joh B. Philby, who was now sent by Cox to Riyadh.

By November 1917 it had become more urgent for the Britis military and political authorities that Ibn Saud should take a mor active role. Quite apart from the fact that the Turks still held Medin in spite of the spectacular achievements of T.E. Lawrence in damag ing the Hejaz Railway and taking Aqaba, there was the loomin danger that Russia would fall out of the Allied coalition after th 1916 disasters and the success of the Revolution in February 191 followed by the Bolshevik coup in early November 1917. Philby wa given instructions by Cox relating to his mission to Ibn Saud i Riyadh which he proceeded cheerfully to ignore in ways which wer to have more than trivial effects on the future career of Ibn Saud.

Having quarrelled in Riyadh with Hamilton, the British militar officer who could not accept being junior to him in status, Philb settled down to spending as much time as possible alone with Ib Saud as a result of which he formed the opinion of him which he wa to urge upon the British throughout the remaining years of hi service with the British government. For him it was crystal-clear tha bn Saud was far greater in stature than any other Arab leader and certainly a better bet than Hussain bin Ali. Within two years he was o see the authorities in London abandon their high opinion of Hussain when the matter came to armed conflict between Hashimite orces and Wahhabi elements in the Khurma–Turaba area on the Nejd–Hejaz borders. For the moment, however, he was content to ndulge his passionate interest in matters Arabic, genealogical, geographical, financial and personal and it is because of the quite accidental presence of Philby in Riyadh that we have the first detailed description of Ibn Saud in his native environment which Philby was o publish to the world in 1922 in *The Heart of Arabia*.

Although Philby is reported by many Saudis who knew him to have had defective Arabic and in particular to have caused needless disputes through misunderstanding discussions taking place in Ibn Saud's *majlis* he had the priceless advantage of having remarkable linguistic flexibility and a readiness to learn Arabic in whatever way seemed feasible. On arriving at Basra from India, for example, he had settled down to read the Bible in Arabic and on the other hand had plunged into whatever Arabic conversation he could arrange with all classes of society. The result was that we have the first published record in English of lengthy one-on-one conversations in Arabic with Ibn Saud, and the first detailed account in English by a remarkably qualified observer of the status of the leader of the Al Saud in early 1918.

Philby comments with great discernment on the position of Ibn Saud as the heir of the former Saudi states and on his position among members of the Al Saud.

> I always felt at every turn the presence of a skeleton in the cupboard – the skeleton of the nightmare history of the royal line. Neither Ibn Saud nor the members of his family could ever forget the past which might repeat itself at any moment in the future . . . . Ibn Saud alone stood between order and chaos.

Philby also describes the unique atmosphere of Riyadh at this time.

'Before us in the folds of the grey valley below,' he says, describing how the British mission first came to Riyadh, 'lay a streak of emerald green; it was the gardens of Riyadh. The clay towers of the Wahhabi capital showed dimly through a screen of palms.' The members of the mission were sharply aware of the deathly stillness in the air, but 'suddenly there was a stirring, as of rustling leaves; somehow it was known that the gates had been flung open; life resumed its sway over a world that had seemed dead'.

He goes on to give us a picture of how he first met Ibn Saud, but without at first realising that he was present. He describes how Prince Abdul-Rahman, Ibn Saud's father, received the delegation with much cordiality. He describes how 'a little old man, somewhat inclined to stoutness, sharp-featured and bright-eyed' engaged all their attention while 'Ibn Saud himself, sitting apart in a far corner, humbled and effaced himself in obedience to the laws of God'.

When he comes to describing Ibn Saud himself he emphasises above all what most struck him as a man of action and vigour himself. Ibn Saud was 'a man of inexhaustible energy', a man who put the affairs of his State above all other considerations'. We learn that Ibn Saud habitually at this stage of his life had four hours' sleep a night and rested during the day, usually for two hours.

Philby noted shrewdly with what great attention to detail Ibn Saud observed relations with and between members of his family. Philby himself met many members of the immediate family: Turki, his eldest son, now aged about 19 who had been a warrior, he said, since the age of 8; the young sons Muhammad and Khalid, the future King of Saudi Arabia; the sons of his dead brother Saad whom Ibn Saud was bringing up as his own children having married their mother; Ibn Saud's younger half-brother Abdullah bin Abdul-Rahman, who was to become one of his closest advisers to the end of Ibn Saud's life; and Ahmad bin Thunayan, a descendant of a collateral branch of the Al Saud, who stood out as having a knowledge of the great world since he had been brought up in Constantinople where he had even learned French. With Ahmad bin Thunayan, accompanying Ibn Saud when he visited Philby in his guest quarters, was another person with links to the outside world: Abdullah Damluji, born in Mosul, qualified in medicine, with a knowledge of French and destined to be Ibn Saud's first Foreign Minister.

Philby learned of the complexities of Ibn Saud's position in many ways, especially in relation to his having dealings with the British. He read out to Philby a letter he had received from one of his subjects warning him of the selfish aims of the British. They would 'eat him up when it suited their purpose to do so'.

Ibn Saud's approach to his responsibilities in the area of cementing ties with the tribes through marriage was a subject of which he did not fight shy: 'Wallah, in my lifetime I have married 5 and 70 wives and inshallah I have not done with wiving yet. I am yet young and strong.' Ibn Saud even explained to Philby the administrative details of arranging to take a wife when on a journey or a campaign. If he wished to take a new wife when away from Riyadh he would arrange for a letter to be sent to Riyadh divorcing one of the incumbents, so as to keep to the Sharia limit of four wives.

Philby heard from Ibn Saud himself an exposition of the benefits of his policy of 'musahara', that is, marrying into the tribes but Ibn Saud was frank enough to describe how the best-laid plans can go astray.

He told Philby of an occasion when he divorced one of his wives by letter when away from Riyadh only to discover, after the new marriage had been consummated, that the new bride was the sister of an established wife, indeed the mother of his eldest son, Turki. Ibn Saud himself was horrified since such a marriage was unacceptable in Islamic law.

We learn a little, also, of the potential size of the extended family of Al Saud in the fact which Philby learned, that Ibn Saud's favourite sister was one of 16 sisters, that is, daughters of Abdul-Rahman.

In all, Philby calculated, he spent no less than 34 hours in informal talks with Ibn Saud in the first period which he spent in Riyadh as the British Government's official representative, quite apart from his official discussions.

As to his actual mission Philby was now to show how he was given to creative interpretations of his instructions, not for the first time nor the last time in his life.

He proposed to Ibn Saud that he should be allowed to cross the Peninsula from east to west to call on Hussain bin Ali in Jedda since Hussain was making much of his claim that British representatives could not possibly be allowed to cross in the other direction. Hussain averred that he could not guarantee their safety once they had crossed into the territories nominally under Saudi rule where the beduin tribesmen made life totally insecure. Ibn Saud accepted the idea and Philby left for the Hejaz where he arrived safely.

Hussain bin Ali was infuriated at this demonstration that the territories of Ibn Saud were at least as safe as his own but exacted his revenge in forbidding Philby to return by the same route. Eventually Philby made his return journey to Riyadh via Cairo, Bombay and Basra, meeting up with Ibn Saud again in the spring of 1918, having made a contribution to Saudi–Hashimite relations which the British could well have done without. Not only had he enraged Hussain by

crossing the Peninsula but he had taken pleasure in arguing furi
ously with the King, commenting that it was not every day that one
had the opportunity of making a fool of a king. Hogarth, the founder
of the Arab Bureau, had come to Jedda to negotiate with Hussain in
more serious vein in the light of the new situation in the area caused
by the fall of Jerusalem to the Allies and a possible advance on
Damascus. Now he had to forbid Philby to attend his talks with
Sherif Hussain.

In his second encounter with Ibn Saud, Philby worked on the
question of getting him to advance on Hail but also had the oppor
tunity to note many conversations which he had with him and to
record many incidents which are a revelation of the facts of Ibn
Saud's overall situation.

Philby relates the incident of one of the Ikhwan who had refused
to travel with Philby since he was an unbeliever. The man took
refuge with bin Jiluwi in order to avoid the wrath of Ibn Saud when
he heard of his story.

'See, thou dog!' Philby quotes Ibn Saud as saying, 'See these clothes
nay the food I eat! All these I have from the English. How darest thou
then abuse them! Go, dog! The pleading of bin Jiluwi has saved thee
from death.'

In other conversations Philby learned from Ibn Saud that he would
never marry a Shia woman nor a woman from Mecca. In private
conversation he would also admit to an intense dislike of Jews. He
confirmed the common Wahhabi view of the people of Mecca, that -
in a rising crescendo of Arabic rhyming verbs – they fornicate, betray
people, carouse drunkenly, engage in unnatural sex and are poly
theists.

On practical everyday matters Philby spoke to him at length on
roads, on railways, on the development of the country's mineral
resources and when Philby got on to the subject of an attack on Hail
he learned of aspects of Ibn Saud's policy other than direct combat

He told Philby that

'I have long been undermining the position of the House of Rashid
by *siyasa*', a word frequently translated as 'politics' but more cor
rectly understood in this context as subversion, espionage and psy
chological warfare.

On another occasion Philby had a remarkable demonstration of
many of Ibn Saud's qualities when he told Philby one evening that
'the standard of the Al Saud will start at dawn' but that he was
taking a bride from the Damir section of the Ajman tribe. The mar

riage ceremony took place but Ibn Saud delayed consummation because of pressing work with his staff. Between 9 and 10.30 p.m. he was dictating to two secretaries in completely systematic manner without ever losing the thread, as Philby was able to observe as he was summoned to the tent while this was going on. Ibn Saud then detained Philby in conversation till 11.30 p.m. before going to his bride. Philby confirms that Ibn Saud broke camp at 2 a.m. and that he later confided to him that the bride had not pleased him and that he was going to divorce her.

Philby then moved with Ibn Saud's retinue to Riyadh where he spent nearly three weeks till 6 May 1918. Back in the palace Philby had a conversation where he learned of Ibn Saud's approach to personal security. 'Ibn Saud', he was told by a Sudanese slave, 'trusts no one very far except the royal slaves, whose fidelity is above suspicion.'

That Ibn Saud was personally alert to matters of security and intelligence is shown by another incident related by Philby when he heard of a mendicant, a *derwish* wandering through Riyadh. Ibn Saud was suspicious and had the man detained, whereupon they discovered that he was a spy working for the Turks.

His sensitivity to long-term considerations is shown by his attitude to yet another of Philby's urgings for him to attack Hail. Ibn Saud startled Philby by saying that when the time came for him to attack Hail he would have to declare his intentions publicly so as to allow time for friendly elements to get out of the way.

Throughout Philby's encounters with Ibn Saud in this period he had plenty of occasion to study his approach to finance and revenue. It was quite clear that 'Ibn Saud is his own finance minister and personally supervises the disbursements of his Treasury in every detail'.

Philby noted, too, the shrewdness of Ibn Saud in the collection of taxes due to him. He quotes the instance of where, when he was entitled to taxes of 25 per cent on corn and dates, he exacted only 5 per cent. This is one aspect of his policy of gaining friends:

For many years now I have been applying all the resources of diplomacy to detaching the adherents of my enemy to my side and now my efforts are beginning to bear fruit.

Ibn Saud was also aware of the need to motivate his troops if he were to make a successful attack on Hail, and told Philby of his plans to work on the morale and attitudes of his new model army, the Ikhwan.

I have summoned a great gathering of the Ikhwan for a few days hence when I will explain matters to them and work them up to a great enthusiasm for the assault on Hail.

In spite of this, Ibn Saud still had reservations about whether he should make the final commitment to an assault on Hail. He was remarkably frank to the representative of the British Government when he said, 'I want to be assured that the British Government will not withdraw their support for me once the die is cast.'

Eventually Ibn Saud made the commitment to an advance on Hail in September 1918 but the enterprise was a failure if not a farce. Ibn Saud did not allow Philby to go all the way with the headquarters staff in the approach to Hail for reasons which can only be guessed at but which may have had to do with other factors than a wish to avoid having another of His Majesty's representatives killed in tribal fighting.

At any event, among the factors which led to the failure of the attack was that before Hail the Ikhwan, among whom Feisal bin Duwish had a leading role, after capturing '2000 camels and sheep innumerable' declared that they had no real quarrel with the Rashid and it was time to go home.

Curiously enough Ibn Saud was disarmingly frank on the subject of motivation to Philby. 'Remember,' he admonished him, 'we are fighting Ibn Rashid for your sake only, for we have no unsatisfied claims upon him. . . . The real enemy of Nejd, high and low, is the Sherif', that is, Hussain bin Ali.

Philby was witness to a striking incident of the growing bitterness of the relations between the Hashimites and Ibn Saud when he was filling in time waiting for news of Ibn Saud's campaign. He had, he said, plunged into Anaiza society, and after the experience of that frantic scene Ibn Saud had rejoined them. An Utaiba tribesman then told Ibn Saud of the attitude of Hussain bin Ali to him.

If you surrender the whole of Nejd to him he will not relent; if you give up to him all your women and children and your men he will not relent. It is your religion that he is bent on crushing.[17]

Relations between Jedda and Riyadh were now approaching an explosive climax but by then Philby had left Riyadh. He returned with Ibn Saud to the capital to discover that his instructions had been changed. Cox had come back from London apprised of the whole strategic situation which no longer required an active role for Ibn Saud in Central Arabia. Philby had to break the news that he was not even to get the 1000 rifles and their ammunition which he had been promised.

> Who after this will put their trust in you? I wanted not to attack Hail and you pressed me to do so. And now you tell me to stop. And you hold me up to the ridicule of my own people by supplying me with worthless weapons.

Philby's comment is engaging in its frankness: 'I had no leg to stand on and nothing to reply.'
Before Philby left for the coast Ibn Saud had a final breakfast meeting with him at which he puts his position with perfect frankness to him:

> I am nervous of my subjects for hitherto I have stood alone against their natural inclinations, persuading them that British friendship was to their ultimate advantage. But what can I say to them now?

What he was to say to them was to become clear very shortly and the direction of his thoughts could be gathered from his remark to Philby the night before his departure.

> It is the Sherif who is responsible for this blow at me – he has utterly deceived the rulers of Egypt and I will attack him if, to humour him, your Government persists in treating me so ill.

The British Government moved swiftly to make amends by issuing an invitation to Ibn Saud to visit London as one of a series of goodwill visits by wartime allies, an invitation which had an increasingly serious purpose since after much petty skirmishing between Hashimites and forces loyal to Ibn Saud a full-blown engagement had been fought and the forces of Hussain bin Ali had been massacred.

The engagement took place at Turaba in the borderlands between Nejd and the Hejaz and involved no less a commander on the Hashimite side than Hussain's son Abdullah, later to be the King of Jordan. The area of the village of Khurma near Turaba had been in dispute since even before the local Emir, Khalid bin Luai, had thrown off his allegiance to the Sherif after adopting the religious principles of the Sheikh. In May 1919 Abdullah arrived on the scene with 5000 men, supported by machine-guns and field-guns. Furthermore Abdullah proceeded to boast that his mission was not confined to Khurma and Turaba: with the approach of the Pilgrimage season he planned to celebrate the Eed in the heart of Nejd. Such provocative talk brought a determined reply: Ibn Saud ordered a force of the Utaiba Ikhwan from their settlement at Ghot Ghot to proceed to Turaba.

The Ikhwan made their way speedily over the 300 miles to Turaba and made a night approach march to the Hashimite camp. They fell upon the sleeping camp before dawn and slew every one they came upon. Abdullah himself managed to escape in undignified fashion in his night-clothes. For the first time the war-cry of the Ikhwan had been heard, 'The winds of Paradise are blowing, where are ye who seek it?' and for the first time in Ibn Saud's lifetime the murderous power of blind faith when armed had been demonstrated.

Ibn Saud declined the British invitation to London since the situation in and around his dominions was now too disturbed but deputed his son, Feisal, now aged 14, to travel to London in his stead. He arranged also for Ahmad bin Thunayan to accompany him as political adviser and to engage in discussions on his behalf with the British Government. Ibn Saud also sent a prominent Nejdi merchant with Feisal to London, Abdullah Gosaibi, with a brief to import the new technology to Nejd in the shape of motor cars.

The visit of Prince Feisal to Britain has often been described and has indeed much interest of its own. After a false start when Government hospitality arrangements failed and the intervention of George V was needed to restore wounded pride with an invitation to Buckingham Palace, the son of Ibn Saud had a fascinating introduction to the Western world in the immediate aftermath of the First World War. Besides London he had visits to the Peace Conference at Versailles, to the battlefields of northern France, to Phoenix Park in Dublin and to the cities of Marseilles, Cologne and Strasbourg. As to the immediate object of the exercise, the improvement of Saudi–British relations, there were discussions with Curzon, now become Foreign Secretary, which were less than beneficial since Feisal and Ahmad bin Thunayan left enraged at having been treated like children. Discussions in Versailles were similarly disastrous since the attempt to bring the Saudis and the Hashimites together almost resulted in an armed brawl. Feisal bin Hussain made a slighting reference to the Ikhwan by asking, 'Who are these Ikhwan? I am told they are not allowed to cut their beards.' Fortunately the respective aides-de-camp were at hand to bring the discussions to an abrupt end.[18]

When Feisal returned to Nejd in February 1920 Ibn Saud was at Hofuf to welcome him back and the scene was described by a knowledgeable observer who was to come to know Ibn Saud extremely well in the next 33 years, Harold Dickson, who had been recently appointed Political Agent in Bahrain. Ibn Saud was delighted to see how well his son looked after his visit abroad and was moved to see the letter which George V himself had written to him and which Dickson had to read out in translation a number of times so that Ibn Saud could properly relish it. A celebratory feast was ordered and all fell-to when the slaughtered sheep were placed before them.

However, there was a noticeable change in the atmosphere after lunch when Ibn Saud sent for Dickson. He had had time to hear from Ahmad bin Thunayan of the tenor of his discussions in London and Versailles and was depressed and outraged to learn of the continued disparagement of the Al Saud and the unreasoning support given to the Hashimites.

'You are supporting a broken pillar',[19] he told Dickson. 'As sure as I hold this stick,' he said, indicating his camel stick, 'so surely do I know the Shareef's days are numbered.'

But the out-and-out conflict with Hussain bin Ali was not to be yet. Ahmad bin Thunayan is reported by one writer to have given an assurance in Paris on behalf of Ibn Saud 'that no matter what the provocation there shall be no war for 3 years'.[20] Bray goes on to say that Ibn Saud honoured the word of his envoy given without consulting him. This may not be the case: it is equally probable that Ahmad bin Thunayan had been thoroughly briefed and understood as well as his master the imperatives of his overall situation, above all that it would not be politic to make an assault on the Hejaz at this time. The British were too closely committed to the Hashimites and in any case the Muslim world was not ready to accept the Wahhabis being in charge of the Holy Places.

Ibn Saud had in any case many other issues to deal with, principally Kuwait and Mesopotamia and the border region of the Yemen in the Asir, not to mention the continuing problem of the independent power base of the Rashidis in Hail. In all of these areas the Ikhwan were to play a crucial role.

There had been clashes in 1919 and 1920 between Kuwaiti tribesmen and the Ikhwan of the Mutairi tribe based on Artawiya. They in their holy zeal had no respect for borders and had tried to establish a settlement on territory traditionally regarded as Kuwaiti. When the Kuwaitis expelled them the Mutairi Ikhwan returned in larger numbers and eventually launched a full-scale raid on Kuwait Town. The Kuwaitis were able to erect town walls in sufficient time to hold off the Ikhwan but not before 200 Kuwaitis were killed in October 1920 at Jahra. There was no resolution of this problem until the death of Sheikh Salim bin Mubarak. The new ruler of Kuwait Jabir bin Ahmad – who had travelled to Europe with Feisal in 1919 – met Ibn Saud in April 1921 and an announcement was made that there was no need to define a frontier between the countries which had such intimate relations as Kuwait and Nejd. Ibn Saud had taken due note that the British had made military moves to protect Kuwait if necessary.

A similar situation had arisen in relation to Iraq, as Mesopotamia now came to be called. The British had from 1920 assumed responsibility for the Mandate and had immediately been faced with a revolt of the tribes and towns from July to December 1920. The Ikhwan had begun to cross the newly-conceived borders between Nejd and Iraq, which it was impossible to define precisely, and anarchy and insecurity now prevailed. The British eventually used a combination of police and air-control to deter raids, largely through the personal initiative and energy of the young Lieutenant John Bagot Glubb, but the borders remained porous.

The Asir region presented a quite different problem since this area was almost a clearly-defined political entity. It had been ruled in semi-independent fashion since the mid-nineteenth century by the Idrisi family but after the departure of the Turks Hussain bin Ali had attempted to impose his own rule on the coastal plain of the Asir region. The Ikhwan had been summoned from the Turaba region where they had annihilated the Hashimites in 1919 and within a short time the Idrisis were happy to acknowledge the suzerainty of Ibn Saud. Feisal, his son, had been the nominal commander of this warlike expedition, which apart from the knowledge of the area of the Yemen border which it gave the future King Feisal, is a telling demonstration of Ibn Saud's policy of delegating responsibility.

Ibn Saud himself, however, took personal control of the movement against Hail in November 1921 which finally ended the rule of the Rashidis at Jebel Shammar. The prelude to the move against Hail was that there had been yet another bloodletting among the Rashidis.

In the spring of 1920 the ruler of Hail, Saud, was engaged in an impromptu shooting-match with members of the family when he made an incautious remark about the aim of a cousin Abdullah bin Talal who, in a rage, shot him dead. Although the murderer was immediately despatched by the late ruler's retainers, the future of the Rashidis was now in jeopardy once again, since the new ruler was a mere thirteen years old.

Ibn Saud joined a force of the Ikhwan under Feisal bin Duwish, of the Mutair, outside Hail and proceeded to carry on the same kind of debate (and with the same man) as had puzzled Philby in 1918. This time the Ikhwan were for not going home but for assaulting Hail frontally. Ibn Saud prevailed in the argument for using more subtle methods. A secret agreement was made with the Deputy Governor of the town whereby in return for his opening the gates the town and its inhabitants would be spared. The gates were duly opened and the power of Hail was at an end.[21]

The policy of Ibn Saud in showing clemency and urging reconciliation with the Rashidis was clearly not the result of pure altruism but was undoubtedly a policy demonstrating the greatest political wisdom and far-sightedness. Reconciliation and good behaviour were assured by Ibn Saud's marrying the widow of the murdered ruler and by his policy of keeping the Rashidis as his honoured guests at Riyadh.[22]

By taking Hail, Ibn Saud had extended his dominions to the north in a way which brought him into immediate contact with British power and influence in another of its aspects for, since March 1921, a new order had prevailed in the Near and Middle East thanks to Winston Churchill.

The new Secretary of State for the Colonies had assimilated the arguments raised by numbers of MPs who had questioned the multiplicity of British jurisdictions in the area and the potential for conflicting commitments since, as was frequently pointed out, Britain was subsidising two rulers in the Peninsula who were at daggers drawn. Churchill had summoned a conference of military and civilian specialists on the area in Cairo and had with great vigour laid down the lines of the new arrangements. Feisal bin Hussain, having lost the throne of Syria after the French had defeated him at the battle of Maisalun in 1920, was to receive the throne of Iraq; Abdullah bin Hussain, having during the Cairo conference, made an armed *démarche* in the direction of Syria, was rewarded with the Emirate of the new entity of Transjordan, and Ibn Saud was left to fume that the

British had now arranged for him to be entirely surrounded by his enemies.

Nonetheless Ibn Saud had, by conquering Hail, ensured for himself a great deal of attention from the British. His proclamation of himself now as the Sultan of Nejd and its Dependencies naturally gave rise to discussion as to what precisely were Ibn Saud's ambitions. Were they boundless? Did he seek to spread Wahhabi doctrines as his forefathers had done? Was Transjordan safe from his attentions? Was Kuwait safe? Could the new monarchy of Iraq survive the continuing raids by the Ikhwan across the borders from Nejd? Did Ibn Saud have control of the Ikhwan? If he did not, was he happy to use the lack of control as a pretext and enjoy any benefits which might accrue?

An attempt was made to regularise the situation across the Iraqi border when Saudi delegates negotiated the Treaty of Muhammerah in May 1922 but Ibn Saud would not ratify what his delegates had agreed.

The raids across the border with Transjordan led to violent British reaction. In one raid by the Ikhwan in November 1921 the Royal Air Force pursued and caught the raiders in the open with the result that only eight of the 1500 Ikhwan returned to Nejd.

The concept of a Transjordanian border was very far from realisation indeed, as was shown by a bizarre incident involving Philby, who was at this time Chief Administrator for Transjordan. In May 1922 Philby once again exceeded his instructions on an official expedition to Jawf, where he found himself and his party hostages of the Ruwalla tribe. In order to negotiate his release, he committed His Majesty's Government to an offensive and defensive alliance against Ibn Saud. Philby secured the release of his party but his Government's need to disown this new departure in its policy was among the last nails in his coffin. He was soon to leave official life and after various vicissitudes attach himself to Ibn Saud's court.

Clearly, from the point of view of the British Government, there were too many loose ends and the potential clearly existed for serious hostilities to break out. It was therefore decided to call another conference, which turned out to be as momentous in its way as the Cairo Conference. Ibn Saud was invited to meet Sir Percy Cox, now High Commissioner in Iraq, at the port of Ujair, along with representatives of Kuwait and Iraq.

This conference, which lasted for more than a week, was remarkable in its incidents, in its consequences and in the fact that we have eye-witness accounts of more aspects of it than would be normal at a formal international conference. Dickson, who was present in his formal capacity of Political Agent, wrote at length about what he observed of many aspects of the conference, and almost anything which he may have missed was described by a total outsider, the Lebanese–American writer Amin Rihani.

Rihani had developed a great commitment to the idea of Arab unity and had undertaken to visit all potential leaders of such a movement in the Peninsula, whom he was describe in several books in English and Arabic. We owe to him colourful descriptions not only of the events of the Conference but of many sides of Ibn Saud's personality and private and public life as well as of Riyadh to which Ibn Saud invited him after the Conference.

Rihani was present at Ujair to await the arrival of Ibn Saud from Riyadh. The caravan of Ibn Saud could be heard approaching from a great distance away as they intoned the chant of the Al Saud endlessly: 'Yaa su'ayyid . . .'. Eventually Ibn Saud and a bodyguard of 300 men appeared and Rihani described his impressions.

'What an unearthly charm had the cry I heard at that moment coming from behind the dunes in waves of assurance and awe across the meadows of night . . .'.[23] He goes on to describe how the sound of over 200 camel-drivers tapping the necks of their mounts with their bamboo canes was 'like the patter of rain in a grove of palms'.

His first encounter with Ibn Saud was clearly a matter of some awe for even this well-travelled and sophisticated man.

We first met on the sands under the stars and in the light of the many bonfires that blazed all around. A tall majestic figure in white and brown, overshadowing, overwhelming – that was my first impression. . . . (He) took my hand and held it in his own as we walked into our little tent. . . . He sat on the sheepskin leaning his right arm against the saddle and the fire outside of our open tent lighted up his rugged countenance which is offset by a mobile mouth, full but not heavy and soft brown eyes.

Later that night when summing up his impressions Rihani confided to his diary:

I have now met all the Kings of Arabia and I find no one among them bigger than this man. He is big in word and gesture and style as well as in purpose and self-confidence. His personality is com-

plex. The shake of his hand and the way he strikes the ground
with his stick proclaim the contrary traits of the man.

Having contrived to be on the scene, Rihani played a role in
the conference proceedings, often acting as a translator and com
mentator to Ibn Saud.

The main object of the convening of the conference was to reach an
understanding on Nejd's border with both Kuwait and Iraq. Here
two different concepts clashed, that of European-style borders and
the inclination of the tribesmen to opt for tribal boundaries and
allocation of wells. After a week of discussion,[24] with Ibn Saud
backing the latter option, Cox finally lost patience and in a private
meeting reprimanded Ibn Saud in somewhat schoolmasterish
manner for his preference for a tribal boundary, at which Ibn Saud
declared in tears that Cox was his father[25] and that he would leave
entirely to Cox the decision as to the marking of boundaries. Dickson
describes what happened next.

At a general meeting of the conference Sir Percy took up a red
pencil and very carefully drew in on the map of Arabia a bound
ary line from the Persian Gulf to Jabal Anaizan close to the
Transjordan frontier. This gave Iraq a large area of territory claimed
by Nejd.

Obviously to placate Ibn Saud, he ruthlessly deprived Kuwait of
nearly two-thirds of her territory and gave it to Nejd, his argument
being that the power of Ibn Sabah was much less in the desert than
it had been when the Anglo-Turkish agreement had been drawn up

South and west of Kuwait proper he drew out two zones which he
declared should be neutral and known as the Kuwait Neutral Zone
and the Iraq Neutral Zone.

And then came one of the most revealing exchanges in all the
dealings between Ibn Saud and the British. Cox was urged by one of
the advisers to Ibn Saud to allocate more grazing room for the Saudi
tribes than he had done.

'Why, pray,' asked Cox, 'are you so anxious that this area should
go to Nejd?'

'Quite candidly,' was the reply, 'because we think that oil exists
there.'

Cox was firm in his reply.

'That is exactly why I have made it a Neutral Zone. Each side shall have a half share.'

Before the end of the conference at Ujair Ibn Saud and Cox were to be in tears, as Dickson himself bore witness.

Cox was asked by Ibn Saud to come and see him and, when he came, Ibn Saud broke into tears lamenting the loss of land to Iraq. Cox was thereupon himself moved to tears and trying to comfort his old friend said, '"My friend I know exactly how you feel and for this reason I gave you two-thirds of Kuwait's territory. I don't know how Ibn Sabah will take the blow."'

Amin Rihani offers another insight into the deals which were made at this conference in describing his own role in translating certain documents for Ibn Saud.[26] He mentions a cable sent by Cox to Churchill proposing allotting to Ibn Saud territory between Nejd and Transjordan, near Jawf and comments, 'This is part of the compensation made to (Ibn Saud). . . . We take from Ibn Saud to satisfy Iraq and we take from Trans-jordan to placate Ibn Saud.'

As a result of the Ujair Conference a *modus vivendi* had been reached and certain arrangements made which were to be of long duration, such as the new Neutral Zones. Furthermore Ibn Saud had, by the end of 1922, established control of all the major oases of the Arabian Peninsula, from the Fertile Crescent to the Empty Quarter. In addition he had made a new departure in ensuring the switch of the movements of goods to and from Nejd through Hasa ports rather than through Kuwait, a move which symbolised the deterioration of relations between Kuwait and Nejd. The major change brought about by this conference, however, was that the concept of modern frontiers had been brought to Nejd and its neighbours, but without the prior agreement of all parties. In the next decade there were to be the most severe problems when the tribesmen, and in particular the Ikhwan, demonstrated their rejection of this new concept, and in so doing almost brought about the ruin of Ibn Saud.

The conference had a sub-theme which was eventually to dominate all thinking about the area in which the conference took place, namely oil.

Since the discovery of oil in Persia in 1908 and the conversion of the Royal Navy to oil-burning ships, the British had focused in determined fashion on ensuring guaranteed access to oil, of which the nearest major source was the Gulf region and Iraq. The allocation of territory to Britain's mandate for Iraq took full account of the presence of oil at Mosul, which was carefully excluded from the claims of both France (which had the mandate for Syria) and of the successor to the Ottoman Empire, the new Turkish Republic. The possibility of discovering oil in the Arab lands bordering the Gulf was a major consideration for British policymakers, given the nature of the exclusive treaties which they had with the Gulf sheikhdoms, and so Cox was extremely sensitive about the presence at the Ujair conference of an oil concession-hunter, Major Frank Holmes.

This New Zealander deserves a place in the history of Ibn Saud because he not only managed to get himself to Ujair at the right time and get himself included in the photographs taken to commemorate the event but managed as a result of the conference to get the first concession to explore for oil in Saudi territory.

In August 1923 Ibn Saud wrote to Rihani to tell him that he had granted a concession to Holmes. This was a highly significant event since Rihani knew better than anyone what pressure Cox had put on Ibn Saud in Ujair to reject Holmes' pleas for a concession. Cox had even drafted a note for Ibn Saud to sign, informing Holmes that no concession could be granted until the British government had been consulted. Ibn Saud had resisted signing until the last possible moment but had to agree in the end, because in the last analysis the British were the paymasters. The annual subsidy of £60 000 was still indispensable to Ibn Saud's budgeting.

On 31 March 1923 the British Government announced that the subsidy to Ibn Saud would end in one year's time and thereby absolved Ibn Saud of the need to be apprehensive about British economic sanctions. The first beneficiary of the new situation was Major Frank Holmes but more importantly Ibn Saud felt freed from any inhibitions with regard to dealing with the other protégés of the British, the Hashimites in Jedda.

The British called a conference in Kuwait which met from November 1923 to April 1924 in an attempt to resolve border disputes between Transjordan and the newly-extended Nejdi territories (which now reached to the north of the Wadi Sirhan) and in order to resolve all outstanding territorial issues between Ibn Saud and the Hashimites. Ibn Saud accepted the idea of Saudi participation, and delegates arrived from Feisal bin Hussain in Iraq and from Abdullah bin Hussain in Transjordan. The key figure, however, did not attend or send delegates, namely King Hussain bin Ali, King of the Hejaz. Although the conference sat for months it was doomed to failure for the two excellent reasons that Hussain, the principal Hashimite figure, refused to take part, and that Ibn Saud no longer had any financial inducement to be amenable. The issues between Ibn Saud and Hussain bin Ali were to be resolved in 1924 by force and Ibn Saud was to replace Hussain as Lord of Mecca in October of that year.

As Ibn Saud said to Rihani

No one can force anything upon us.[27] No, by God! What was the right of our forebears is our right. And if we can not get it by friendly means we shall get it by the sword.

FAMILY LIFE

In this period the following bore Ibn Saud children:

1.   Bazza, whom he married in about 1919 and who bore him Nasir, who was to be Governor of Riyadh until removed in 1947.

2.   Jawhara bint Saad Al-Sudairi, who was the widow of his full brother, Saad. She bore him 3 sons.

3.   Hassa, of the Sudairi family whom Ibn Saud married twice, for the first time in 1913 when she was about 14 and in 1920 after divorcing her. In the intervening period she married Ibn Saud's brother Muhammad. She was to bear Ibn Saud seven sons, the eldest being King Fahd, born 1921. She also bore him seven daughters. Her last child was born in the 1940s.

4.   Shahida, who bore him Mansour, who became Minister of Defence and died in 1951. She is touchingly described by the wife of one of the American medical missionaries, Mrs Dame, who describes her Christian origins.[28]

5.   Al-Fahda, who was the widow of one of the Rashidis defeated in 1921. She bore him the Crown Prince Abdullah, born in 1923.

6.   Bazza, the second wife of that name, who bore him Bandar and Fawwaz.

Apart from the marriages noted above, the year 1919 was a year of great drama in family terms. Ibn Saud's beloved wife Jawhara bint Musaid, the mother of Muhammad and Khalid, died in the great influenza epidemic, as did his eldest son Turki and two other young sons.

A number of Ibn Saud's half-brothers were born in this period: Ahmed, Musaid and Saad of all of whom Philby comments that they 'played no part in public affairs'. The same can be said of the last brother to live to adulthood, Saud, who was born about 1890.

5

The Imam in Mecca, 1924–28

In 1925 I heard the late Dr. Hogarth, a keen and wise observer of Arabian problems, declare that nothing would surprise him less than to find, within five years or so, the Wahhabis deposed from the Hejaz and the Sharifian family again in authority there.

K. Williams, *Ibn Saud*, 1933, p. 7

The holy land is ruled today by a house nurtured in rapine and robbery, raids and aggression and bloodshed.

King Abdullah of Jordan, *Memoirs*, 1954 on the Al Saud

Beware, o Ikhwan! Encroach not upon the rights of others. If you do your value and that of the dust are the same. . . . We took you by the sword and we shall keep you within your bounds by the sword, if God wills.

Ibn Saud, quoted by A. Rihani, *Ibn Saud*, 1928, p. 214

In telling the story of Ibn Saud we can remain a while longer in the company of Amin Rihani, since he had the priceless opportunity to observe and talk with Ibn Saud over a six-week period after the Ujair conference. He travelled in the Sultan's retinue riding across the desert to Riyadh, observing and making notes. What makes the observations of Rihani worthy of remark is that he resisted the temptation to be carried away by unadulterated admiration. To him Ibn Saud was a truly great man, who would have been, had he been born in Europe, a monarch of great historical stature, but he can at the same time note that Ibn Saud was capable of being a bore when he allowed his words to carry him away.[1]

Although Rihani was a Christian he was able to take pleasure in the sound of the Koran being recited as the great retinue moved along on the way back to Riyadh, with some 300 Arabs riding behind Ibn Saud, and chanting the verses in chorus: 'The camels

themselves seemed to keep time with the rhythmic human movement of body and voice.' Ibn Saud himself stood out with his silk
agal (head-cord) and with his great height towering above all the
rest. Even his red Omani camel had a higher hump than the other
camels.

In the context of religion Rihani notes how Ibn Saud would take
delight in constantly having read to him extracts from three particular books: (i) collections of the Prophet's sayings; (ii) Tabari's
great history of the Arabs and (iii) the life of the Prophet. These
readings would take place in Ibn Saud's more open assemblies and
one can only note with admiration, in addition to Ibn Saud's piety,
his great skill in what today would be termed public relations and
promotion of that image. He had a natural skill in choosing the most
effective means for broadcasting the message which he wished to
propagate.

Riding along with Ibn Saud's retinue Rihani had time to talk to his
retainers and quickly learned that most of them had been very
restless at having been so long away from Riyadh and at having to
wait around so much at Ujair. The reason was explained to him with
charming frankness: 'We desire women all the time.' This would
have been no great surprise to anyone familiar with the conditions of
desert life but what makes Rihani's observations more pertinent is
that his informant goes on to say: ' . . . and he whose desire is the
strongest is the Imam,' namely Ibn Saud.[2]

When the caravan eventually reaches Riyadh, Rihani is surprised
to find that he finds the Great Mosque to be an original work of
architecture, sublime in its very austerity.[3] 'I have not seen its like
anywhere.' Austerity is, however, the dominant feature of this unusual capital: Rihani notes that in the entire time of his stay he does
not see a single flower or aromatic plant within the mud walls of
Riyadh.

Nor does he find the people of Riyadh as agreeable as their ruler:
'The good cheer and geniality of the Sultan have taught the natives
of the capital nothing.'[4]

He notes also the surliness of the Ulema, even towards Ibn Saud
himself. Indeed Ibn Saud confides to Rihani: 'The Ulema do not
condescend to speak to us.'[5]

Ibn Saud does not appear to have let this peevishness get him
down, for Rihani records an incident when he rides out on a pleasure
jaunt with Ibn Saud and his retainers and when the group is some
way from the walls of Riyadh Ibn Saud looks round and says:

'There are no Ikhwan with us. He who has a good voice will now let us hear it.'

In spite of his relaxed manner Ibn Saud does not let his guard down for a moment, as Rihani notes. His concern for security has evidently now become instinctive and part of his routine and that of his retinue.

When Ibn Saud prays, notes Rihani, his principal bodyguard remains erect.[6] And as Ibn Saud says to Rihani:

'I have to be aware of my own people – the nearest to me. Treachery we have discovered among the closest of our allies.'

When camp is set up for the night Ibn Saud's tent is placed in the centre of the encampment, indistinguishable from the many others of camel hair and canvas surrounding it.

Nor was Ibn Saud alone in his concern for security, for Rihani relates how the populace of Riyadh was thrown into turmoil on one occasion when Ibn Saud failed to return for the evening, having left in the late afternoon by car with his guards and companions. For some reason the cars were delayed and Ibn Saud was reprimanded on his return by the elders for perturbing the breasts of his loving subjects.[7]

Ibn Saud did not reciprocate the love, or at least not love for Riyadh. Rihani quotes him as saying that he feels like a stranger in his own capital. He would not live in Riyadh for a single day if he were not the ruler of the country.[8]

Riyadh was the capital of the Al Saud but it was also the gilded cage for his 'guests,' the members of the family of the Al Rashid. Rihani meets a number of them, including Feisal bin Rashid and Abdullah bin Mut'ib and notes how freely they get up and walk out of the *majlis* of Ibn Saud while he is holding forth.

Rihani notes carefully how closely Ibn Saud keeps the Rashidis under observation while affording them every courtesy.

On one remarkable occasion Rihani is present when Ibn Saud addresses members of the house of Rashid in his *majlis*:

You of the House of Rashid, all of you, are as dear to me as my own children. You live here as I live, neither better nor worse – your clothes are like mine, your food is like mine, your horses are even better than mine.

By this time, Rihani notes with astonishment, some of those listening were in tears.

I give you the pledge of security on the book of Allah and the life of the Prophet on condition that you be loyal to us and that you lend not your tongue nor your hand nor your presence to such as would intrigue and plot against us.[9]

For the life of politics went on and Rihani had the good fortune to be present in Riyadh to witness the unfolding of one particular aspect of Ibn Saud's plans.

In February 1923 the Sultan's son Feisal rode back into Riyadh at dawn at the head of the troops which he had been leading in another campaign in the Asir region. Following the 1920 Ikhwan campaign, the Saudis had strengthened their hold on the region by another military action commanded by Feisal. On his return, Ibn Saud was overwhelmed by fatherly pride and wheeled his horse into line behind Feisal, charging at the head of a detachment of horsemen and shouting,

'Allah is One! There is no God but Allah!

'He was stern of aspect and full of the importance of the moment'[10] as the Commander-in-Chief welcoming back one of his generals.

Ibn Saud was later to confide to Rihani that he could not have simply stayed on the reviewing stand: if he had done he would have simply burst into tears of pride.

Rihani also witnessed the implementation of another part of Ibn Saud's policy, in relation to the Ikhwan for, while he was in Riyadh, raids still continued by the Ikhwan into Transjordan. We have an account of one particularly savage raid[11] to the neighbourhood of Amman and witnessed by Philby: after massacring tribesmen of the bani Sakhr the Ikhwan tribesmen were caught out in the open by Royal Air Force planes and were almost totally wiped out. Rihani saw the sequel in Riyadh when Ibn Saud jailed the leaders of the raid for three months for acting without his authorisation.

Rihani quotes the eloquent words which Ibn Saud addressed to the Ikhwan:

Do not forget that there is not one among you whose father or brother or cousins we have not slain. Aye, by God! It was by the sword that we conquered you, and that same sword is still above your heads. Beware, o Ikhwan! Encroach not upon the rights of others![12]

A good part of the story of the next four years of Ibn Saud's life is taken up with the complications caused by the actions of the Ikhwan both when they were acting on his authorisation and when they were apparently out of control.

Before dealing with the events of the period it may be worth looking at another account of Ibn Saud written by an Englishman with a knowledge of Arabic and of the area who encountered him at just this period in 1924 before the assault on the Hejaz.

R.E. Cheesman, OBE, was a slightly eccentric individual, deeply interested in bird-watching and surveying, who came to Hasa in early 1924 where he encountered Ibn Saud and had lengthy and sometimes bizarre conversations with him.

Cheesman was present in Hofuf in January 1924 when Ibn Saud arrived two hours before sunset with an escort of some 350 men mounted on camels, and noted with admiration how with characteristic energy Ibn Saud held a *majlis* until a late hour of the night to receive all those who wished to greet him.

When it came to Cheesman's turn to speak to Ibn Saud he found himself being questioned about the likely result of the General Election in England and whether the question of reparations between France and Germany had been settled. He says forlornly, 'I could give him no information on either subject.'[13]

Cheesman soon learned that not all was solemnity in Ibn Saud's court. As was usual when Ibn Saud came to Hasa, Abdullah Gosaibi was charged with the task of providing sustenance and, as was not uncommon, found himself caught short because of the large numbers of mouths to feed. At a certain moment in the victualling crisis when he thought he had retrieved the situation by getting hold of a supply of peach jam he found himself besieged with complaints of lack of bread to go with it. Abdullah Gosaibi thereupon scuttled out in alarm, but was pulled back and told they were only teasing him.

Cheesman spent some days in Ibn Saud's company and came to certain conclusions which harmonise with what we know of Ibn Saud's caution and care for security.

He spoke at some length to Cheesman about the murderous dissension among brothers eager to secure the succession for themselves. That this could occur, and not only with the Al Saud, had made him cautious and this was, according to Cheesman, the reason why Ibn Saud always took care to have his sons with him at all times so that he might detect any untoward ambition amongst them.[14]

Ibn Saud always had a capacity until his declining years to divert himself from major preoccupations with a wide variety of interests and occasions for light relief, and this is shown clearly in Cheesman's account of these few days.

He was asked to show his bird collection to Ibn Saud who thereupon proceeded to astonish Cheesman with the depth of his knowledge. 'He displayed more knowledge of the different species than any educated Arab I had yet encountered.'[15]

Ibn Saud then discussed with Cheesman the qualities of various motor cars: he was expecting delivery of a Citroen with caterpillar tracks for desert-going and told Cheesman that he had several cars in Riyadh, several Fords and one big car.

Cheesman then relates how, having received his London *Times* from Hofuf he rushed off to give Ibn Saud the British General Election results on which he felt he had failed his *viva voce* examination. Ibn Saud thanked him politely and informed him that he had already heard the news as he took the Damascus papers.

Cheesman then relates his disappointment at not being able to visit Ibn Saud since he was not receiving at a time when he was fasting before Ramadan. Since he would be travelling in Ramadan it was his duty to make up for it in advance.

Before Ibn Saud left for Riyadh, however, he did receive Cheesman and was able to tell him that the first Labour Government in British history had just taken office.

No sooner had Ibn Saud returned to Riyadh than an election of a different kind occurred which was to preoccupy his attention and indeed that of the whole Islamic world and was to signal the beginning of the end of Hashimite rule in the Hejaz: namely the election of the Caliph.

The Ottoman Caliphate had been ended by the proclamation to that effect by the new leader of the Turkish Republic, Mustafa Kemal (Kemal Ataturk) early in 1924. In March 1924 Hussain bin Ali, visiting his son, the Emir Abdullah of Transjordan, in Amman was urged by him to make a response to this proclamation and on 5 March the Islamic world was astounded to hear that Hussain had proclaimed himself the Caliph; that is, the spiritual and temporal leader of the Islamic Umma. Nowhere except in the immediate entourage of Hussain was there any enthusiasm for this idea, but among the Nejdi tribesmen there was outrage.

The Wahhabis had already sufficient cause for outrage on spiritual grounds since the King of the Hejaz had forbidden them to perform the *Hajj* out of fear of allowing into the Hejaz the warriors who had

massacred the army of Abdullah at Turaba. A conference was hel
in Riyadh in June 1924, attended by the main tribal chiefs and th
Ulema, and the decision was taken to invade the Hejaz. Ibn Sau
was now to be allowed to show whether his judgement was correc
that if the English had allowed him to he could have conquered th
Hejaz within one week.

In late August the Ikhwan of the Utaiba tribe and those led b
Khalid bin Luai moved towards Taif, which was garrisoned b
Hashimite troops commanded by the last of Hussain's sons in th
Hejaz, Ali. The judgement of T.E. Lawrence, on the lack of strengt
in his character,[16] had been endorsed by successive British repres
entatives who had made his acquaintance and he now gave the mos
telling proof of their perceptiveness by leaving Taif under cover c
darkness on the night of 4 September with his forces. Taif wa
abandoned and lay defenceless before the Ikhwan.

There now took place an appalling massacre among the civilia
population of the town in which as many as 300 were slaughtered i
a matter of hours. Homes were looted and destroyed, throats wer
cut and even the *qadi* and religious men of Taif, sheltering in th
mosque, were dragged out and murdered.

The extent of the slaying lost nothing in the telling as the new
reached the other cities of the Hejaz. There was widespread pani
and many who could afford it fled across the Red Sea to Port Suda
which saw a large increase in population through the flood of refu
gees in the period until Ibn Saud had completed his conquest of th
Hejaz and brought stability to the area. This process was to la
many months, however.

The first major consequence of the capture of Taif and the ensuin
massacre was that the citizens of Jedda led by Abdullah Alireza, th
city's most prominent merchant, consulted together and agreed t
form a deputation to wait on Hussain bin Ali. The delegation wa
received by the King on 3 October 1924 and made its case to him, tha
he should abdicate and hand over to Ali. The hope was that A
would be less obnoxious to Ibn Saud than his father and that
would be possible to arrange for the Nejdi tribesmen to return whenc
they had come with a mixture of inducements and the threat of forc

Surprisingly for such an obstinate old man, Hussain accepted th
proposal for abdication the same evening and within two weeks h
had left the Hejaz for ever, taking with him large quantities of gol
the balance of funds paid to him by the British since he had declare
the Arab Revolt in June 1916.

The British attitude to Hussain had been hardening throughout he period since it had become apparent that their protégé was not nly objecting in the strongest terms to the postwar settlement – and 1 particular to the plans for a national home for the Jews in Palestine but that he was now become a fallen idol, not even able to keep the espect of his sons ruling in Iraq and Transjordan. As early as June 922 a senior British official dealing with Gulf and Peninsular mat- ers wrote that 'the feeling is growing that it would be a good thing [Ibn Saud did establish himself in Mecca.'[17]

Now that Ibn Saud was on the verge of taking over Mecca it was lear that the British were not going to send gunboats to protect Iussain bin Ali. The Ikhwan were able to enter Mecca without esistance on 16 October 1924 to find a town largely deserted since 1any of its inhabitants had fled. Almost one month later Ibn Saud 1ade his departure from Riyadh, for almost the last time on camel- ack. The journey to Mecca took 23 nights, in the course of which Ibn aud found relaxation in listening to the Koranic recitals of Sheikh bdullah bin Ahmad Ujairy. When word came to him that he could ely on the neutrality of the powers,[18] he gave heartfelt thanks with pecial prayers to God, for now the results of the campaign could be retold.

Hussain bin Ali, in his indignation over Palestine, had left himself efenceless as he had refused to join the League of Nations because f the Mandates policy. There could therefore be no use in appealing Geneva. The Islamic countries had no urge and no mechanism to ome to his assistance and the only action the British were prepared take was to send a cable to Ibn Saud reminding him of the need to nsure the safety of British pilgrims.

Ibn Saud was completely aware of the overwhelming importance the Muslim world of the performance of the *Hajj* in conditions of afety and stability and himself entered Mecca in early December 924 in the traditional dress of the pilgrim, two seamless lengths of hite material. He made his way on foot to the Great Mosque, roclaiming as he moved along,

'Labbaika! Allaahumma! Labbaika! . . . . . '
'O God! Here am I, come at your call to do your service!'

Although he had taken Mecca without bloodshed and although ere was hardly even the slightest chance that the Saudis could enceforth be removed by force, it was essential that Ibn Saud should

win the approval of the Muslim world for the change of regime and
reassure Muslims that the new custodianship of the Holy Mosque
was a change for the better. He was assisted in this regard by the fact
that the custodianship of Hussain bin Ali had been marked by inse
curity and exploitation of the worst kind. The pilgrims fortunat
enough to arrive at Mecca without suffering the depredations of th
Bedu on the way would certainly fall victim to the extortion of th
Sherif's tax-gatherers. There was also the likelihood of dying on th
Hajj since Hussain would not allow proper medical or quarantin
services. The result had been frequent outbreaks of contagiou
diseases.

Ibn Saud moved discreetly forward and immediately on capturin
Mecca made a proclamation to the Muslim world, asking for repres
entatives to come to the Hejaz to discuss the future of the Hol
Places. This was in line with the statement he had made to Rihar
that he did not plan to establish his rule in Mecca and Medina, whic
indeed may have represented his intentions. He made numbers c
statements to the effect that he was not planning to establis
Wahhabism in every place that his forefathers had reached. This ha
made one writer propose the thesis that a clear distinction can b
made between the foreign policy of Ibn Saud and that of his for
bears on the basis that Ibn Saud realised during his exile in Kuwa
that he must modulate the religious element[19] in the spread of Sauc
influence and must conform with the restrictions imposed by th
dominant influence of the British. It has also been proposed that Ib
Saud calculated that no matter what form of pan-Islamic guardiar
ship might be proposed for the Holy Places the end-result would b
absolute Saudi control over them. For lack of proper documentatio
we shall never know the exact state of mind of Ibn Saud at th
time,[20] as indeed at many other times in his career, with the resu
that it becomes just as feasible to argue that his policy at this an
many other points was to probe forward, testing for response an
reacting in the light of such response.

There can be little doubt, however, of the sincerity of Ibn Saud
view that it was a point of virtue to institute great changes in th
Hejaz and in particular in Mecca. He had particularly strong view
on Mecca and its citizens, which have often been quoted:

'ahl Makka dabash'
The people of Mecca are rubbish!'[21]

He also confided to Rihani that he would never marry a Shia woman nor a woman from Mecca, and he shared the views of most Nejdis that Mecca, the place which above all others should be distinguished by high morals, was in fact a sink of iniquity.

It is noteworthy, however, that Ibn Saud acted with discretion and clemency in the process of cleansing. There was not a wholesale dismissal of the religious establishment but care was taken to ensure that the Nejdi divines and the men of religion of Mecca should reach understanding.

On the international scene there was response to his call only from the Indian Muslim community, from the Indian Caliphate Committee in particular. The Committee sent representatives to Mecca but they achieved little, becoming embroiled in futile efforts to reconcile the Saudis and the Hashimites.

This was a hopeless cause: a trial of arms would decide the matter of relations between Ibn Saud and the last of the Hashimites in the Hejaz, Ali bin Hussain.

Ali was to be besieged in Jedda for fully 12 months[22] since, as always, Ibn Saud preferred to achieve victory without resort to frontal assault if there was the slightest possibility of this.[23] His brother Abdullah bin Abdul-Rahman was put in charge of the siege of Jedda which proceeded by a combination of desultory shelling from the Saudi side and farcical attempts at the use of the Royal Hejazi Air Force to raise the siege. This force was unlikely to achieve any of the aims of the use of air-power since its pilots, White Russian and German mercenaries, were committed almost exclusively to the cause of staying out of danger.[24] Nor were the Hashimite forces sent from Transjordan of the slightest use for two excellent reasons: their armoured cars could not even withstand rifle-fire and they themselves were not paid. The siege was broken if at all only by Ibn Saud who carried on secret negotiations and may have arranged for food to be smuggled in to the beleaguered inhabitants and thus to lay the groundwork for his being accepted by them when eventually the siege was ended.

Ibn Saud also took action in respect of the other main centres while the siege of Jedda went on. He dispatched Ikhwan forces to besiege Medina and its port Yenbu, but with careful instructions to avoid bloodshed, and proceeded to consolidate his position in Mecca. In January 1925 he proclaimed the establishment of a *majlis Shura*, or Consultative Council which thereafter became the instrument

for ruling Mecca during 1925. His policy of providing for th
next year's *Hajj* was farsighted and ultimately an overwhelmin
success.

In February 1925 Ibn Saud proclaimed that in the absence of Jedd
as a port for the pilgrims new *Hajj* terminals would be established a
what were then tiny fishing villages, Lith, Rabigh and Qunfudh
For the *Hajj* that year, although the numbers of pilgrims, mostl
from the Indian sub-continent, were very small, the reports whic
they carried back of thoughtful organisation and security togethe
with lack of extortion, did much to confirm the good standing of Ib
Saud in the world and to dispel the panic effect of the massacre a
Taif.

In the context of international politics it was clear that the Saudi
would triumph in the Hejaz and the main parties to be affected b
the new situation began to take precautionary measures.

Abdullah of Transjordan moved in the summer to take the area c
Maan and Aqaba, thus removing them from the suzerainty of th
Hejaz and therefore from the successor-state, the new Saudi entit
which was to emerge. This question was to become a major issue i
relations between Ibn Saud and the British Government withou
whose approval Abdullah could not have acted. In October 1925 Ib
Saud sat down to negotiate for the first time with Clayton, the Britis
representative who was assisted by George Antonious, the futur
author of *The Arab Awakening*.

For the British it was now clear that Ali was finished and therefor
negotiations must take place with the new regime. Clayton kne
Arabic from his experience in Intelligence in Egypt and the Suda
and had wide experience in the Arab world. He took to Ibn Sau
immediately.

> A fine-looking man – very tall and strongly built . . . he has a clea
> handsome face . . . a striking and commanding figure. His expres
> sion in repose is rather sad . . . but his face lights up attractivel
> when he smiles.

The night of their first meeting Ibn Saud was the generous, consid
erate host as the small group of Arabs and one Englishman sat dow
to 'three or four sheep, roasted whole and stuffed with rice, almond
raisins, etc.' Ibn Saud himself was 'most hospitable, selecting sa
voury morsels and tit-bits' for his guests.

'I should say that he was a strong character but the expansion of his dominions is bringing him up against problems and influences which are new and strange to him and I fear that in his ignorance he may fall into the hands of unscrupulous advisers.

The occasion for this doleful conclusion was that Clayton had for the first time[25] come upon a new phenomenon not only in the Peninsula but probably in the Arab world, that of foreign advisers to the ruler whose background was of strong opposition to the presence of the Western powers in the Arab world.

Detailed negotiations took place not with Ibn Saud but with Hafez Wahba and Yusuf Yassin. The former was an Egyptian who had had to leave Egypt because of his opposition to the British and indeed was a fugitive from justice. He was to become one of Ibn Saud's most trusted and longest-serving advisers and was for many years his ambassador in London. Yusuf Yassin was from the Latakia area of Syria who had fled the French Mandate and was to become the closest of Ibn Saud's domestic confidantes, nearly always by his side and so intimately in touch with Ibn Saud's every thought and action that it was said of him that even if he were in China he would still be able to tell you exactly what Ibn Saud was thinking and doing. The talks at Bahra and Hadda with Clayton were his first direct dealings with the British which would continue for fully 30 years until the climax of the breakdown between the two countries over the Buraimi oasis in 1955.

Clayton fought a rearguard action against Ibn Saud's advisers, trying to maintain Transjordan's control of the north of the Wadi Sirhan where the Ikhwan had been raiding for so long, but eventually gave in. He signed with Ibn Saud the two agreements of Bahra and Hadda which dealt respectively with relations between Nejd and Iraq (and particularly questions of tribal allegiance and boundaries) and Nejd and Transjordan by which Ibn Saud gained recognition of his control of the Wadi Sirhan and agreed to accept, through unwillingly, the *fait accompli* of the loss of Aqaba and the Maan area.

Having settled with the British, Ibn Saud could now proceed to bring to an end the military presence of the Hashimites in the Hejaz. On 5 December Medina surrendered to his son Muhammad, who thus acted on Ibn Saud's direct instructions – to make sure that the Ikhwan did not take too prominent a role. Yenbu surrendered on 21

December but Ali bin Hussain had already announced his with
drawal from the Hejaz.

Jordan, the British Consul on 21 December accompanied Jedd
officials to Ibn Saud's camp where the city was formally surrer
dered. The next day the last Hashimite King of the Hejaz, Ali, saile
for Iraq to join his brother Feisal.

Ibn Saud himself entered Jedda formally on 23 December and o
Christmas Day 1925 it was announced officially that the Nejd–Heja
war was over. Ibn Saud was proclaimed King of the Hejaz an
Sultan of Nejd and its Dependencies on 8 January 1926, when h
received the allegiance of the notables of the Hejaz, following noor
day prayers.

And so it came about that Ibn Saud extended his rule to the wes
coast of the Peninsula, almost exactly 24 years after the successft
commando raid on Riyadh. Within the next three months he was t
receive international recognition, firstly from the Soviet Union, the
from Britain, France and the Netherlands, the main powers wit
large Muslim communities under their protection. Domestically
however, Ibn Saud was just entering on the most dangerous four
year period of his reign.

Even as he entered Mecca, events were taking place on the borde
with Iraq which demonstrated the fragility of the system of goverr
ment. On Christmas Day 1924 the young Lieutenant Glubb in hi
capacity as 'SSO Ikhwan Defence' was so alarmed at the threat fror
the Mutair tribesmen to the shepherd tribes in the border region tha
he gave up his holiday-entitlement to survey the situation.[26] He rod
far into the night with his companions in dread of the slaughte
which he knew the Ikhwan were capable of committing. Soon afte
dawn his worst fears were realised as his little party came over a hi
and surveyed the desert below them: 'A whole shepherd natio
seemed to be moving northwards, the entire face of the desert bein
covered as if by swarms of ants.' 'Oh Allah! Oh Muhammad! Oh Al
Oh Allah protect us.' The pathetic cries of the shepherds and thei
families rose as Glubb and his companions strained their eyes to spc
their attackers. Soon they could make out the Ikhwan closing on th
shepherds and as bullets flew all around them Glubb saw that ther
was nothing he could do except to summon help from the Royal Ai
Force. It was two days before Glubb had the satisfaction of seeing th
Ikhwan attacked by aircraft but by then they had scattered widel
and were able to make their way across the frontier with their booty

This episode in itself sums up the problems which were to assail bn Saud until 1930, for British armed force had now been brought nto the question of defending the borders drawn by Sir Percy Cox at Jjair in 1922.

Although Glubb himself suffered agonies as he saw the peaceful ribesmen whom he loved being murdered and robbed, and ılthough he fumed at how little understanding he found among the ase-wallahs whom he was urging to action against the Ikhwan, it is oossible that action would have been taken sooner or later whether Glubb had been there or not.

The Ikhwan became a force out of control once the Hejaz had been aken. After Ibn Saud had been proclaimed King of the Hejaz and iultan of Nejd and the Dependencies in early 1926 it soon became lear to the Ikhwan that they were not to be rewarded for their war ffort as they imagined they should be. Ibn Saud made it clear that 10 Ikhwan leader was to be governor of any Hejaz city, thereby nfuriating the main tribal leaders, especially Ibn Bijad of the Utaiba ribe who had hoped to become Governor of Mecca and bin Duwish vho had similar ambitions for Medina.

As they made their way back to Nejd, the Ikhwan were an in-creasingly angry and dissident force and raids across the frontiers ncreased. What made these raids so dangerous for Ibn Saud was hat in 1927 and 1928 they met determined action from the Royal Air Force, even to the extent of raids in hot pursuit into Nejd. ıbn iaud had to take a stand now in defence of his subjects as they vere being attacked on their own territory. Negotiations were re-umed with the British in 1928 and Clayton had to return to the Hejaz to attempt to deal with the situation. In their negotiations n May 1928 Ibn Saud pleaded eloquently against the attacks from he air on his subjects. He made the case which they urged upon him or resisting the building of forts designed to limit their freedom to aid but there could have been little doubt in Ibn Saud's mind that he Ikhwan were exposing his new regime to collapse and were apable of presenting an image to the world of unrestrained avagery.

Clayton was accompanied to Jedda for the negotiations by Glubb vho now met Ibn Saud for the first time.

The king's frank and open manner and princely hospitality im-ressed him enormously but, as was the case apparently with all British officials who encountered them and wrote their memoirs, a

much less favourable impression was created by the King's counsel-
lors. The Egyptians, Syrians and Palestinians around the King struck
Glubb as being excessively legalistic, a comment which may be
compared to Ibn Saud's view of the proceedings.

Glubb relates the end of the negotiations.

> Yesterday we again met Ibn Saud. His manner was much changed
> since our first meetings and he seemed depressed and bitter. To
> Clayton he said,
>
> 'When the English first came to Iraq I congratulated my people.
> They were surprised and asked me why. I had always abused the
> Turks as unbelievers, they said, yet here were people who were
> even worse because they were not Muslims at all. I told them the
> English were honest and my friends. Now I must admit that we
> have despaired of the English and their hair-splitting.'[27]

The British delegation left without any great progress having been
made but with Glubb convinced that Ibn Saud could no longer
guarantee control over the Ikhwan.

Glubb also ran a professional soldier's eye over Ibn Saud's security arrangements and though he was scathing about the tendency
of the guards to wear rather gorgeous uniforms he could not help
admiring the thoroughness of the searching of the building to which
the King was due to come, even down to ascertaining where Ibn
Saud was to sit.

Even in the heart of the Holy Places, Ibn Saud had direct personal
experience of the Ikhwan problem as early as the pilgrimage season
of 1926. This was the first *Hajj* attended by Muslims from all over the
world but in the midst of the ceremonies there was bloodshed caused
by the attitude of the Ikhwan.

The problem arose over the traditional ceremonies relating to the
Kaaba, the centre of the *hajj* rites. The covering of the Kaaba, called
the Kiswa, a richly-decorated brocade drape in black and gold, was
changed every year and by long tradition the covering, made in
Egypt, was brought with great ceremony and fanfare by the Egyptian pilgrims' procession, with an armed escort and accompanying
band. As the *kiswa* was brought through the throngs of pilgrims in
Mecca, borne aloft on the *mahmal* a commotion arose as the assembled Ikhwan voiced their disapproval of the intrusion of music.
Stones were thrown at the procession, the escort replied with fire-
arms·and no less than forty pilgrims were killed before Ibn Saud

himself intervened to end the bloodshed. One consequence of this spilling of blood at the Kaaba was that diplomatic relations were broken off with Egypt for ten years.

Ibn Saud returned from the Hejaz to Riyadh after the *hajj* of 1926 and it is significant that he returned by car. It was to be another nine years before camels for the royal retinue were abandoned but the use of motor cars was to be one of the most important elements in Ibn Saud's ensuring his survival against the Ikhwan.

In October 1926 the leaders of the three tribes which were to represent the great rebellion against Ibn Saud had met at Artawiya to enumerate their complaints against him. He had sent his sons to lands where infidels were dominant, namely Egypt which Saud had visited and England, which Feisal visited once again in 1926 with Ibn Saud's adviser on foreign affairs, Abdullah Damluji. Ibn Saud was guilty of using innovations of the devil and witchcraft, namely cars, telegraph and telephone. He was allowing tribes from Transjordan and Iraq to graze in Muslim territory, that is, in the grazing lands of the Ikhwan, and he was being remiss in his Islamic duties in not enforcing the doctrines of the Sheikh among the Shia of Hasa.

Ibn Saud's response was to convene in January 1927 a conference at Riyadh of Ikhwan leaders of Ulema, which was attended by the main figures with the exception of bin Bijad of the Utaiba, who declared a boycott. Some of the Ikhwan complaints were addressed directly, such as forbidding the Egyptians to enter the Hejaz with the *mahmal* or an armed escort, and arranging for the Shia to receive special teaching by Wahhabi missionaries but, in effect, Ibn Saud was postponing final confrontation with the dissidents.

There were international matters to be cleared up and the decisive step was taken in May 1927 when the Treaty of Jedda was signed with Britain. This gave Ibn Saud confirmation of the contents of the treaties of Bahra and Hadda but above all gave explicit recognition to his status as a totally independent and sovereign ruler and annulled the impact of his treaty of protection with Britain of December 1915.

Later in 1927, however, the British thrust upon Ibn Saud the issue of the need to restrain the Ikhwan by their interpretation of another treaty, that of the Protocols of Ujair from December 1922. By the terms of Article 3,[28]

The two Governments mutually agree not to use the watering places and wells situated in the vicinity of the border for any

military purpose, such as building forts on them and not to con
centrate troops in their vicinity.

In September 1927 work began on a police fort at Busaiya wells
115 km within the Iraqi border. By the British interpretation of both
the English and Arabic texts such action was perfectly legitimate, bu
for the Ikhwan this was intolerable provocation. On 5 November
1927 the Mutair, led by Feisal bin Duwish, attacked the fort under
construction and massacred everyone there, mutilating the corpses
in particularly loathsome ways as if to draw their gesture to Ibn
Saud's attention as a warning to him as well as to the British and the
Iraqis. The Ikhwan also caused panic in Kuwait Town by a raid on
Kuwaiti territory.

The developments on the border with Iraq and Kuwait represen
the culmination of a number of separate issues: Saudi–Hashimit
rivalry, the clash of the mandate system with existing native institu
tions such as tribal rights, and, most pressing of all, the growth o
dissension within Nejd which was based on the growing disenchant
ment of the Ikhwan with Ibn Saud.

It should be emphasised that not all of the Ikhwan were to take
part in the revolt against Ibn Saud, which was to come to an end in
January 1930, but even those of the Ikhwan who did not resort to
armed revolt expressed their dissatisfaction with many of the pol
icies of Ibn Saud. The involvement with a Christian power – the
'*Ingleez* – was a highly suspect relationship to many Nejdis, as Philby
had found in 1918, and in 1922, even during the negotiations at Ujair
as we have seen, Abdullah Gosaibi had warned Ibn Saud not to put
his neck in the British noose. That the *Ingleez* had proceeded to
maintain the family in Transjordan and Iraq which they, the Ikhwan
had thrown out of the Hejaz was proof of their duplicity. And that
they were now restricting the freedom of the tribes to have access to
wells was final proof that there was no end to British manoeuvring
to ensnare the Arabs. And these were the people that Ibn Saud was
relying on, in bringing in new and devilish devices such as the
telephone, the motor car and wireless transmission. Throughout
1927 and 1928 Ibn Saud had to face frankly-expressed opposition to
almost all of the changes which were being introduced, even though
he was able to control the final campaign in the Asir region in 1926
through a wireless station built by Marconi at Qunfidha.

Ibn Saud was by frequent protests made aware of the opposition
to even the simplest elements of modernisation: in 1926 there were

probably only a dozen or so cars in the country but the mentality was everywhere prevalent which many years later led to the burning of the first lorry to be seen in Hauta.[29]

By 1928 Ibn Saud was compelled to take note of, and respond to, the vocal protests of the unreconstructed Ikhwan. He summoned a conference of the tribal elders in Riyadh in November 1928 to which about 800 of the Ikhwan leaders, the Ulema, and leaders of the settlements came. Ibn Saud invited them specifically to present their grievances and over several days he listened to them and debated with them.

Careful planning had gone into the preparations for the conferences in terms of the logistics of catering and seating for 800 people, for it was clear to Ibn Saud that this was a crucial meeting. The fact that the main Ikhwan leaders – bin Duwish, of the Mutair, bin Bijad of the Utaiba and Hithlain of the Ajman – had boycotted the meeting made it clear that in one way or another the conference must be a turning-point in Ibn Saud's handling of relations with the Ikhwan.

His strategy was of a sensational nature since he proceeded to offer to abdicate, to free his subjects from their oath of allegiance to him and to allow them to choose whomsoever they wished from his family to succeed him. The response of those present is described by Zirikli as follows:

The Ikhwan shouted out,
    We are innocent before God of what Duwish has done . . . . We have boycotted both him and those who are with him . . . . We are ready to attack him and to punish him . . . . Abdul-Aziz, we pledge our allegiance to you in obedience. We will fight against those whom you wish us to fight on both your right and your left . . . . Even if you drove us to the sea we would plunge in . . . . We pledge our allegiance to you, to fight against those who oppose you and to swear enmity to your enemies . . . . We shall stand with you so long as you uphold the Holy Law among us.[30]

Possibly the most important result of the conference was that it meant the rejection of the claim of the Ikhwan that they could proclaim Holy War, *jihad*, without the permission of the Imam, that is to say ibn Saud.

Ibn Saud had now fully inherited the title of Imam since his father had died in June 1928 in Riyadh while Ibn Saud was in Mecca. When the news was brought to him the scene was observed by a remark-

able man, a Polish Jew and former foreign correspondent, who had
become a Muslim and was to become not only a chronicler of Ibn
Saud's life but the ambassador of Pakistan to the United Nations
Muhammad Asad wrote that he would 'never forget the
uncomprehending stare with which he looked for several seconds at
the messenger and the despair which slowly and visibly engulfed
the features that were normally so serene and composed.'

He looked on as Ibn Saud

jumped up with a terrible roar,
'My father is dead!'
and, with great strides, ran out of the room, his abaya trailing on
the ground behind him . . . . he bounded up the stairway past the
awe-struck faces of his men at arms, not knowing himself where
he was going or why, shouting, shouting,
'My father is dead! My father is dead!'

That Ibn Saud had a deep respect for his father has often been
related by observers. We have the incredulous description of an
experienced observer, the Dutch consul in Jedda in 1926, who was
present when Abdul-Rahman arrived there after Ibn Saud had taken
its surrender. Van der Meulen looked on as the conqueror of the
Hejaz knelt in the dust beside his father's horse and witnessed the
old man ease himself down on to Ibn Saud's shoulder before step-
ping on to the ground. When Ibn Saud returned to Riyadh he would
always send ahead to ask permission of his father to enter the Saudi
capital. And, as Muhammad Asad relates, he had such humility
towards his father that he would refuse to enter a room in the palace
if he knew that Abdul-Rahman was on the floor below.

'For how can I allow myself to walk over my father's head?'
The shock of his father's death was so great that, for two days
afterwards, he refused to see anyone or to take food and drink but
spent day and night in prayer.

Even more striking is the fact, related by Zirikli, that Ibn Saud
would visit his father's grave frequently in Riyadh since, by Wahhabi
custom, graves were not marked in any way, even by the simplest
headstone.

Ibn Saud had always consulted his father on all important matters
and he was now deprived of that possibility in facing the crisis

which was developing with the Ikhwan. Immediately after the Riyadh conference of November 1928 the issue of Ibn Saud's own position was thrown up in the most brutal way when the Ikhwan for the first time attacked Nejdis.

In December 1928 a group of the Utaiba attacked defenceless camel traders from the Qassim area, massacred them all and took away their camels as booty. This was the final challenge, for in attacking Ibn Saud's subjects they were striking at the very basis of the Saudi state and of law and order themselves. The time for negotiation had now ended.

FAMILY LIFE

In this period Ibn Saud married no wives who bore him children who survived. It should be recalled that until the end of Ibn Saud's life there was an extremely high infant mortality rate in Nejd: in 1918 Philby estimated it at 75–80 per cent.[31]

We have no reason to think that Ibn Saud slackened off in his policy of marrying into the tribes and keeping his full complement of wives.

The following sons were born in this period:

1. Abdul-Muhsin, the last son of Ibn Saud born to Jawhara, the widow of his brother, Saad.

2. Mish'al, who succeeded his brother Mansour as Minister of Defence in 1951, on Mansour's death.

3. Sultan, who has been Minister of Defence since 1962.

4. Mit'ab, born 1928.

From this period also we can note increasing numbers of not only Ibn Saud's sons but of his grandsons. The future Kings Saud and Feisal had sons and daughters born in the 1920s.

6

Ibn Saud at Fifty

I have conquered my Kingdom with my own sword and by m
own efforts; let my sons exert *their* own efforts after me.

> Ibn Saud, quoted in M. Asad, *The Road to Mecca*
> London, 1954, p. 17

He who obeys God has no difficulty in exacting obedience t
himself.

> Ibn Saud, quoted in D. van der Meulen, *Wells of Ibn Saud*
> London, 1957, p. 6

Go into battle sure of victory from God. Have no doubt of hi
sustenance and support.

> Ibn Saud, quoted in K. Zirikli, *Arabia in the time o*
> *King Abdul-Aziz*, 4 vols (Arabic) Beirut, 1970, p. 98

Ibn Saud 'is very conscientious in the fulfilment of his religiou
duties but the fanaticism of the first representatives of the Wahhabi
is foreign to his nature.'

> *Encyclopedia Britannica*, 14th edn, *Nejd*, p. 30

The year of the death of Ibn Saud's father may be taken as a conven
ient point to reflect on the character, achievement and prospects o
our subject, the more so since at this time 25 years had passed sinc
he had become the effective leader of the Al Saud and another 2!
years would pass before his death.

On the assumption that he was born around 1876, he had jus
passed his fiftieth birthday, a significant date in the life of anyone
though one which probably had little significance for Ibn Saud sinc
he would have calculated his age, if at all, in the Islamic calendar. H
would, however, have had much occasion in precisely this perio
around 1926 to 1928 to ponder on his position as a ruler since by 192!
he had passed through what in one respect could be regarded as th
final phase of establishing his kingdom: he had just made a treaty

with Britain whereby the total independence of his dominions was recognised. He could ponder on the significance of changes in this particular relationship since at the beginning of the 25-year period the British had thought fit to ignore the approach of the Al Saud aimed at achieving a protectorate status while now British power was much exercised to prevent incursions from Nejd and the Hejaz into Hashimite territories which had now become British mandates.

Ibn Saud could reflect also on the transient nature of power, since he had witnessed the demise of the German, Austro-Hungarian and Russian Empires and had been party to the collapse of the Ottoman Empire. ('Were the millions of Abdul-Hamid of use to him?,' he was quoted as asking.)[1] The irony would not have escaped him that the first country to recognise the new Kingdom of the Hejaz-Nejd in 1927 was the godless, communistic regime of Soviet Russia. As we have seen on a number of occasions, Ibn Saud always had a fine sense of the overwhelming importance of the application of the force of money and weapons at the right time. The success of the Bolshevik coup in achieving the termination of a great empire would not have been lost on him, as on many other rulers and politicians. He had preoccupations of a similar kind because of the turbulence in his own dominions caused by instability on his borders and the discontent of several of the tribes. The great trial of strength with the Ikhwan was yet to come and 1928 was the most decisive year in producing a frank challenge to his rule by the three major dissident tribal leaders, the chieftains of the Mutair, the Utaiba and the Ajman.

In none of the frontier areas was there stability. There was continuous raiding across the border with Iraq. With Kuwait there were longstanding differences, embodied at present in a Saudi blockade of trade with Kuwait. The borders with Qatar and Abu Dhabi could hardly have been less defined and would present major difficulties with both the British and the local rulers until the day of Ibn Saud's death. With Oman there was a potentially volatile relationship since the interior of Oman was itself unstable while the Saudis had historic recollections of extending their influence well towards Muscat itself. In the south-west of Ibn Saud's domains there was continuous instability both in the Asir province and on the border with Yemen itself.

Ibn Saud could look back with satisfaction to having defeated the Turks in Central and Eastern Arabia, to having expelled the Hashimites from the Hejaz and to having overcome the alternative seat of power, that of the Al Rashid in Hail, but only in the case of the Turks could he feel totally secure from irredentist ambitions. The

Hashimites made no secret of their enmity until the day of Ibn Saud's death and the Rashidis of Hail, for all the magnanimity of the King, could not be assumed to have abandoned all ambition: those members of the family still alive would be kept as honoured guest and always close to Ibn Saud.

He had become the most powerful ruler of the Peninsula but i was far from being a foregone conclusion that the Kingdom of the Hejaz–Nejd would be the beneficiary of 'manifest destiny,' extend ing from sea to shining sea and emerging triumphant as 'the King dom.' In addition to the internal problems and external pressures which Ibn Saud faced, there was the seemingly eternal problem of the lack of resources, financial and natural, of his expanded domains.

The wonder is that Ibn Saud, faced with such a range of problems could be as relaxed and as impressive as he was frequently described at this time. His deep religious faith explains a great deal of his apparent imperturbability and there can be little point in querying as some writers have done, the nature of his belief and the relation ship between faith and patience. It seems to one observer that the evidence is overwhelming that Ibn Saud never wavered throughou his life in the simplicity of his views that Islam was the final revela tion of God to mankind, that the happiest state for any human being was to be a true Muslim, that God wished for the triumph of Islam and that anyone supported by God would not be defeated. (Even when agreeing to sign the oil concession with the Americans in 193: he was to say to his Finance Minister, 'Put your faith in God, and sign.') Ibn Saud took genuine pleasure in hearing the Koran continu ously recited, in reading and having read-out collections of Hadith and the life of The Prophet, and was himself always ready, as Amin Rihani noted, to launch into a homily on religious matters. Until almost the last days of his life he would, in his *majlis*, announce a religious subject for discussion and then lead and 'chair' the discus sion. It was the simplicity and spontaneity of his religious beliefs which would impress all observers all his life, even Presiden Roosevelt, when he met him in 1945. The President must have found it a novel approach to have the products of Hollywood questioned fundamentally as being unacceptable because they would divert the King's subjects from their religious observances.

It is in no way to question Ibn Saud's sincere religious nature to point out that he was still a human being. By 1928 he had lived 25 years of tension and of frequent combat in which he had personally taken part: the last occasion on which he was to take the field in person was still two years into the future. It would be astonishing if the evidence of this continuous tension were not to be seen in his behaviour from time to time.

Amin Rihani gave some of the most vivid account of Ibn Saud's tendency to fall into a rage so violent that the observer felt revulsion. 'His mouth becomes like iron, the lips shrunk and taut, white and trembling. . . . All the charm of his features gives way to a mordant, savage expression.'[2] Rihani goes on to say that he was appalled to see Ibn Saud in such a fit of rage but that the storm would always pass quickly.

The rage might pass quickly but while it lasted it was something quite exceptional, since it might even extend to Ibn Saud physically maltreating the object of his rage. Philby, in his first encounter with Ibn Saud in 1918, was amazed to see him ferociously beat Fahd, the son of his most trusted governor, bin Jiluwi for having struck one of his own guards.[3] Zirikli, the chronicler of Ibn Saud's life in four volumes, did not see it as part of his role to gloss over Ibn Saud's fits of rage and his beatings of servants but emphasises that such beatings would be frequently followed by gifts.[4]

It is not to invite charges of blasphemy to mention in a human context that The Ninety-nine Most Beautiful Names of God[5] which Muslims revere and adopt as personal names can be divided into those qualities which inspire awe and those which inspire affection. Ibn Saud might usefully be viewed under the two headings of awe and affection.

Undoubtedly the most awesome quality of Ibn Saud was his reputation for imposing his rule with the ultimate sanction. Bin Jiluwi might be given the credit for imposing law and order in the east[6] by striking examples of severity but it was the will of Ibn Saud which bin Jiluwi was imposing. He never had the slightest doubt of the deterrent effect of the most severe, indeed spectacularly harsh, punishment. His view was expressed in a declaration which Rihani heard him make in 1922 to a group of Ikhwan. 'Do not forget,' he exclaimed, 'that there is not one among you whose father, or brother or cousin we have not slain. Aye, *billah*, it was by this sword that we have conquered you!'[7]

Doctor Dame of the American medical mission from Bahrain once had occasion to minister to a man found in a dead faint after witnessing a beheading for the first time in Riyadh. The beheading took place when a man was being led out, as he thought, for a flogging to which a court had sentenced him. He was unaware that the King had overruled the court and had ordered his head to be struck off.[8]

It was without question the knowledge of Ibn Saud's ruthlessness in inflicting punishment which persuaded so many of his opponents to accept the smile and handshake of reconciliation which he offered to them. Such was the case with dissident members of the Al Saud family, with many tribal leaders, with the Al Rashid in the period before 1928 while those of the Ikhwan who did not appreciate his readiness to be utterly merciless were to experience brutal repression and a refusal to take prisoners.

By the year 1928 Ibn Saud had had time to impose on the Hejaz the regime of law and order and strict deterrence to wrong-doing which Nejd and Hasa had known for many years. His biographer and interpreter, Muhammad Almana, gives many examples of the imposition of the new regime on the Hejaz which had been, even in the days of the Hashimites' greatest strength, peculiarly vulnerable to the depredations of the Bedu against pilgrims and ordinary travellers. One example among many may suffice.

The forces of law and order at the disposal of the Saudi Amir of Medina eventually captured a notorious brigand who had for years robbed pilgrims openly. The man had his legs bound together, he was handcuffed and was then thrown into a thorn bush where he was left to die slowly in the sun. The decomposing body was then left at the side of the road.[9] It was in this way that Ibn Saud was able to give pilgrims to the Holy Places at last the feeling of complete security.

Ibn Saud's bravery and endurance of hardship were qualities not invented by image-makers but were clearly shown in many instances of hand-to-hand combat in the years of his many campaigns before 1930. Questions of image and motivation are, curiously enough, made difficult to answer because of the recorded comments of Ibn Saud himself.

Amin Rihani records him as saying that he flung himself into the attempt to capture Riyadh in 1902 because of the grief he felt at the loss of his first wife.[10] 'So I left Kuwait and came to Nejd to seek solace in distance and oblivion.'

Ibn Saud was distinguished throughout his life by the pleasure he found in the company of those women who had won his affections whether wives, concubines or sisters or other relatives and it is probably in this context that his remark to Rihani is best understood. The need to forget grief may well have been a contributing factor (although Ibn Saud was wrong in speaking of his first wife: it was his second wife with whom he had two years of happy marriage before she died). It seems clear, however, that the dominant motive in Ibn Saud's leading the assault which led to the recapture of Riyadh was the need to restore the patrimony of the Al Saud. 'No, by God! What was the right of our forebears is our right. And if we cannot get it by friendly means we will get it by the sword.'[11]

Having resolved that the power of his own right arm and his skill as a leader must resolve the issue of claiming the rights of the Al Saud, Ibn Saud displayed remarkable courage on many occasions. At his death the evidence of the many wounds he had suffered was still to be found and, although the chroniclers differ in the exact tally of the wound-marks, he was indeed wounded on many occasions from as early as 1902 and, on occasion, severely. We have already encountered the story of the famous occasion during the First World War when Ibn Saud, having been wounded in the stomach, had to demonstrate to his warriors that he was still fit and able to command and therefore took a bride in the heat of the battle. His physician, Rashad Pharaon, further testified to the courage and hardiness of Ibn Saud in telling the story of how he removed two spent machine-gun bullets from the lower abdomen. As the doctor prepared the anaesthetic Ibn Saud asked what he was doing and when he was told he laughed and, taking the scalpel himself, cut away the flesh above the bullets so that Pharaon could remove them.[12]

Ibn Saud freely acknowledged, however, that a great role in his life was played by *Hazz*, a word which may be loosely translated as 'luck' but which had implications of 'good fortune provided by the Almighty' and which is recognised by those who do not have it as being attached, always, to its fortunate possessor.

The greatest good fortune in the material sense was to be the happy coincidence that his realms lay above the world's greatest petroleum reserves but during the years of Ibn Saud's campaigns his *Hazz* was to be shown in a number of remarkable episodes,[13] which became widely-known and lost nothing in the retelling.

The greatest example of all was his success in capturing Riyadh from the Al Rashid in 1902. Whatever the truth about the details of the final capture it is clear that, for all the careful planning and watchfulness, in the final bold stroke a part was played by good fortune. It is quite possible that the whole enterprise might have failed had Ibn Saud been more severely wounded or indeed killed or if the gate to the fortress had not been forced.

Quite apart from Ibn Saud's escaping fatal injury in his many campaigns in the period before the First World War he enjoyed good fortune in one particular assault on a fortified place when he was fighting against his cousins in 1912. His foot, instead of entering his stirrup, became entangled in his robe with the result that his horse bolted towards the enemy, whereupon his soldiers, emboldened by his audacity, surged forward behind him and captured the stronghold. Following this triumph the word soon spread that 'Abdul-Aziz won a victory because of the mistake made by his mare.'

In his campaign against the Hashimites in 1919 Ibn Saud was the gainer from the incident when the future King of Jordan, Abdullah bin Hussain, was unwise enough to slap across the face the future Ikhwan leader, Khalid bin Luai. Again an incident became part of the legend of Ibn Saud's *Hazz* and people spoke of a throne being lost because of a smack across the face.

Towards the end of the siege of Jedda in 1925 Ibn Saud was faced with the restiveness of his troops because of the lack of supplies, especially food. With no means of making good the deficiency Ibn Saud addressed his troops: 'Those of you who wish to depart, may do so. As for myself, I stay. God will relieve this situation.'

At precisely that moment, according to legend, a merchant of Rabigh came into view leading 20 camel-loads of food. This man's brother had been killed by Ibn Saud's enemy, Hussain bin Ali. The food crisis was resolved.

A similar tale is told of another ultimatum to the tribal leaders during the siege of Jedda. In the final days, the leaders wanted to end the siege by assault but Ibn Saud replied that there was to be no violence and they were free either to go or to stay and maintain the siege. Again there was a *deus ex machina* dénouement, as the news came in at that moment that King Ali bin Hussain had at last surrendered.

The long siege in the Hejaz produced numbers of other similar incidents which may or not be true but which served to reinforce the legend of Ibn Saud's good fortune. Several tales are told of Ibn Saud's escape from air-attack[14] when the Hashimites made use of their military aircraft and mercenary pilots.

Well might Ibn Saud say, 'If God sends my children the same luck as he has sent me, they will be able to rule the whole Arab world.'[15]

Among the best-known of Ibn Saud's qualities inspiring affection was his generosity. In this context truth would seem clearly to be stranger than fiction since he was always given to the bold, generous gesture which would resound throughout his domains, even when his resources were at their lowest. The element of calculating in his giving cannot be denied since he spoke often of the need to give to the Bedu in times of plenty so that they would give him their all in time of need. Moreover Ibn Saud himself laid down the criteria for grades of presents to be made to his guests. Nonetheless he evidently took simple pleasure in the act of giving throughout his life.

Ibn Saud's simplicity of conduct and his lack of pretentiousness impressed all who met him, from the highest to the lowest. His food was always of the simplest and he always ate in moderation, according to an almost totally unvarying menu. For breakfast he would take bread, honey and curdled milk, while lunch would consist of rice and meat, boiled together, with a little vegetable. His evening meal would be almost identical with lunch with the addition of a dessert. His milk would always be camel's for preference[16] and his preferred water was that of a well in Mecca, used since the days of the Prophet. He drank large quantities of coffee and almost never drank tea.

The simplicity of Ibn Saud charmed Philby from the moment of their first meeting in 1917 and his many books give countless instances of an unaffected nature. Perhaps one of the most charming episodes comes from 1918 when Philby was present at what might be described as a royal garden party[17] in Riyadh, were it not that the occasion was a mange-treating session for camels. Food and drink were served to the workers while Ibn Saud and his family moved among them, Ibn Saud being easily the most relaxed and gracious person there.

Ibn Saud could not, however, have achieved supremacy and independence by charm, simplicity and generosity. He had a most unusual range of qualities which equipped him to perform the many tasks which enabled him to become sole ruler after possessing only a foothold in Riyadh with only meagre resources and support.

Above all he had great intelligence, native shrewdness and the ability to think widely and with great speed. Ibn Saud always had an enquiring mind and with very little formal education gave evidence of very wide knowledge and varied interests. We have already seen many instances of how he had impressed in this way the foreigners who had made his acquaintance, whether Gertrude Bell, Percy Cox, Cheesman or Philby. Although convinced that the Koran contained all knowledge, he was very far indeed from the mentality of that member of the Ikhwan who boasted of two things he had never done, to smoke a cigarette and to read a newspaper. Ibn Saud was always eager for the latest news and used the appropriate means to acquire it, human messengers and the foreign press before the First World War and radio and Reuters after the war, to supplement the other means.

That he thought widely we have seen in his actions in the area of world politics. From 1903 he was in touch with not only the British but with the Russians while his actions in Central Arabia in relation to the Turks were always based on a shrewd calculation of the limits of their ability to retaliate because of difficulties throughout the Empire. His attack on the Hasa region was timed for maximum effect to coincide with Turkish difficulties in the Balkans and North Africa.

Apart from great ability in strategic thinking Ibn Saud had remarkable skill and intuition at the tactical level. In the pre-automobile age, when the deciding factor was the speed of the fastest camel, Ibn Saud was uniquely qualified to make optimum use of all factors of speed, mobility, concentration of force, economy of effort, planning and communications. His ability to survive on little sleep and food, his restless energy, quick thinking and resolute action, his ability to motivate his followers and to use a combination of force and what might be called psychological warfare – all of this constituted a package of qualities and advantages which were never found in his opponents in the period of Ibn Saud's military campaigns.

Philby was to complain in later years that it seemed that the King had become so used to a routine of sudden action and swift departures that the Court was constantly irritated by his sudden whims to go hunting which involved orders out of the blue to pack up at a moment's notice. It seems reasonable to read into Philby's complaints annoyance at frustration of his own inclination to pursue his interests undisturbed. Two factors should be mentioned to correct the picture.

Sudden changes of plan would not surprise anyone familiar with the life of the Bedu. Furthermore, what is truly distinctive of Ibn Saud is not the sudden changes of plan but the way in which he settled on a routine for getting through business and managed to maintain this routine wherever the court was, whether in Riyadh, making to or from the Hejaz (an annual event) or out hunting, which became more attractive when cars became more freely available.

Ibn Saud can in some ways be regarded as a master of time-management, making due allowance for an Arabian approach to the subject being fundamentally different to that of, say, a multinational corporation.

As we shall see later, the routine for Ibn Saud's performing the many roles he had to perform – monarch, tribal leader, military commander, paterfamilias, religious leader, world statesman, welfare state, teacher, foreign minister, finance minister – became established at about the period at which we have paused to take stock of the man. What is striking is the way in which the routine was maintained even when the Court was on the move. It was Ibn Saud who dictated the pattern of keeping to a routine and it was his deep religious feelings which underlay his predisposition to such a routine.

Ibn Saud's daily routine was dictated by the calls to prayer. From the early-morning prayers at about 4.30 a.m. to the final late-evening prayer there were fixed points about which Ibn Saud arranged his many activities, the least important of which was sleep. He would sleep for some four hours after midnight, for another hour after dawn prayers and for about an hour after lunch. The combination of light sleep, healthy diet, deep religious feeling and absorption in his many tasks allowed Ibn Saud at the age of 50 to maintain a level of activity and of leadership which would have been remarkable in one 15 years younger.

Physically Ibn Saud was by no means at his peak,[18] since he had a chronic eye complaint which almost totally impaired vision in the left eye, and had lost some mobility because of knee problems caused by his wounds. However, it is not the case that he wore spectacles all the time and his difficulty in moving seems to have been a condition which came and went. The medical missionaries who visited him in the 1930s paint a picture of one in very good shape indeed, who was subject to spells of being off-colour, especially when in the Hejaz other than in Taif. Glubb Pasha who visited him in 1928 found him in very good form: he was 'a tremendous personality. He would have ended up as Prime Minister in any country in the world.'[19]

The next two years of his life, from 1928 to early 1930, were to be possibly the most dangerous of his reign, when his authority was challenged by revolts of important sections of the Ikhwan which led him, as we saw, to make an offer to abdicate and when his relations with the British, because of the Ikhwan revolt, were at their most delicate.

Ibn Saud was to need to exercise all the skills and experience which he had been accumulating for the last 25 years, in particular as military strategist, tribal leader and diplomat.

7

The Kingdom Established, 1928–32

Saud, I have left my desert, and my sheikhship and sacrificed my wealth in seeking the gifts of God and fighting the infidels.

> Feisal bin Duwish to Saud bin Abdul-Aziz, 6 June 1929, in
> Helms, *The Cohesion of Saudi Arabia*, p. 261

I believe that he was in his heart hostile to all Western influences including that of Great Britain but he knew that British friendship was a condition of his survival.

> Sir A. Ryan, first British Minister to Court of Ibn Saud,
> *Last of the Dragomans*, p. 83

If anyone would offer me a million pounds now he would be welcome to all the concessions he wants in my country.

> Ibn Saud to Philby, 1931 in Philby, *Arabian Days*, p. 291

In November 1928 Ibn Saud had been given the explicit pledge of allegiance of large numbers of leaders of the Ikhwan against Feisal bin Duwish and his allies. He was well aware, however, that there was what might one call the 'Ikhwan multiple': the numbers of the rebel Ikhwan should be multiplied by an indeterminate factor to represent the impetus given to them by their fanaticism. They had in the past defeated larger bodies of troops, as at the battle of Turaba in 1919, and they were masters of the art of achieving and fully exploiting surprise. They frequently exercised, as has been noted, battle-drills such as night-marches and dawn-attacks. They were also totally unafraid of death, especially in combat against other beduin: they had learned to have a healthy respect for aircraft and machine guns and to take cover as appropriate but against other beduin troops they had a blind disregard for the possibility of being killed.

Ibn Saud therefore took all prudent precautions in making ready to confront the rebels. Contact was established with the British in India and requests were made for assistance in the form of arms and ammunition. The result was that in February 1929 Ibn Saud received, by way of the Awazim tribe in the east of the Peninsula, one thousand five hundred serviceable rifles and the appropriate ammunition. The British had apparently decided that the previous instability and raiding were dangerous to all and that the best way of ending such a situation was to enable Ibn Saud to crush the rebel Ikhwan.

By the spring of 1929 there was widespread insecurity in Nejd and beyond. Muhammad Asad, the converted Polish Jew who was in Riyadh at this time, describes the atmosphere:

> Mysterious emissaries rode on fast dromedaries from tribe to tribe. Clandestine meetings of chieftains took place at remote wells. . . . Central and Northern Arabia became the scene of widespread guerrilla warfare; the almost proverbial public security of the country vanished and complete chaos reigned in Nejd; bands of rebel Ikhwan swept across it in all directions, attacking villages and caravans and tribes that had remained loyal to the King.[1]

We can follow some of Ibn Saud's actions and journeys at this time, as the young Muhammad Almana had recently joined his retinue as a clerk and administrator/interpreter, having acquired knowledge of English in India. He later wrote an account of the years 1929 to 1935 which, in spite of many errors probably caused by relying on memory, has many insights into the methods of work and planning of Ibn Saud.[2]

Almana describes how the King made his dispositions, having ensured that he had obtained the necessary arms from the British. He sent letters to the amirs of each town and village requiring them to make for Riyadh with their men under their *jihad* flags and took the important step of absolving the warriors thus recruited from having to observe the Ramadan fast. This was in line with Muslim practice in time of war which even prescribed that it was sinful to continue to fast once the dispensation had been granted. When some of the warriors insisted that they would continue the fast Ibn Saud ordered them to be stoned, in line with the punishment prescribed for such recalcitrance. However, he ordered that the men should be stoned symbolically so that they should be shamed into obedience, not humiliated, let alone killed.

Ibn Saud then proceeded with a large retinue from Riyadh to the Qassim province to ensure that he had control of Buraida. Almana notes that although the bulk of the force was mounted on camels, the King himself was now travelling by car, at least as far as Buraida: thereafter the ground was more suitable for camels than for cars.

In addition to acquiring weapons and cars, Ibn Saud needed intelligence above all, and the process by which he acquired such battle-information as he needed is described, perhaps a little naively, by Almana.

He described the large assemblies the King held for the tribesmen at which he would talk and joke freely among them. 'Each tribesman . . . might give an opinion about the strength and whereabouts of the enemy or the allegiance of a particular tribe or tribal section . . . in this way the King gained a mass of information . . . to obtain an accurate picture of the overall military situation.'

The process was continuous:

> While we travelled (Ibn Saud) continued to speak to as many of the chiefs and tribesmen as he could. This was in order to keep up the continual process of encouragement at which he was so expert, and also to satisfy his own voracious appetite for news.[3]

Almana goes on to describe the preliminaries to the battle of Sibilla in March 1929 and makes it quite clear that Ibn Saud, on this as on so many other occasions, wished to avoid open conflict and tried to get the rebel tribes, the Mutair and the Utaiba, to accept the judgement of the Shari'a court in respect of the acts of murder committed against the camel-traders and others. He describes the tension in the King's camp as messages were exchanged between the loyal and the rebel camps until it was agreed that the leader of the Mutair, Feisal bin Duwish himself, would come unarmed to Ibn Saud's camp and would discuss means of resolving the situation.

Bin Duwish arrived in the morning with a bodyguard of eight men. Almana who had the tent next to the King's tent where the talks were to take place describes the actions taken, familiar to all devotees of films showing negotiations between Mafia chieftains.

> The King's tent had four openings, one at each corner. Two men from Duwish's bodyguard went to each opening; with military precision, they lifted all four tent flaps simultaneously so as to

satisfy themselves that the agreement had been kept or, if it had not, to dispose of any potential assassin.[4]

Ibn Saud and Duwish then talked alone for one hour, after which Duwish came out and told his bodyguards to surrender their arms as a truce had been agreed. He was then invited to lunch with the King as an honoured guest, after which he was treated to a martial display by the tribesmen loyal to Ibn Saud. One particularly fierce loyalist who was eager to have done with the talking and to finish off the rebels rode by, crying out, 'Woe to the enemies of the Shari'a; let them beware of our wrath!'

As the sun went down Ibn Saud and Duwish prayed together and Duwish slept that night in a tent next to that of Ibn Saud. All next day talks went on, with Ibn Saud trying to persuade Duwish to accept the judgement of the Shari'a court. Duwish's answer was,

> I will speak with Ibn Bijad (of the Utaiba) and tomorrow we may return. But I warn you that if we do not come our absence will mean war.

Almana later on heard from the enemy camp of how Duwish reported to his fellow rebels on the atmosphere in the King's camp. The King's army, he said, was full of fat townsmen who would be of no value if it came to a real battle. 'They are about as much use as camel bags without handles!'[5]

Ibn Saud's instinct for security is evident from the extra guards which he posted to guard against surprise attack. When dawn came and no attack had taken place the King prepared for battle. He dressed for combat and ordered in fresh supplies of water to guarantee staying-power for the coming battle and supervised the payment of money to the tribal chieftains and their fighting men: six gold pounds to each chief and three pounds for each warrior.

The King was mounted on his war-horse and when a last attempt to hold talks had failed he called out, 'Trust in God and prepare to fight!'

Ibn Saud then bent down, took up handfuls of sand and hurled these in the direction of the enemy, the traditional gesture among the desert Arabs to announce the beginning of combat, said to have been performed even by the Prophet Muhammad.

The battle itself was over within thirty minutes and was settled by the use of machine-gun fire at the decisive moment when the rebel

Ikhwan were caught out in the open. They suffered a thousand casualties, of whom half were killed, while the loyal troops lost only 200 dead.

In the fighting Duwish disappeared as did the Utaiba leader bin Bijad, and it was only after the battle that Ibn Saud learned that, even though surrender had been indicated by the fact of the Mutair women being placed in Ibn Saud's care, Duwish had taken refuge in the Mutair colony of Artawiya. Ibn Saud made ready to attack Artawiya but was visited by Duwish's son, Abdul-Aziz (normally known by the friendly diminutive form of Azaiyiz) who pleaded with him not to assault the colony. In return he would arrange for his father to be handed over to Ibn Saud.

The King's camp was astonished the next day to find that Duwish was brought in on a stretcher. He had been wounded by a bullet through his generous paunch and Ibn Saud ordered his doctor to tend his wound. He addressed Duwish,

'You are no match for me. I am too powerful. I pardon you. You may go wherever you wish and I will give you whatever you need. But your future actions and behaviour, good or bad, will be judged by me and dealt with accordingly.' When Duwish indicated that he wished to go to Kuwait, Ibn Saud wrote out letters to his own agent in Kuwait to ensure that his requests were met.

The pardon for Duwish was not matched by Ibn Saud's attitude to the Utaiba leader. When bin Bijad eventually came to Ibn Saud, possibly lured by the leniency shown to Duwish, the King had him arrested and sent to Riyadh in chains. He was imprisoned there and did not emerge alive.

The Ikhwan rebellion now seemed to be over, since Ibn Saud's governors had ensured that there were no disturbances in Hasa or in Hail, where there might have been risings by former enemies of Ibn Saud, the Ajman and the Shammar. Ibn Saud now prepared to move to Hail and then to Hejaz for the *Hajj* season but not, as Almana relates, without giving a demonstration of his policy of cementing relationships.

He moved to Buraida and Anaiza to express his gratitude for their solidarity with him and in Anaiza took a bride from a prominent family, the Al-Shibailis of that town.

The King's court then moved north to Hail before proceeding to Mecca for the performance of the *Hajj*, but Ibn Saud was not to stay long in the Hejaz. Word was brought to him in Jedda that the Ikhwan rebellion had broken out again.

In May 1929 the Ajman had decided that the victory of Ibn Saud at Sibilla meant that they had better make terms with the victor. Their chief, Dhaidan bin Hithlain, arranged a meeting with Fahd, the son of Abdullah bin Jiluwi, Ibn Saud's cousin and faithful governor of Hasa, and negotiations began. Before any conclusions could be reached bin Hithlain declined Fahd's invitation to stay the night, saying that if he did not return his men would come for him. Fahd became enraged at these words which he regarded as a threat and ordered bin Hithlain to be put in chains. In spite of bin Hithlain's caution to him that he was acting unwisely Fahd persisted and even gave orders that if the Ajman should come for their chief he was to be slain. Soon after midnight the Ajman duly arrived to the sound of gunfire. Bin Hithlain was dispatched at Fahd's orders but Fahd himself was killed almost immediately since many in his entourage were of the Ajman.

The circumstances of the killing could not have been worse from Ibn Saud's point of view since bin Hithlain was carrying safe conduct papers signed by the King himself as well as by Abdullah bin Jiluwi and his son who had had him killed. To make matters worse, the leader of the Mutair, Duwish, had not only not died from his wounds but after recovering was once more leading his tribe against Ibn Saud. The Utaiba also, even though their major colony, Ghot Ghot, had been razed to the ground and their chieftain imprisoned, had risen against Ibn Saud and since they controlled the territory between the Hejaz and Nejd, Ibn Saud was in effect trapped in the Hejaz.

From this point the situation could have developed into a total catastrophe for Ibn Saud. It is going too far to say, as a biographer of Glubb says, that 'it would now only be a matter of time before Ibn Saud brought the Ikhwan to heel.'[6]

Ibn Saud had first to make his way back through hostile territory to Riyadh and his safe arrival was by no means a foregone conclusion. He would have to make the most careful use of his advantages and resources and avoid falling victim to the manoeuvres of his enemies. Access to water on the route was the first essential, but the Utaiba were able to delay Ibn Saud for days – not by military means, but by the simple device of dropping into the wells a dead man and a dead donkey. Ambushes on the way were an ever-present danger, especially on the mountainous sections of the route. To avoid the danger Ibn Saud ordered a detour of hundreds of kilometres to reach the next oases on the road to Riyadh.

The advantages which Ibn Saud could exploit were his great experience as a leader in war; the money by which he could ensure the loyalty of tribesmen on the route; the weapons and ammunition which he was able to obtain through the British in India; the use of wireless to coordinate his operations and the use of motor vehicles. By the exercise of due caution, Ibn Saud was able at last to reach Riyadh.

Having arrived in the capital, Ibn Saud was still surrounded by enemies. Hasa was in a state of total insecurity because of the revolt of the Ajman and even his most trusted lieutenant, Abdullah bin Jiluwi, was a spent force, having suffered a collapse on hearing of the death of his son Fahd. Nejd itself could not be guaranteed: Riyadh was now 'an island in a sea of rebellion. The city itself was overrun by bedouin tribesmen and no one could be certain where their loyalties lay.'[7]

Ibn Saud moved to try to guarantee his hold over Hasa by sending his son Saud in a motorised convoy to take over from bin Jiluwi but the Ajman laid an ambush for the convoy and took many prisoners. Saud himself, according to Almana, reached safety only because of the success of the first recorded escape in Arabia by custom-built Mercedes. This vehicle Saud had borrowed from his father and in it he made his get-away to Hofuf.

From his base in Hofuf, Saud had to face the combined forces of the Ajman and the Mutair under Duwish himself, who was determined to take over the whole region. There can be little doubt that Duwish was moved by different ambitions from those of the other Ikhwan leaders since there is a great deal of evidence of his plans to establish a separate Ikhwan state in the north-east[8] of the Peninsula for which he attempted to obtain the endorsement of the British and the ruler of Kuwait.[9]

Feisal bin Duwish was defeated in the Hasa region by the Awazim tribe, which had a fierce loyalty to Ibn Saud since he had freed them from the status of being an inferior tribe obliged to pay tribute to more powerful tribes. They had also the advantage of being equipped with ample arms and ammunition from supplies shipped from India. The result was that Duwish was forced to retire from the oases region to the north in the direction of the Kuwait border.

In the height of the summer of 1929 Duwish adopted another tactic by dispatching his son Azaiyiz to raid the northern part of the country at the head of many hundreds of raiders. They harassed all the tribes which were loyal to the King and took huge quantities of booty but their eventual fate was a horrible one.

In order to return to their base in the east of the country, and this in the height of summer, they had to use routes which were easily predictable via the few wells available. At Umm Urdhuma the force remaining to Azaiyiz (after the defection of those who refused to face the inevitable dangers from taking this route) found themselves confronted by loyalist Shammar tribesmen. They had no choice but to make a frontal attack on the wells against defenders in concealed positions. There was enormous slaughter on both sides but the Ikhwan were halted: four hundred and fifty were killed, among them Azaiyiz and two hundred and fifty were taken prisoner, too exhausted to fight on. As the fighting came to an end, the governor of Hail came on the scene, having been summoned to give help. He gave orders for all the prisoners to be beheaded on the spot.

During the great raid carried out by Azaiyiz his father was conducting operations again in Nejd. The resources of the Duwish family were clearly not inconsiderable and it was to the origin of his resources that Ibn Saud addressed himself during that summer while he was in Riyadh.

Muhammad Asad was sent for late one summer night in Riyadh to go to see the King and found himself given a remarkable assignment.[10] He describes Ibn Saud's thinking about the problem of Duwish.

> The Sharifian family hates me. Those sons of Hussain who now rule in Iraq and Transjordan will always hate me, for they cannot forget that I have taken the Hejaz from them. They would like my realm to break up, for then they could return to the Hejaz . . . and their friends, who pretend to be my friends as well, might not dislike it either . . . they wanted to cause me trouble and to push me away from their frontiers.

Muhammad Asad knew enough about the background to territorial arrangements made in the 1920s not to need reminding about suspected plots by the *Ingleez* to carve out an amenable buffer-state in the north of the Peninsula to guarantee land contact between the Mediterranean and the Gulf and possibly even a Haifa–Basra railway.

He goes on to relate the King's careful words on 'those mysterious sources of Duwish's supplies. I have my own suspicions about them;

perhaps even more than suspicions – but I would like thee to find out for thyself all thou canst, *for I may be wrong.'* [11]

We see now, once again, not only Ibn Saud's care for acquiring information but also his sense for broadcasting information. He wants Muhammad Asad to make his way secretly to Kuwait, find out the source of Duwish's guns and money and 'tell the world of the crooked truth behind Duwish's rebellion . . . I think thou will be able to find out the truth.'

If Muhammad Asad's account is to be believed, he duly made his way to Kuwait Town with the help of Sulubba guides who demanded handsome recompense for the risks they were running in territory controlled by Duwish. There he exercised his investigative journalist's skills, knowledge of the area, of Arabic and of Islam to make the necessary enquiry. He established to his own satisfaction a picture of the source of Duwish's guns and money and the network of connections between a dissident Ruwalla leader and the Hashimites, if not with the *Ingleez* themselves.

Ibn Saud used the information provided by Muhammad Asad to protest to the British about the freedom Duwish had to buy arms and ammunition in Kuwait but according to Muhammad Asad he received the answer that Kuwait was sovereign territory, not British territory, and the British Government could not be held responsible.

The issue could only be resolved on the battlefield and the final act of the campaign against Duwish was the battle of Hafr Al-Batin in which loyal Harb tribesmen used the most typical Ikhwan tactics against Duwish himself. They took his force completely by surprise by night and caught them fast asleep. Feisal bin Duwish himself was forced to flee for his life and took refuge in Kuwait.

Ibn Saud now moved northwards, with his sons Muhammad and Khalid commanding motorised columns. A number of savage engagements were fought in which no prisoners were taken: there were several instances of Ikhwan prisoners being machine-gunned and beheaded. [12]

The refugee Ikhwan were now between the forces of Ibn Saud and the armed might of the British, based on both Kuwait and Iraq. After some 10 days of negotiations, agreement was reached on the many questions of compensation for looting and damage by the Ikhwan and losses suffered by the Nejdis through RAF raids as well as of the eventual fate of Feisal bin Duwish. The British at last surrendered Duwish to Ibn Saud once he had placed his womenfolk in the safekeeping of Dickson, the Political Agent. The Ikhwan rebellion was over.

The British now moved very swiftly to resolve a situation whose complexities had become very dangerous. During the final stages of the negotiations between British representatives and Ibn Saud's officials (among whom Yusuf Yassin was yet again the most uncomfortable person for the British) a message was passed to the King, asking if he could agree to meet for the first time in his life Feisal bin Hussain, King of Iraq.

Ibn Saud agreed to this gesture of reconciliation and meetings took place aboard HMS *Lupin* and two other vessels moored in the Gulf off Kuwait. Although amicable words were exchanged and commemorative photographs show two smiling monarchs, there were many moments of tension which threatened to turn the occasion into disaster. The memory of the loss of the Hejaz could evidently not be erased, as could be seen from Feisal's later addressing Ibn Saud in such a way as to avoid naming him 'King of the Hejaz.' It was only after Ibn Saud refused to receive any letters which did not so address him that correspondence was able to proceed.

As a result of this meeting, the first of only two occasions in Ibn Saud's lifetime when he met face-to-face any of the Hashimites, treaties were later signed which gave some substance to the words of reconciliation which the two rulers exchanged. The Treaties of Friendship and Good Neighbourliness established mutual recognition of Iraq and Hejaz–Nejd and formalisation of diplomatic representation, outlawed tribal raiding, established extradition procedures and a Permanent Frontier Commission and made provision for reparations for past raids. There were to be many other issues of contention between Bagdad and Riyadh in future years but the significance of the meeting of Ibn Saud with Feisal on board ship was that Ibn Saud by his realism and magnanimity gave the indication required that the two countries could deal with each other at arm's-length and not as sworn enemies.

Immediately after the meeting with Feisal, Ibn Saud returned to Hasa via Bahrain, having made another gesture of reconciliation. He had been asked by the British representative in Iraq if he would receive Glubb and had refused. He had always considered that Glubb had a bad influence on the Iraqis and on the tribesmen but when Humphreys tried again to have Ibn Saud see Glubb, he relented and a meeting took place. As Almana comments, however the two men did not get beyond the stage of formal courtesies.

Ibn Saud in 1910. Taken by the British representative in Kuwait, Captain Shakespear, this was probably the first picture ever taken of Ibn Saud (seated, left). Note the binoculars: Ibn Saud never travelled without them. His strong, graceful hands were a notable characteristic.

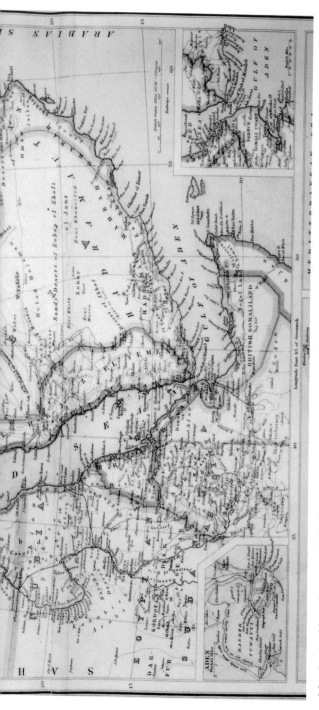

Map 1 Arabia as known in 1900. The map shows the lack of detailed knowledge on the part of the general public and specialists alike. Note the strong British presence. Note also 'East India Company' (!) between Qatar and Abu Dhabi.

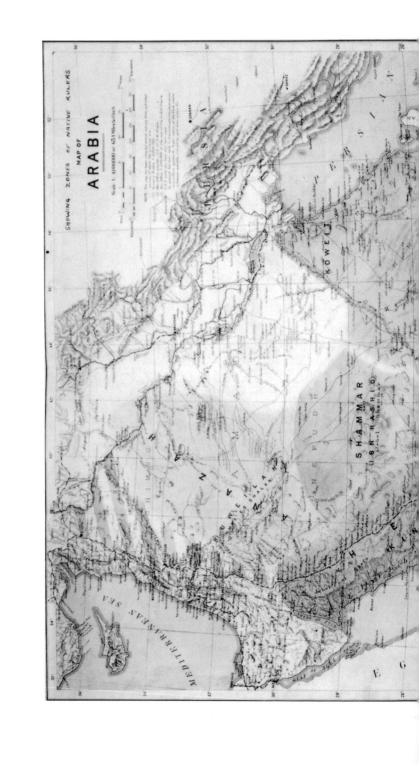

SHOWING ZONES OF NATIVE RULERS

MAP OF

ARABIA

Scale 1: 4,000,000 or 63.1 Miles to 1 Inch

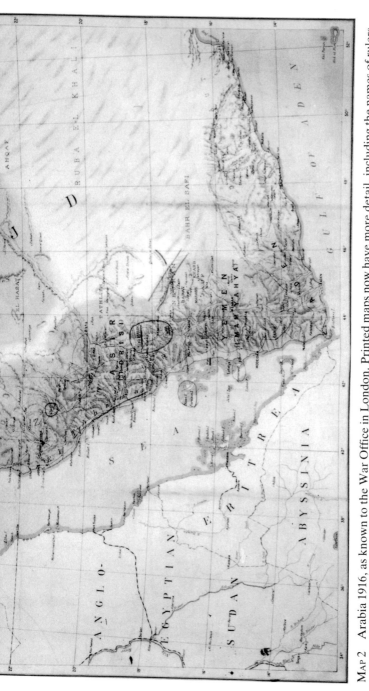

MAP 2   Arabia 1916, as known to the War Office in London. Printed maps now have more detail, including the names of rulers and tribes. The anonymous user in the War Office has marked, inter alia, for special attention TAIF and KHAMIS MUSHAIT.

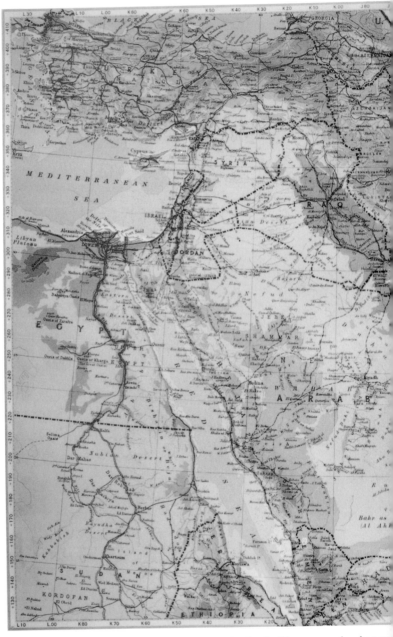

MAP 3   Saudi Arabia at the time of Ibn Saud's death. The map maker has ass
the Abu Dhabi tribal homeland, the Liwa, to Saudi Arabia.

King Abdul-Aziz in his last years. Although by now almost totally chair-bound Ibn Saud preserved an appearance of strength and grace until shortly before his death. The telephone makes clear the Kingdom's command and control system. The Saudi flag behind the King bears the words 'There is no god but God'.

On arriving off Bahrain (according to Almana) Ibn Saud was told in response to his telegram to the British representative that the Ruler was ill and could not receive him. Having slept on board overnight the party was preparing to sail for Ujair when the sons of Sheikh Eisa came aboard, having heard that Ibn Saud would not be landing. They insisted that their father was well and would not rest till he had seen Ibn Saud.

Ibn Saud therefore went ashore and saw Sheikh Eisa, whom he had not seen since he had gone to Bahrain as a young man for medical attention. The Ruler said that now that he had seen Ibn Saud he felt he could die in peace, to which the King replied that after the death of his own father he had no one to consult but Sheikh Eisa.

Muhammad Almana, who was close to the King throughout all these proceedings, relates that the King resented the British representative's gesture but that he could understand why he had tried to deceive Ibn Saud. The arrival of a great Arab leader in Bahrain could at that moment have been very inconvenient for the British since there was a growing nationalist movement on the main island. Nonetheless he recalls that in 1931 the King had occasion to pay the British back in kind.

A request was allegedly received for the Earl of Athlone and his wife Princess Alice to cross the country from Jeddah to Ujair. Almana was commissioned to send the King's reply refusing the request on the grounds that elements of rebel tribes made the journey unsafe and adds that the King ordered him to add words to the effect that the British themselves were to blame for this rejection. At this, according to Almana, the British realised the depth of the King's feeling over the Bahrain incident and a letter was sent apologising for the Bahrain representative's attitude and asking if all the local British representatives might call to pay their respects to Ibn Saud. Such a meeting was arranged and relations on a more friendly basis were resumed.

The Bahrain incident as related by Almana is wildly inaccurate in its detail but the significance of it is as an instance of the continuing sensitivity of relations between Ibn Saud and the British which Almana, as Court Interpreter, was well placed to observe. As the first British Minister to Jedda, Sir Andrew Ryan, was to say, 'I believe that he was in his heart hostile to all Western influences including that of Great Britain but he knew that British friendship was a condition of his survival.'[13]

Among the manifestations of the *Ingleez* was Philby, who now re-enters the story of Ibn Saud with full force, as he had left the service of His Majesty's Government and become established in Jedda since 1926.

Having, as we have seen, made the acquaintance of Ibn Saud in 1917–18, Philby had never wavered in his profound admiration for him and had consistently forecast that he would defeat the Hashimites. When the siege of Jedda was in progress Philby managed to get himself to the Hejaz with sponsorship from a British newspaper and ill-advisedly attempted the role of mediator between the Saudis and the Hashimites. His attempts were in any case frustrated by his falling seriously ill, with the result that he had to be medically evacuated. By the time his ship reached Aden he was well enough to land and visit the US Consul who had been advising Washington that Ibn Saud was a Shia. The result of Philby's lectures to him was that the official was honest enough to advise Washington 'that he is not outside the pale of Islam as erroneously reported in a previous despatch'.[14]

By 1926 Philby was ready to make a totally fresh start and moved himself on a permanent basis to Jedda with a view to earning a living through trading so as eventually to be able to realise his long-held ambition to explore the Empty Quarter.

He was able to develop his relations with Ibn Saud because of their previous contacts but was not able to spend with the King the time that he would have wished since he was not a Muslim. He knew from his conversations with Ibn Saud that had he been a Muslim he would have been able to accompany him on his travels, even to Mecca, and would always have the *entrée* to his Court. He eventually took the step of proclaiming his conversion in the summer of 1930.

A rather charming touch about this occasion was that he was summoned to make this step by telephone when the King called from Taif to tell him to proceed to Mecca. The King had detailed Fuad Hamza and Abdullah Sulaiman to accompany him and by the light of the moon over the Great Mosque, Philby proclaimed his acceptance of the Pillars of Islam. The following day, 8 August 1930, the King himself introduced Philby to his court as Abdullah and so began a relationship with the Al Saud unique of its kind which was to end only with Philby's death 30 years later.

The Court which Philby was now able to attend had become relatively sophisticated, with a number of functions quite efficiently allocated, and with Ibn Saud at the very heart of it and fully in control of all its operations.[15] He had by now, as we have seen, engaged the services of a number of advisers from other Arab countries who had come to him by processes of self-selection, or had been recruited and by 1930 Ibn Saud also had numbers of officials in his administration from both the Hejaz and Nejd. Muhammad Almana was in a sensitive and important position but was quite young, whereas Abdullah Sulaiman, from Anaiza was rapidly assuming control of all financial and commercial operations, having demonstrated his ability in the campaigns of 1929–30 which had required considerable administrative ability for the control of logistics and movement. Ibn Saud's second Foreign Minister – to use the term very loosely – Abdullah Damluji had succeeded Ahmad Thunayan, who had died young, but he had himself retired, totally exhausted, to his native Iraq in 1928. From then on for foreign affairs Ibn Saud relied very heavily on the advice of the Egyptian Hafiz Wahba, whom we have already met, and Fuad Hamza, who was a Druze. Yusuf Yassin, whom we have met dealing with negotiations with the British, was from an Alawite area of Syria – for which he was roundly abused by King Abdullah in his *Memoirs* – and among his many responsibilities was the editing of the Mecca newspaper *Umm Al-Qura*, which took the place in some respects of an *Official Gazette*.

Ibn Saud had, as we have seen, great respect for medical men and two foreign physicians were the beneficiaries of his respect for them. Doctors Pharaon and Khashoggi, having made the intimate acquaintance of Ibn Saud, found themselves relied on more and more for advice and Rashad Pharaon in particular was still a trusted adviser on foreign affairs long after the death of Ibn Saud.

Administration of the country in the broadest sense was delegated by Ibn Saud to his two sons, Feisal and Saud. Feisal was Viceroy for the Hejaz, and Saud was Viceroy to his father when he was absent from Riyadh. But Ibn Saud ensured that he kept fully in touch with everything that was happening in the country through a highly personalised system of control.

We have a picture of the routine of Ibn Saud's day in Muhammad Almana's memoirs which can be supplemented by information from other writers to give a picture which illustrates an excellent system of time-management.

Ibn Saud would arise as much as two hours before dawn and say the dawn prayers with great devotion. So intense was his feeling that he would often be heard to sob.[16] His prayers have often been

described by observers and many have pointed out how frequently
Ibn Saud would perform additional prayers to those which fulfilled
the strict requirement. He would then retire for a further hour or so
of sleep before rising for the day.

Work would begin at 8 a.m. when Ibn Saud would begin seeing
his important visitors, graded according to importance by Ibrahim
Al-Jum'a. Following this, he would deal with correspondence while
simultaneously receiving in his private *majlis* individuals of lesser
importance. Many writers have noted Ibn Saud's skill in dictating
letters on different subjects to different secretaries simultaneously
without losing the thread.

By late morning a general *majlis* would be held, which Ibn Saud
would begin with a recitation of the Koran. He would then frequently announce a topic for general discussion, on which he would
pronounce and invite questions. Those who attended his *majlis* would
receive gifts which Ibn Saud would himself personally authorise,
checking the ledger himself.

A key figure in Ibn Saud's court administration for many years
was Shalhoub, who was in charge of his stores where were kept the
full range of goods which would be given out as Ibn Saud's gifts.
Having been with Ibn Saud since he left Kuwait in 1901 he was in a
unique position to comment on the state of the King's finances. He
told Almana that when they left Kuwait for Riyadh he had the entire
Treasury in his purse.[17] Now, nearly 30 years later, he could comment wryly that the King had painted himself into a corner by his
generosity. 'Every King in the world is supported by his people but
the people of Nejd are supported by their King.'[18] The King was
throughout his life noted for fabulous generosity but managed at the
same time to have a system of grading gifts according to status.

The noon prayers would provide a natural break in the proceedings after which there would be the daily meeting of the political
committee, where, Almana notes, the King alone proposed the topic
for discussion.

The meeting of this committee would be followed by lunch, after
which the King would sometimes retire to the women's quarters.

In the afternoon there would be a short drive around Riyadh with
the sunset prayers often being said at a rocky outcrop, Abu Makhrouq,
which was that time surrounded by the bare desert floor, and was a
favourite place for excursions for the Court. There the King would
relax, laughing and joking with his retainers, many of them compan-

ies for over 20 years, before returning to the palace for the Isha prayers.

There would then be an evening *majlis* of a less formal kind with readings from some religious book by Sheikh Abdul-Rahman Al-Quwaiz, during which a bowl of camel's milk might be passed around.

Following this, Ibn Saud would make a tour of the Court, usually visiting the Political Section – that is, Foreign Affairs – and would often call in at the interpreters' office, discussing individual matters and commenting on the frequently bizarre commercial propositions being sent to him for consideration. The King would then pay a call on some close relative before, late in the evening, retiring to his private quarters.

Almana comments on the way in which Ibn Saud kept contact with his large and growing family also. On a daily basis at 7 a.m. he was open to receiving the family elders, sons and other relatives. Once a week he would hold a *majlis* for all the male members of the family while once every two weeks there would be a *majlis* for the females. Children were free to come to any *majlis* without permission.

Almana comments that a striking feature of Ibn Saud's routine was that he kept to it even when the Court was moving around the country while Philby says that Ibn Saud was 'a man of rule and habit':[19] apart from accidents he 'always observed with punctuality and punctiliousness the regimen which he expects his courtiers, officials, boon-companions and myrmidons to follow in his services.'

As part of his observations on Ibn Saud's addition to routine, Philby describes the King's approach to dealing with the female members of his household. He gave it as his opinion that it is permissible for women to listen to the Koran and to scriptural literature but for them to be able to read and write is 'an accomplishment regarded as unsuitable in a woman, though not forbidden.'[20] Another aspect of his dealings with the opposite sex was that he had never seen a woman eat in his presence.

As to conjugal relations Ibn Saud was able to be very factual and told Philby that by 1930 he had had relations with 135 virgins and about 100 others but that he planned from now on to have only two new wives annually. This would mean that he would be able to maintain the standard of having four wives, four concubines, wives in all but name, kept in the Shubra palace and four slave-girls, to say nothing of his right to select from the damsels at his disposal.

Philby makes an observation which is possibly the kind of observation which only a complete outsider could make, but may have some validity for all that, in relation to Ibn Saud's dealings with his family. The King, he says, 'held himself free to absent himself from all domestic festivities occasioned by normal events like marriage and births'[21] and comments that for such events he would generally take himself off to camp. He would indeed see new-born babes only some days after their arrival and as for relations with their mothers these would resume after an interval of 40 days.

Philby nowhere says so but it could be argued that it was probably essential for Ibn Saud to maintain the kind of detachment displayed in the last quotation in order to deal with the many calls on his time. He had to provide means of handling the many problems raised by increasing responsibilities of government for a huge country with limited financial resources.

Ibn Saud had by now acquired many taxable assets: in Nejd and Hasa, in the territories formerly controlled by the Rashidis, and in the Hejaz which gave access to not only the normal tax revenue but to the taxes on pilgrims. Philby calculated that in the 1930s his income was between 4 and 5 million pounds a year while it had been before the First World War only about £100 000 annually.[22] Ibn Saud was, however, now about to enter upon a very difficult period financially because of the world financial crisis.[23]

Following the crash on Wall Street in late 1929, it was 1931 before the world recession began to show itself in the Peninsula. The most dramatic manifestation was in the numbers of those able to make the Pilgrimage to the Holy Places. While the average from 1926 had been 100 000 annually,[24] the numbers fell after 1930 to 40 000 and in 1933 reached 20 000. Ibn Saud was forced to commandeer the customs receipts and Abdullah Sulaiman paid the merchants who supplied the Court by means of drafts on these sums. Even Philby found that he enjoyed no special status: Abdullah Sulaiman confiscated the goods destined for his company Sharqieh worth £4000.

Ibn Saud had ended one huge drain on his resources by crushing the Ikhwan rebellion but had growing overheads in running his administration and his Court and palaces. The Court alone at this time, for instance, ran no less than 85 motor cars and 800 camels. The advent of modern technology represented net outgoings, not profits:

at this time four de Havilland aircraft with foreign crews were acquired and Philby was commissioned to instal Marconi wireless equipment to cover the country and to arrange for training of nationals as operators. There was also a continuous call on his financial resources for the purpose of satisfying the demands of the tribesmen who had to be pacified and kept happy in the cause of long-term stability. It is therefore completely understandable that Ibn Saud should unburden himself as he did to Philby on the need to sell concessions for prospecting in his country.

An outsider's view of the demands on Ibn Saud's purse is provided at just this time by a medical missionary from Bahrain, who was summoned at short notice to Taif by the King. Doctor L. P. Dame and his team set off via Riyadh, travelling by car, and treating anyone who wanted treatment until he arrived at Taif. The journey had taken two-and-a-half days, where a camel caravan would have taken anything from 30 to 45 days.

> We were within sight of the Palace when a car came to meet us and half an hour before sunset we were ushered into the marble-floored vestibule and up the marble staircase into the King's reception room.[25]

Having known Ibn Saud personally since the early 1920s, the doctor was in a position to make comparisons and comments on the appearance of the King in this, only the second year in which he had not been engaged in combat since he conquered Riyadh in 1902.

> The King has changed but little since I last saw him. He was most cordial in his greetings and all during my two months' stay he was ever kind and cordial. Physically he is a bit stouter than he was a few years ago and now has a sprinkling of grey hairs. He still captivates his callers by his very charm and graciousness. One day as I was sitting in his reception room a white-bearded old religious leader called. As the visitor was crossing the room to the royal seat the King arose, took several steps towards him, extended his hand, smiled most graciously and led him to his seat at his right, saying he had not learned of the old man's arrival until that very morning but that had he known he would have called on him. 'We are duty bound and rejoice to honour you. You are our father in age, also in wisdom and we respect and honour you,' etc, etc.

Doctor Dame was not, however, unaware of what was happening
in the country and makes some comments based on what he had
seen and heard.

Too much money has been and is spent on motor cars, petrol and
personal expenses. . . . The government budget is the same as it
was four years ago and not till this year have they begun to cut
down on expenses.

He has praise for the King's integrity and lack of avarice. 'It would
be unthinkable for the King to amass unlimited quantities of gold as
did his predecessor in the Hejaz.' But clearly the marble halls in
which he visited Ibn Saud had given him pause. Doctor Dame quotes
approvingly a remark said to have been made by Ibn Saud to some
Hejazi merchants at this time: 'Rob me as much as you can, others
are doing it too, but I do not want you to put heavy burdens on the
people.'[26]

He comments with perception on the King's role in bringing his
people forward and, after regretting that he has still been able to do
nothing for primary education or for sending bright young men
abroad, says,

The King is far in advance of his citizens and it means pushing or
pulling them where they have no interests. Then, too, men who
can really help him in guiding and executing governmental affairs
are rare in his own land. Nearly all his chief advisers and department heads are at present Syrians with a smattering of Egyptians,
Nejdis and Hejazis.

Doctor Dame's comments were published at the time and even
though the Medical Mission's reports were for limited circulation
there is the faint possibility that he wrote with an eye to the comments coming to the notice of the King. On the whole, however, it
seems fair to regard his published views as the unbiased views of a
qualified observer speaking as he finds.

His comments on both the King and the advisers around him may
be compared to comments forwarded to London by Dickson from
Kuwait after he had a visit from another of his informants in 1933.

Ibn Saud is the greatest present-giver and the most wonderful
man in the world to win a man's confidence if it suited him. At

the same time in treachery, cunning, cruelty and revengefulness he has no equal in all the world. . . . In making the English dance to his tune he is entirely first-class and unmatchable in all the world.

The advisers around Ibn Saud such as Fuad Hamza and Yusuf Yassin were nothing but adventurers who had him completely under their control and had taught him that it was nothing to break his word to the Bedu.

The force of these remarks is somewhat diminished when it is realised that the speaker was one of the chiefs of the Ajman[27] but they do at least have the value of neatly covering the main heads of expenditure which were troubling Ibn Saud at this time and explain why he was so desperate for additional income, even from selling concessions for exploration in the country.

It was from this source that salvation was to come, or rather the assurance of income for the future for in 1931 Ibn Saud first met the American philanthropist Charles R. Crane. This gentleman had long connections with the Middle East and deep sympathy for the Arabs having been one part of the King–Crane Commission which on behalf of President Wilson had taken soundings of Arab opinion in Egypt and the Levant before the allocation of mandates in the Arab world to the victorious Allies.

He had continued his contact with the Arab world in the 1920s and visited many areas of the Peninsula. He had offered to help the Imam Yahya of Yemen with surveys of potential water resources, had visited King Hussain in Jedda to discuss agricultural development and had nearly been killed by the Ikhwan. This had occurred near the Kuwait border one day in 1928 when he was driving with an American missionary, Henry Bilkert. As they approached a body of Bedu in white turbans they were fired on and Bilkert was killed on the spot. Crane had nonetheless pursued his humanitarian travels and in 1931, having visited the *majlis* in Cairo of Ibn Saud's representative Fawzan Sabiq, he asked for permission to visit the country so as to perform, gratis, a survey of the mineral potential. Ibn Saud replied to his representative's cable with an immediate acceptance and Crane was welcomed personally by the King at Jedda on 25 February 1931. The visit resulted in Crane sending a list of the names of American engineers capable of performing the survey. From these the name of Karl S. Twitchell was selected and in April 1931 Twitchell arrived in the country for the first time and began energetically surveying in the Hejaz, then in the north and finally in the winter of 1931–2 in the Hasa region.

It was while he was in Hasa that he heard of the prospecting for oil being done in Bahrain which was to result in the discovery of a commercial source there in the summer of 1932. He reported to Ibn Saud in suitably detached and objective terms that he was not overly hopeful but that since the geology of Bahrain and the Hasa coast opposite were very similar there were prospects for oil in Hasa if oil were to be found in Bahrain. Before 1932 was over the necessary connections had been made between an American oil company (Socal), Twitchell and Philby for a serious bid to be made to gain an American concession to explore for oil in the dominions of Ibn Saud. We shall follow the *dénouement* of this particular plot in the next chapter.

Before 1932 was out, Ibn Saud had also put down a rising in the Hejaz which was fomented from Transjordan and carried out by bin Rifada. It was thanks to his excellent information service and his wireless network that Ibn Saud was able to suppress this rising so swiftly and demonstratively. Ibn Saud learned at an early stage of the possibility of a rising and contacted the chieftain of the Bili tribe of the northern Hejaz to urge him to write to Rifada encouraging him to stage his rebellion, which was armed and financed by the Emir Abdullah of Transjordan. When the uprising began, Ibn Saud's commander, forewarned, was able to intervene decisively with armoured fighting vehicles and cavalry, block off all escape routes and slay 350 rebels including Rifada and his two sons. Rifada's head was given to children to play with and was then hung in the bazaar.[28]

The Kingdom of Saudi Arabia itself was proclaimed on 23 September 1932 and a curiosity of the naming of the country was that the *Ingleez* seem to have had a role in making the eventual choice of name.[29] Hafez Wahba, Ibn Saud's Ambassador in London, consulted the departmental head in the Foreign Office dealing with the Peninsula on his view of the name 'Saudia.' Rendel gave it as his view that such a name was one which no one would understand and that there should be much more emphasis on 'Arabia.' And so it came to pass.

FAMILY LIFE

In this period Ibn Saud married several wives who would bear him sons destined to have important roles in the Kingdom after his own death.

In 1930 he married Munayir who gave birth to Talal and has always been referred to as Umm Talal. At the time of writing she is still alive.

Talal has throughout the 1980s performed important work internationally in connection with child welfare and in the 1960s was one of the Princes who declared their rejection of the regime and left the Kingdom.

Another of these Princes was Badr (now Deputy Commander of the Saudi National Guard), who was the son of Haiya Sudairi, whom Ibn Saud married in 1932. Haiya Sudairi was the sister of another of Ibn Saud's wives, Jawhara bint Saad Sudairi.

Another wife whom Ibn Saud took in this period was Bushra. She gave birth to Mishari, whose head his father was to demand after he shot dead a British subject in 1951.

The other son born in this period was Abdul-Rahman, full brother to King Fahd.

Among the new wives taken by Ibn Saud in this period was one of the widows of Azayiz, the son of Feisal bin Duwish. The other widow became the wife of Ibn Saud's younger brother, Abdullah. This was 'a great honour to the widows and a sure sign to the world that the King was the conqueror.'[30]

8

The Locust Years, 1932–38

Several babies arrived this year to add to the number of 29 boy
and 30 girls.
> Princess Alice, March 1938 on visit to Saudi Arabia, quoted i
> Lacey, *The Kingdom*, p. 25

Incomparably therefore the least malleable problem confrontin;
King Abdul-Aziz lies in economics . . . the land is not blest o
Heaven in the material sense.
> K. Williams, *Ibn Saud*, p. 29(

The King, still apparently more dictator than sovereign, refreshe(
himself during the first part of August by slaughtering gazelle a
the purifying risk of being thrown from his Mercedes-Benz.
> British confidential report on Ibn Saud in the Hejaz, 1932, i
> *The Jedda Diaries*, Vol. 3, p. 14.

In 1933 the spy Kim Philby made his first contribution of substanc(
to the world's knowledge of the Kingdom of Saudi Arabia. For it wa
in that year that Abdullah Philby published his account of his cross
ing of the Empty Quarter in 1932. The 21-year old Kim was engage(
by his father to do the proof-reading, a task which he performe(
with care but not without error.[1]

The book is, like so many of Philby's works, over large tracts quit(
unreadable but it is a treasure-house of information which is stil
used by experts in many scientific fields making comparative studie
of aspects of Saudi Arabia. This is its true significance, for it was th(
first book published in English to describe, however imperfectly, th(
extent of the dominions of Ibn Saud.

Philby had left Riyadh in December to begin the trip, reachin;
Hofuf on 25 December, when he enters in his diary, in spite of hi
recent conversion: 'XMAS!' His party of exploration left Hofuf on :
January 1932, and 90 days later after the party had spent 68 day;
exploring the Empty Quarter, he arrived in Mecca. They ha(

travelled by way of Jabrin oasis, then on to the site of what the Bedu assured Philby was the fabled city of Wabra mentioned in the Koran. Heading south they touched on the route taken the previous year by Bertram Thomas who had, without Ibn Saud's permission, made the first crossing of the Empty Quarter from south to north. After resting at the oasis of Naifa they pushed on south until the Bedu said they would go no further. Philby therefore made the best of it by heading west with his Bedu, eventually reaching Sulayyil in early March 1932. He then spent three weeks making his leisurely way to Mecca by way of the battlefield of Turaba where he could still see the bones of the soldiers of Abdullah bin Hussain slaughtered by the Ikhwan in 1919.

Ibn Saud had resisted for a long time Philby's pleading to fulfil his ambition to be the first person to be allowed to explore the Empty Quarter. Having, through his conversion, gained access to Ibn Saud's *majlis* at almost all times Philby lost no opportunity to press his case despite the King's obvious reservations. Clearly Ibn Saud was taking account of the lack of security in some parts of his territories in rejecting Philby's pleas, but Philby tried frequently to override such objections until Ibn Saud was one day so infuriated that he roared at Philby 'Oh shut up!' and stormed out of his own *majlis*.

Philby sank into a depression throughout 1931[2] bewailing not only his position but the situation of Ibn Saud. 'At the actual present moment his show is worse than Hussain's, which is enough said.' But in late 1931 deliverance came suddenly when Ibn Saud was discussing in his *majlis*, with his close advisers, plans for the trip to Europe planned for Prince Feisal for 1932 when it was hoped that he would be able to raise loans to ease the dreadful financial situation of the country. Philby's name was mentioned as possibly being useful on the trip but Ibn Saud interrupted to say 'No, Philby shall go to the Empty Quarter.'[3]

The King was not given to making such decisions lightly, especially as he had been advised by Abdullah bin Jiluwi himself of the compelling reasons for putting off Philby's planned explorations. Now, however, it seems plain that Ibn Saud could see advantage in having Philby make the trip in order to establish basic facts about the country. There were no maps of huge areas of Ibn Saud's dominions quite apart from the Empty Quarter, and Ibn Saud having imported cars, aircraft and wireless to consolidate his rule, was intelligent enough to realise that he needed information and maps. Even had there been native-educated personnel, Philby was the ideal person to provide such information, for he was the true polymath, with detailed knowledge of not only Arabic and the history of Arab countries and tribes but of several sciences and techniques, such as geology, zoology, botany, meteorology, palaeography and surveying.

Detailed information about the country would evidently be crucial now that Ibn Saud was involved in questions of surveys of his mineral resources and the search for water and oil in particular. And so Ibn Saud gave his permission and sent instructions to Abdullah bin Jiluwi to give Philby all necessary assistance for the journey. After only slight delay, which Philby characteristically found intolerably frustrating and malicious of intent, the party set out remarkably well-equipped, with tents, beds, tinned foods and even packages of the London *Times* for Philby to do the crossword.

This expedition marks the beginning of the accumulation of scientific knowledge of the Kingdom of Saudi Arabia and Philby was to continue to play a role in this field, especially in carrying out surveys and making maps, even after the death of Ibn Saud.

The Americans also were to play their part in mapping Ibn Saud's lands because they made their definitive entry to the country early in 1933 when negotiators for Standard Oil of California (Socal) arrived in Jedda. Socal had been brought into the Middle Eastern oil scene by none other than Major Holmes, the same man who had obtained a concession to explore for oil from Ibn Saud just 10 years before but had allowed the concession to lapse by not paying rent of £2000 p.a. after the first two years. He had continued his activities in the Gulf region and had obtained a similar concession for Bahrain. Socal made an agreement with him via a Canadian subsidiary and following the discovery of oil on Bahrain in commercial quantities in the summer of 1932 the American oil companies had taken the major step which would lead to the American dominance of the Saudi oil scene and to the scrapping of the Red Line agreement. This had till now obliged the major oil companies to work in concert and within the bounds of what was allegedly the sphere of influence of the Ottoman Empire in the Peninsula.[4]

In the summer of 1932 Philby had agreed with a representative of Socal to act as its consultant, while not revealing this important step to the British oil companies, the most important of which at this time for the Gulf region was the forerunner of BP, the Anglo-Persian Oil Company (APOC). By the time Philby returned to Saudi Arabia,

ollowing his triumphal visit to London in the summer of 1932 and
a leisurely holiday tour on his way back, Socal had also engaged the
services of the other man with the ear of Ibn Saud, the American
engineer Twitchell. Having had the optimistic forecasts of Twitchell
for the oil prospects in Hasa being as good as those for Bahrain, the
company was ready to enter serious negotiations and on the advice
of Philby sent a team of negotiators led by Lloyd N. Hamilton who
came ashore at Jedda on 15 February 1933.

Philby had now advised APOC that he considered himself a free
agent in the matter of oil negotiations, which had the result of
APOC, the main British shareholder in IPC (Iraq Petroleum Company), sending its own negotiator, Stephen Longrigg, to Jedda. The
bidding was now on, but the end came only three months later when
the oil concession agreement was signed by Ibn Saud's representative, Abdullah Suleiman.

The King was in desperate need of money by now. A major source
of income, the *Hajj*, was reduced by 80 per cent compared to 1930.
There were also growing expenditure problems, not only (as we
have seen) in connection with his administration and his family, but
also with the campaigns being fought in the west of the country, first
against the Rifada rebellion in 1932 then against rebellion in the Asir
region. This was undoubtedly fomented by the Yemen under the
Imam Yahya and was to occupy him throughout 1933 until it came
to open war against the Yemen early in 1934.

The prospect of ready cash in down-payment for the granting of
the concession was a major factor in the thinking of Ibn Saud and
some writers have suggested that the Americans won the concession
against the British for this reason alone. It must also be taken into
consideration that there was on the British side some lack of commitment, since many in the oil industry were sceptical of the prospects
for discovering oil in the country. The story is well-known of the
director of one major oil company who said that he personally was
ready to drink all oil found in Saudi Arabia. In addition Ibn Saud
himself may have been more prepared to deal with an American
company than a British one on the basis that the more distant country was less likely to interfere directly than the British. It is hardly
surprising that there is no documentation of the thinking of Ibn Saud
on this particular point and such evidence as exists is contradictory.
The King kept the British representative, Andrew Ryan, informed of
the negotiations and actually consulted him at the last moment on

whether to accept the American bid. Ryan seems to have advised the
King to accept the American bid, since it was unlikely that there was
oil anyway.[5]

In May 1933 the King gathered his advisers around him to discuss
the offer: Yusuf Yassin, Abdullah Sulaiman, Fuad Hamza, Philby
and others had all taken part in the discussions. After Abdullah
Suleiman had read out the details of the agreement the King said,
'Put your trust in God and sign,'[6] and the way was open to riches
beyond the dreams of avarice.

The terms that Ibn Saud had agreed seem modest enough in
retrospect: an annual rental of £5000 plus an immediate loan of
£30 000, and a further loan of £20 000 in 18 months' time, all these
sums to be paid in gold, while subsequent annual rentals and royalties of 4 shillings a ton would be paid in agreed foreign currencies.
In return Socal obtained the exclusive right to explore a vast area
defined in not entirely precise terms as the eastern part of the Kingdom. The Kuwait Neutral Zone was not included in the main agreement but came into a secret annexe by which additional money
would be paid should oil be discovered there in commercial
quantities.

However, the £35 000 in gold sovereigns which Abdullah Suleiman
personally received and counted in August 1933 represented salvation, since sources of income for Ibn Saud were practically negligible. Dickson, the British Political Agent in Kuwait, has much to say
of Ibn Saud's plight in these years and for 1933 in particular seems
almost to rejoice in news or especially rumour of the evil days on
which he has fallen. The observer, when reading Dickson's dispatches,[7] cannot help thinking that there is not a single rumour of
Ibn Saud's imminent fall which he is not ready to pass on to London,
usually with a note at the end for his protection to the effect that the
source of the news is not noted for his sympathy for the country he
continues to call Saudiya. In Dickson's dispatches we can read of the
Ikhwan chieftains detained in Riyadh being shipped out by night to
be delivered to bin Jiluwi in Hofuf and murdered; news of the
spread of syphilis among the tribesmen; the spread of immortality in
the King's palace where one of his wives has been caught *in flagrante
delicto* with one of his sons; the attempt of Ibn Saud to demand
protection money from the ruler of Kuwait to guarantee the safety of
Kuwaiti pilgrims; the spread of disease as Ibn Saud gathers the
tribesmen in Riyadh for the Yemen campaign and takes no heed for
their welfare; the dispatch of the King's brother Muhammad and

Saud Al-Kabir to Mecca since he did not trust them to stay out of the conspiracies in Riyadh; and much more. The reader looks in vain for confirmation of most of this.

The difficulties of Ibn Saud's situation could be seen from the actions which he and his Finance Minister were obliged to take, such as declaring a moratorium on debts, confiscating merchants' goods, banning the export of gold, cutting down on reception of tribal chiefs and their gifts and maximising customs receipts, especially from the country's Gulf ports, which were operating at the expense of Kuwait. The blockade imposed since 1923 was still in force, on which Dickson comments almost as if he were the representative of Kuwait rather than of His Majesty's Government.

Among the major developments on which Dickson comments in his reports is Ibn Saud's heavy involvement with Saudi Arabia's problems in the region of the border with the Yemen and his reports have value for giving the question of the Asir rebellion more significance than it receives in most accounts of Ibn Saud in the 1930s. From the evidence of Dickson and other sources it becomes clear that the troubles in the Asir region, which we have noted already in 1932, were far more serious than the Rifada rebellion of the same year.

The Asir region had long been a source of problems for successive regimes, for the rulers of Yemen, for the Turks, for Hussain bin Ali and now for the Saudis. A semi-independent fiefdom had been established there by Muhammad Idrisi in the nineteenth century which had been gradually restored to Turkish suzerainty, until finally, in 1911, Hussain bin Ali, acting for the Sultan, gained the upper hand over the Idrisis. An indication of the complexity of the situation and a pointer to problems for the future was that even in 1911 there was intervention by Italy. The Italians knew from their experience in Tripolitania of the significance of the Idrisis since the nationalists they were trying to crush there belonged to a related movement, the Senussiya. As the Italians were at war in 1911 with Turkey they gave armed support to the enemy of their enemy, that is, to the Idrisis. They were unable to impose them on the region and the Asir remained subject to Turkey until Hussain bin Ali revolted against the Turks in 1916.

In the period of the Saudi–Hashimite conflict the Asir region was subdued by the Saudis in campaigns in which, as we have seen, the Ikhwan and Prince Feisal took part. Following the death of Muhammad Idrisi in 1922 there was a power struggle between his son and successor Ali and his brother Hussain who was eventually given Saudi protection, while Ali had the support of the Yemen. As if complications with the Yemen were not enough, the Saudi protégé tried in 1932 to throw off the yoke and thereby involved Ibn Saud in two years of conflict.

From December 1932 in particular there was fierce fighting, in which three distinct Saudi combat groups were involved: the Ikhwan led by Khalid bin Luai, from the Turaba region; the tribal groups led by the Governor of Hail, bin Musaid and troops sent from Riyadh by Ibn Saud himself, who, according to Dickson, accompanied them halfway to the Asir region and saw them off with rousing speeches.

The fighting was very difficult and, even allowing for the *Schadenfreude* of Dickson's informants, it is clear that there were many deaths, including Khalid bin Luai, and that malaria struck many of the combatants in the area of Abha. However, Ibn Saud was able to prevail, one of the contributory factors to his success being once again the use of wireless. From an informant who left Riyadh on 25 January 1933 Dickson learned that 'the King spends much time daily in the wireless operators' rooms.'[8] Weapons purchased abroad also played a role: Ibn Saud's troops used Polish rifles purchased on Feisal's European trip in 1932.

Throughout 1933 there were reports of imminent war between Yemen and Saudi Arabia but it seems somewhat naive of Dickson to report the rumours with such breathlessness, since Philby had in 1930 published in London his *Arabia* in which he said that war was inevitable in the not-too-distant future.[9]

Ibn Saud at this time was known to be either keeping up appearances desperately[10] or else behaving completely naturally since he went hunting whenever possible and took new wives from the tribes.

War did come in February 1934 but in this campaign it is clear that Ibn Saud had learned a number of lessons. The Ikhwan were used only sparingly since they had proved such unwilling and demoralised combatants in the unfamiliar conditions of Asir, so far from home, without the assurance of going to Paradise as martyrs now that they were fighting only for Ibn Saud. The King also made sure that command was given to his sons Feisal and Saud. The Saud column got into difficulties in the highlands region but Feisal forced a way to Hodeida and within two months the Saudis were victorious.

Ibn Saud took up a position with respect to peace terms which literally made Philby weep.[11] Zirikli reports a scene of Philby's tears on hearing of the terms and of Saudi withdrawal. Ibn Saud's response was one of realism: 'You fool! Where will I get the manpower to govern Yemen? Yemen can only be ruled by its own ruler.'

The Treaty of Taif which Ibn Saud accepted on 21 May 1934 provided the basis for a long period of agreement between the two countries since the Imam Yahya got back much of his lost coastal territory, while the Saudis were confirmed in possession of Najran, the uplands of Asir and the port of Jizan.

When Feisal, at the head of his troops, reached the Yemeni port of Hodeida he was made aware of the arrival of warships sent by Britain, France and Italy who all had important colonial interests at stake in the Red Sea region. It is also not without significance that in 1934 Italy began broadcasting in Arabic from Bari and that cultural influence of a different kind began to be exercised with the establishment of the British Council. The British were to begin broadcasting in Arabic only in 1938 when one of their most eager listeners would be Ibn Saud.

At just this time in 1934 we have an account of Ibn Saud from the pen of a British Arabist[12] who appears a number of times in these pages, Gerald de Gaury. Having a knowledge of Arabic, he could speak directly to Ibn Saud and appears to have relished the King's style in speech.

There was speaking before me an Abraham or a Job, the voice of that old Semite wrath. The swirling current of his talk swept one away, cling as one might to the banks of western thought.

De Gaury, like so many other visitors to Ibn Saud throughout his life, listened enthralled as the King expatiated on his religious feelings and in particular on his total reliance on the Koran.

In all things, surely it is well known to you, I am reasonable: in all things will decide on the merits of a case, save only where my religion is touched. By God – I have it here, close in my heart – without it I die – none shall take it from me. By God above I swear it!'

The King's eloquence was not, however, limited to religious matters. He had, in de Gaury's view, a remarkable way with terms of abuse. When angry with his officials, he had scant respect for polite usage. To a provincial governor whom he had weighed and found wanting, 'You are like slaves, the older they become the less their value!' To a senior customs official – one of that band of brothers who appeared to de Gaury to be suitably chastened through having spent considerable parts of their careers in prison – he addressed in terms whose meaning could not be misunderstood. 'O swollen whore! . . .' he begins. Another official is treated to a vivid line in metaphors, 'You are nothing but a strayed beetle!'

De Gaury was particularly struck by the King's style of government and the way in which he listened to his advisers. He quotes Yusuf Yassin: 'The King asks us all our advice and sometimes even when we are all agreed he does the opposite and proves to be right.'

During 1934 questions about the eastern borders of Saudi Arabia began to be raised officially which were not to be settled in Ibn Saud's lifetime. The American Embassy in London responded to enquiries from Socal about the detail of the extent of its concession by consulting the Foreign Office, which responded by saying that the borders were represented by the last borders agreed by the state to which Saudi Arabia was the successor, namely the Ottoman Empire. Britain had made the Anglo-Turkish Convention of 1913, and the blue line drawn on the map accompanying the accord represented the frontiers of Saudi Arabia in the East. When their position came to the attention of Hafez Wahba, Ibn Saud's representative in London, he made the obvious objection that the Convention had not in fact been ratified. This was the first shot in a very extended battle which led eventually to the conflict over Buraimi, which was still in progress when Ibn Saud died although, curiously enough, much of the argument put forward for many years by the Saudis did not even mention Buraimi but was concerned with the areas bordering Qatar and Abu Dhabi.

The Saudi government made an official protest on 20 June 1934 in a Note from Fuad Hamza. As a result of this Note he was invited to London for discussions which were inconclusive, as he had no power to negotiate in the absence of detailed instructions. Ibn Saud kept the threads of all such matters firmly in his own hands, and the next step was taken only in April 1935 when the Saudi claim was formally handed to the British.[13] The line of the eastern frontiers here claimed became known as the Red Line, whose main features were that Saudi Arabia claimed key areas on the western and eastern sides of the Qatar peninsula while also placing its border with Abu Dhabi just south of the Liwa oasis. As protecting power, Britain was clearly to have reservations about loss of its protégés' territory and there now began a period of negotiation and exchanges of visits in which the King's own son became involved until late in 1937.

The details of the exchanges may be omitted from a biography of Ibn Saud but an example of the style of negotiation employed by Yusuf Yassin on behalf of Ibn Saud may be mentioned. The sensitive question of frontiers which, of course, had to do with the possession of potential oil resources, frequently came down to agreeing on the attribution to a particular tribe of a particular well, which meant in turn assigning the land to the suzerain of that tribe. The senior British official complained in March 1937,

> If the Saudi government always claimed as a Murra well the next well beyond the last well we had conceded there would be no reason why they should not eventually claim Muscat Town.[14]

In May 1935 as Ibn Saud was performing the circumambulation of the Kaaba in the company of his son Saud and with his guards nearby he was attacked by three Yemenis with knives. The men sprang out from concealment and would have certainly killed the King if it had not been for the courageous intervention of his son and the guards. Later investigation showed that the three men were regular members of the Yemeni army but there was to be no retaliation against the Yemen.

Ibn Saud's care for security had been put to the test but it is a measure of the care which he always took with personal security that his professional assailants had identified the area of the Kaaba at the time of the Pilgrimage as being their only chance of finding a gap in his precautions.

The King's reaction to the attempt was to complete the rites and to go on to receive congratulations on the Eed at the Mina palace. Among those waiting to greet him was a Yemeni representative and the King specifically ordered that there should be no retaliation against Yemenis. According to an observer, one of those come to greet Ibn Saud wept as he recollected the events before the King. Ibn Saud's response was to say, 'Act like a man!'[15]

After the Pilgrimage and his stay at Taif, Ibn Saud returned to Riyadh, where he received the British representatives in November 1935. These were the British Minister Sir Andrew Ryan, and his Arabist adviser Colonel Gerald de Gaury. This situation of being visited by British representatives who wrote their memoirs was a not uncommon one of which he had no doubt become aware in his later years but this may have been the only occasion on which he was visited simultaneously by two of the species.

The object of the visit was to present to Ibn Saud the British position on the Saudi proposals for marking the eastern frontiers, and to present to the King the greetings of King George V together with the robe, insignia and plumed hat of a Grand Cross of the Bath. The diplomats were given the most courteous and considerate attention by Ibn Saud, several of his sons and three of his advisers, who were personally instructed by Ibn Saud to look after the Minister. Excursions were arranged for them and a ceremonial *razzia* was laid on, all of which made de Gaury conclude that Ibn Saud had achieved the perfect combination 'to follow the law and life of the seventh century while using the amenities of the twentieth.'[16]

De Gaury had the time to appreciate the way in which Ibn Saud lived in his palace in Riyadh. He described how, between the dusk prayers and dinner, the sound was wafted to the King of the reciters of the Koran who sat concealed in the shadows of the archways. He heard the long drawn-out and quavering note of the water-wheels driven by donkeys as they moved endlessly up and down their inclined planes. He observed doves flitting through the sunbeams under the palm-trees and noted the way in which the Royal Body-guard accompanying the visitors trailed their swords through the grass as they walked with them around the guest palace. It did not escape him that, even though princes did not have swords with them in the towns, nonetheless even when preparing to receive the Minister of George V, Ibn Saud has a sword near him. and peering down a corridor de Gaury caught a glimpse of one of the King's grandsons, recognisable by his 'Royal head-fillets of gold.'

Ibn Saud himself de Gaury described with admiration.

> He is well over six feet high and robust in proportion. His left eyelid droops somewhat over an eye now sightless. His nose is fine but prominent. His beard is pointed on the chin and small and close-clipped at the side. . . . His smile is very sweet and reveals well-made teeth. His hands and feet are fine and small for so large a man. His skin is white, much sunburned in the past. His right hand is scarred from an old wound.[17]

Knowing Arabic, de Gaury was in a position to comment on the way in which Ibn Saud spoke.

The King speaks forcibly and well, decorating his conversations with old Arab proverbs, Bedouin sayings and quotations from the Koran. When he is speaking on diplomatic and political business he generally speaks at considerable length, arranging his facts to be noted by the listener in the clearest way, point by point to the climax, whereupon he leans back, shifts his position somewhat and smiles with appealing charm. His freshness and clearness of view would be remarkable anywhere but came with double hitting-power in the heart of Arabia. We were to have many instances of this during our stay. He himself says that he is like the Prophet Muhammad in that '"three things he loved: women, scent and prayer."'[18]

De Gaury's boss used this unique opportunity to form his impressions of the King and his situation since he was given such privileged treatment as the first diplomat to cross the Kingdom to visit Ibn Saud in Riyadh on business. Ryan was detached enough about Ibn Saud, however, to make the observation that the King's famous magnetic smile was switched on and off just a little too readily.[19] It may be mentioned, also, that while Ryan was only one of a long line of British representatives who complained over the years of difficulty of making contact with the King because he was away hunting or was in Mecca it was Ryan who summed up the problem for all diplomats by saying that all countries were represented at Jedda with the exception of Saudi Arabia. His conclusion after this trip, however, was that by now Ibn Saud 'was as comfortably situated as any self-made monarch could wish.'[20] There were nonetheless considerable problems for Ibn Saud and a menacing international situation in 1936. The financial crisis had eased somewhat as the world recession gradually came to an end, but problems of income and expenditure meant that 'The Saudi state lurched from one crisis to another'[21] throughout the years before the Second World War. Even the police could not be paid for long periods and pay for government employees in general had to wait on the income from the pilgrims for that particular year. The international political scene in 1936 was profoundly dispiriting for Ibn Saud as Philby found on one particular occasion when he found the King sunk in depression.[22]

Ibn Saud was now able to follow international developments closely since not only did he have his own diplomatic representatives reporting to him but he followed avidly press summaries made for him by his interpreters and advisers as well as listening to summar-

ies of broadcasts which were now of increasing importance in Arabic
and other languages. What he observed he found disheartening
since events were taking place on his doorstep which gave concern
for the security of his kingdom.

Possibly the most alarming sign for Ibn Saud in the years 1935–6
was to see how Britain allowed Italy to commit aggression against
Abyssinia. Philby observes how disappointed Ibn Saud was with the
British position: he had always taken the view that Britain with its
fleets of ships would never allow Italy to get away with it.[23]

The Palestine question in 1936 began to absorb more and more of
the King's attention since the Arab rebellion which was to last until
1939 had broken out. The Palestine question was to face Ibn Saud
with insoluble problems until his death, especially when the Kingdom came to depend for its entire wealth on income from American
oil companies, but even in 1936 the complexities were sufficiently
striking. The British, who were faced with administering the Mandate and therefore with suppressing the rebellion had still much to
offer Ibn Saud in terms of security guarantees and could not be
lightly offended by too-open encouragement of the Palestinian Arab
nationalists, no matter how deeply Ibn Saud felt the tragedy of the
situation created by the incorporation of the Balfour Declaration in
the Mandate. Ibn Saud therefore made a joint statement with the
rulers of Transjordan, Iraq and Yemen urging the Palestinians to
moderate their rebellion.[24] At the same time Ibn Saud still had a
lively distrust of the Hashimites and particularly of the ambitions of
Abdullah of Transjordan to absorb Palestine into his Emirate. To
balance his public statements Ibn Saud therefore gave his approval
to secret shipments of weapons to the rebels.

At this point in the story it should be said that the truth can only
be fully established, if at all, through access to secret documents but
there are enough indications in published works to show that Ibn
Saud was faced with complex choices and that he investigated various options.[25]

A British note was presented which referred to the activities of
Yusuf Yassin in Damascus. He was alleged to have been telling all
and sundry that Ibn Saud planned to boycott the British and send
arms to Palestine if they did not listen to his pleas for the Palestinians. The note went on to refer to contacts of Yusuf Yassin as terrorist
organisers, including one Nabih Azmeh. Ibn Saud's reply was to
convey the blank denial of Yusuf Yassin of any such contacts. It may
be noted however, as an indication of the complexities of the situa-

tion, that Nabih Azmeh had actually been an employee of Ibn Saud,[26] as a military adviser, as had one of the main organisers of Palestinian military action (in 1936 and 1948), Fawzi Kawukji, who was engaged by Ibn Saud to reorganise his forces in the Hejaz along western lines in the 1930s and served in the Asir operations.

This episode has at least this significance that it was ended by the statement of Ibn Saud to the British of his attitude to Jewish settlement in Palestine.[27]

> If I said to you that there was one atom in my body which did not call upon me to fight against the Jews I would be telling an untruth. . . . I would prefer that my possessions and my offspring should cease to exist rather than that the Jews should establish a foothold in Palestine.

Ibn Saud's attention was not entirely taken up with the question of Palestine in 1937. The British Legation in Jedda noted that 'Ibn Saud has come out strong as a fundamentalist.'[28]

The occasion of this new initiative was a proclamation which the King had published in what amounted to the Saudi *Official Gazette*, the Mecca newspaper *Umm Al-Qura*, for 30 April. He was quoted as attacking those Saudi youths who wanted 'modernisation, progress, civilisation, liberty and what not.' Such as these had been misled by the devil. Special mention was reserved for those women who sought to mingle with men under the pretext of progress, thereby neglecting their roles as wife, mother and housekeeper. The King condemned such groups as these for taking the path of moral ruin.

The Legation puzzled for some time over the strong line which Ibn Saud took on modernisation and westernisation and concluded that the King was being particularly sensitive to the growing discontent in the Hejaz for which the main cause was probably the economic depression into which the province had settled as a result of the world slump. The Legation quotes from a speech alleged to have been made by Ibn Saud to a gathering of Hejazi notables at Mecca.

> O people of Mecca, I am very angry with you. In spite of all the favours I have shown to you you ungrateful creatures are still engaged in mischievous propaganda against me. . . . I warn you to abandon your evil machinations or by Allah I will bring the might of the merciless Nejdis and there will be nothing left in Mecca but decapitated heads.

On the subject of Palestine a further complication, quite unwished
for by Ibn Saud, was Philby. We shall see, in this and subsequent
chapters, the extraordinary fluctuations in the relations between Ibn
Saud and Abdullah Philby but perhaps the most remarkable episode
in their turbulent story was an announcement which Ibn Saud was
obliged to make in the summer of 1937.

Ibn Saud instructed his representatives to have the following announcement published, which duly happened on 18 August 1937.

Some may think that Philby's opinions reflect our own. . . . As for
his personal opinions they are his own and do not reflect our
thoughts at all.

Ibn Saud had to take account of the fact that, although Philby had
no official status as an adviser or employee, many outside Saudi
Arabia could be forgiven for regarding him as some kind of mouth-
piece or agent of influence on behalf of Ibn Saud. The immediate
cause for this disavowal was Philby's persistence in publicising his
views on the need for accommodating the aspirations of the Jews in
Palestine. Ibn Saud's official statement of his views was totally un-
ambiguous: he rejected the proposals of the 1937 Peel Commission
on Palestine which recommended the partition of the country between Jews and Arabs.

It was not only in relation to Palestine that Philby embarrassed Ibn
Saud at this period. The King asked him in early 1936 to undertake
an expedition on the Yemen borders to map in particular the Najran
area. Between May and September Philby was away from Court
carrying out his instructions in the south of the country protected by
armed Saudi guards. From Najran he proceeded wildly to exceed his
instructions and with his Saudi guards made his way across the
British protected areas of the Hadramaut as far as Mukalla. When
word of the arrival of this party reached Aden the British army
commander, Lake, sent him a telegram ordering to withdraw with
his Saudi army party. Philby eventually did so but once again could
not resist cocking a snook by signalling back that he was now retiring to his advanced Headquarters to supervise the evacuation of
occupied territory. This produced not only rage in its recipient but
an immediate change in British policy which led to the Protectorate
being extended by some 70 000 square miles, which did not go
unnoticed by the Imam of the Yemen. Indeed even before reaching

Mecca Philby managed to infuriate the Imam by making a diversion to the Marib dam.

Ibn Saud did manage, however, to get some satisfaction from Philby's journeyings since the maps which Philby produced of the frontier areas were excellent.

Philby was not finished yet, however. On his leave in London in the summer of 1937 he gave a lecture at the Royal Central Asian Society on his recent expedition. He told his startled audience that because he had penetrated the Hadramaut, a British protected area, the British had wanted to shoot him. At this at least one gallant military gentleman rose to his feet and shouted 'Rubbish' and the meeting broke up in disorder.

In the summer of 1937 Philby was able to stay in touch with the Saudi court while in London because Prince Saud (nominated Crown Prince since 1933) and Prince Muhammad were representing their father at the Coronation of George VI. Ibn Saud had been invited as the monarch but, as on the occasion of the British invitation of 1919, he preferred to send a representative. No doubt discontent in the Hejaz was a factor in his decision to remain in the Kingdom. Among the many functions which Saud attended was a dinner of the same society which Philby had outraged but the occasion passed off peacefully.

Philby has become, at this point, as was his wont, somewhat intrusive and it may be instructive to concentrate our attention again on Ibn Saud. There is a series of instructive pictures in words of the King carrying out several of his roles as a ruler, head of family, figure in world politics and devotee of motorised hunting.[29]

The pictures are presented to us by members of the American medical mission based in Bahrain who were visiting the Kingdom at the King's invitation in 1937.

The story opens with the group preparing themselves to meet Ibn Saud (who had left Riyadh on a hunting expedition) and is best told in the words of the missionaries' diary, with spelling and punctuation unchanged.

January 10, 1937.

Yesterday we did very little except go out at about eleven o'clock in the morning to meet the King's party coming home from the hunt. We met them on the open plain outside of the city, and what a sight it was! At first we saw only a cloud of dust on the horizon.

This fast grew in size until we could distinguish a line of cars coming charging down upon us ten abreast. Behind this line came another and another until the whole plain seemed to be covered with speeding phalanxes of motor cars. I was standing on a small hill taking pictures of the on-coming cavalcade when suddenly I noticed the foremost car stop short. All the other cars stopped simultaneously with a great tumult of screaming brakes, and skidding wheels. The King called me over to his car, and after asking about our journey he said, 'And where is Abu Loolua whom I invited to come with you?' I told him that Rev. Van Peursem had not been able to come with me and that I had a letter to His Majesty from him. Ameer Saud, his oldest son got out to give us a hearty handshake and a few words of welcome to Riyadh, over which his father has placed him as governor.

The scene changes to the King's palace next day when the writer of the diary records the story of conversations which the group had with Ibn Saud during which he gave his views on the League of Nations, President Roosevelt and the Jews.

This morning we were called over to the palace to see the King. He was sitting in his office, with Yusef Yesseen, his vizier, Ameer Saud and a few of his advisors. He was in good spirits and talked a good deal, asking about all those who came with Dr Dame two years ago. He glanced through the pages of the book, Paterson-Smith's 'The People's Life of Christ,' that Van Peursem sent him. His only remark about it was, 'It says here that the Jews insulted the Christ. Why don't you treat the Jews as they deserve to be treated and are treated in Germany today?' I replied that to treat them that way would be against the order of Christ, and that 'a nation which returns evil with evil is not Christian.' Soon the radio news of the world was read. The King seems very interested in European news and commented at large on the critical war situation. He sneered at the mention of the League of Nations and said it was as powerless as a mejlis full of old women and that any attempt to revive it now was like the efforts of a physician who tries to give a tonic to a dying man. He admired America for staying out of things and when the last item of news was read 'That Congress of the United States has just passed a law declaring that all citizens who leave America to fight in foreign lands, such as Spain, will lose their citizenship' he expressed his hearty ap proval of our foreign policy. He then said addressing me, 'I love your country and admire your president, and I am very grateful for the services which members of your mission have shown me and my people. You come wanting only to help us.' His cordiality took my breath away and I could say nothing more than that I hoped the friendship would continue.

A week later the diarist is recording news of the state of health of the family of Ibn Saud, mentioning in particular eye complaints from which his sons and daughters were suffering.

17 January 1937

My work so far has been mostly with the royalty here, the endless number of relatives of the King. At home one occasionally hears of a family with enough sons to make up a base ball team but here we find an army in a single family. The first operation that I performed here was a niece of the King, a little girl who had an unsightly and painful eye. We removed this and gave her an artificial one that improved her general appearance tremendously. Several of the King's daughters and younger sons get daily treatment for trachoma and in one week have shown marked improvement. Today I performed several operations for trichiasis (inturning eyelashes which rub against and irritate the eye). My daily rounds take me along the endless labyrinthine corridors of the palace. Each wife, concubine, sister, and son has his own separate establishment within the palace or connected to the palace by overhead passages. One could easily get lost, without a guide, for the passages are as devious as the tunnels of the catacombs.

When the diary writer called on the King to pay his farewells he was able to observe at first hand Ibn Saud's style of conducting business and to note how his advisers and his son Saud fitted into the scheme of things.

Day before yesterday the King left for al Khuffs, his winter hunting encampment in the desert. When I called to say goodbye on the evening previous to his departure he seemed to be in a great stew over a long list of ordinances which had been given out without his official approval. He was sitting in his private mejlis, which is very much like the office of a business executive at home. On the walls hung large maps of the continents, in one corner was a large flat-top desk, with a few neatly piled stacks of paper lying on it. Nearby was a telephone which the King was constantly using, shouting over it in the vehement way, characteristic of an American business man. In another corner stood a cast-iron stove very much like the ones used by my grand-parents. Around the room were arranged overstuffed chairs and lounges and in one of these sat the King, while his six advisers sat mutely in others. The King did not notice me when I entered as he was too agitated by the extravagance of some one. The seat which I was given was behind a pillar, hiding me from the King's view but giving me the opportunity to observe unobtrusively the discomfiture of his ministers. They looked so much like naughty boys being bawled out by a teacher for playing truant. Each one wanted to say that he was innocent but did not dare to. Finally he rang the electric bell that was attached to his chair and in came Ameer Saud. The latter came in very breezily but soon changed his expression when his father angrily asked him why he had authorised the expenditure of so much drygoods and hardware. 'After this,' he said, 'I will see and stamp with my seal every request for expenditures.' After the storm had passed he became more jovial and called for refreshments. Oranges, apples, candies and nuts were brought in on large platters and we were invited to draw up and partake.

Among other features which these diary extracts bring out is the fact that Ibn Saud was clearly the motor force for all that happened in the country, whether affairs of state or the Palace consumption of 'dry goods.' It was his total absorption in all matters great and small which led to Ibn Saud's not accepting the invitation to London for the Coronation of King George VI.

As a result of the Coronation visit to London by his sons, Ibn Saud was in 1938 to make the acquaintance for the first time of a member of a European royal family and indeed of a woman, since in the spring of 1938 Princess Alice had accepted Prince Saud's invitation to visit Saudi Arabia and, accompanied by her husband the Earl of Athlone, landed at Jeddah. Although Ibn Saud had encountered foreign women and had in fact received the wife of Sir Andrew Ryan in Riyadh, this was the first occasion on which he had ever received a woman in public. The party was received everywhere with the greatest friendliness and simplicity, so that Princess Alice was able to visit several of Ibn Saud's wives whom she described in a series of letters home[30] and to note the arrival of new members of the family

A remarkable coincidence was that after crossing the Peninsula by car the royal party arrived at Dhahran where they were received by the American oilmen the day before the well came on-stream which became famous as Dammam No. 7. This was the long-waited proof that oil existed in Hasa in commercial quantities and that the Saudi people would no longer have to eat locusts.

FAMILY LIFE

In this period Ibn Saud married the following wives who bore him sons.
1.   Mudhi, the mother of Princes Majid and Sattam
2.   Nouf, the mother of Thamir. Prince Thamir was to commit suicide in 1959 by setting fire to himself in Miami, Florida.

Sons born to Ibn Saud in this period were:
1.   Turki, full brother to King Fahd. Vice-Minister of Defence to 1978.
2.   Badr, Deputy Commander of the National Guard at the time of writing.
3.   Nawwaf.
4.   Naif, Minister of the Interior at the time of writing. Full brother to King Fahd.
5.   Fawwaz.
6.   Majid, who lived for two only years, 1934–6.
7.   Salman, Governor of Riyadh at the time of writing. Full brother to King Fahd.
8.   Majid.
9.   Thamir.
10.   Abdulillah.

A charming piece of gossip is retailed by Gerald de Gaury from the year 1937 when he was informed by a traveller arriving in Kuwait that two male negroes had carried out the task of counting Ibn Saud's children and had to come to the felicitous conclusion that their number was that of the number of sects in Islam, namely 73.[31]

A somewhat more sinister story is told by Zirikli of the year 1933 when Ibn Saud divorced a Shammari wife who, Zirikli believes, may have been sent away for trying to poison the King.[32]

In June 1938 Shahida, the mother of Ibn Saud's son Mansour,[33] died. Although she was for long a favourite companion, Ibn Saud never married her.

The death of his mother may have accounted for Mansour's taking to drink.[34] The British Legion reported to London that the King personally had beaten his son who had been caught *in flagrante delicto*.

Another son, Nasir,[35] according to the same report, was lucky in that the news was kept from his father that a drinks party which he had arranged had led to the death of at least one guest who had overindulged in the aftershave.

9

The Cup Dashed from the Lips, 1938–45

The United States is a great country but I have learned that it cannot send anything to Saudi Arabia without the consent of the King of England.

> Ibn Saud to Floyd Oligher, quoted in B. Rubin,
> *The Great Powers in the Middle East 1941–7*, p. 44

The English keep enjoining the Arabs to be united. I wonder what is behind this.

> Ibn Saud, quoted in C. Leatherdale,
> *Britain and Saudi Arabia 1925–39*, p. 340

Give them and their descendants lands and homes of the Germans who had oppressed them.

> Ibn Saud to President Roosevelt, February 1945, on resettling
> survivors of the Holocaust, quoted in W. A. Eddy,
> *F.D.R. meets Ibn Saud*, p. 34

When Ibn Saud and his sons received the British royal party in March 1938 the visit did not take place in a vacuum. The invitation was not issued lightly and the British Government in responding to it positively wished to demonstrate its concern for the need to maintain excellent relations with Ibn Saud.

An idea of the British thinking about Ibn Saud at this point can be gained from the minutes of a meeting of the Committee of Imperial Defence of 8 November 1937. The fear was expressed that Ibn Saud could be 'tempted to accept help from some other quarter, for example Italy. His lack of resources might very well tip the scale in turning him against us and the results might be serious.'[1]

The Italian naval presence in the Red Sea, of both surface-ships and submarines, was a cause of concern to British military planners as they studied questions such as access to the Mediterranean and protection of the route to India. Italian dealings with the Yemen raised fears of Britain becoming embroiled in a conflict where the Italians would support the irredentist Yemenis against the Saudis,[2] who would perforce have to be protected by the British.

The fact that Ibn Saud was unhappy over British policy on Palestine and the evidence that his agents, such as Yusuf Yassin, were active in Bagdad and Damascus in so far unfathomable ways meant that British policy would have to be extremely circumspect, especially in view of the growth of influence of Nazi Germany.

At almost precisely the time that the British Imperial Defence strategists were pondering the seriousness of the situation were Ibn Saud to turn against the British, Hitler was addressing his most senior military and foreign affairs advisers on the prospects for the British Empire. On 5 November 1937 Colonel Hossbach took the minutes of the meeting which emerged years later as the Hossbach Minutes.[3] In this secret meeting Hitler made his prognostications for the period to 1945 and in dealing with the British Empire, one of the two 'hate-inspired antagonists' (the other being France) he pronounced that

> there were signs of disintegration in the British Empire: Ireland, India, the threat of Japanese power in the Far East and of Italian in the Mediterranean. In the long run the Empire could not maintain its position.

The British Foreign Office was well aware of the need to be alert to contacts which were developing between Ibn Saud and the Germans, the more especially as there were matters other than Palestine to cloud the horizon.

The Saudi frontiers with Abu Dhabi and Qatar were, as we have seen, a matter which had gone beyond the exchange of notes and maps between officials. The King's son, Feisal, had been entrusted with the issue. The position in which the Foreign Office now found itself before the Second World War could be regarded as a mirror-image of the position of the Foreign Office before the First World War. Whereas in 1913–14 the paramount question for the diplomats was to keep Ibn Saud firmly in his place as a Turkish official or nothing, in order to maintain relations with Constantinople, now the overriding consideration was to maintain good relations with the King, even at the expense of relations with lesser powers such as

Abu Dhabi, Qatar and the India Office. Throughout the period 1937–
there was vigorous debate in London between the India Office
which was still responsible for dealings with the non-sovereign
territories in the Gulf) and the Foreign Office, with a view to resolving conflict over the Riyadh Line in such a way as to satisfy Ibn Saud.
So fierce was the debate and so sensitive the issues involved that in
March 1938 – the moment when Dammam No. 7 came on-stream –
the Foreign Office removed the question of Khaur Al-Udeid[4] – on
the eastern side of the Qatar Peninsula – from the normal processes
and assumed responsibility for the matter itself.

It was against this background that British representatives in Saudi
Arabia paid their court to Ibn Saud. Two of them visited the King
shortly before the royal visit, one of whom later wrote the second-
most entertaining volume of diplomatic memoirs.[5] This largely concerned his experiences in the Peninsula first in the Hejaz when Ibn
Saud was besieging the Hashimites and secondly as British Minister
to the court of Ibn Saud. He was Reader Bullard who was an excellent Arabist. It is the reader's good fortune that London was careful
to send to Ibn Saud as representatives men who not only knew
Arabic and the Peninsula from as far back as 1923 but men who
could write. Reader Bullard's successor, Grafftey-Smith, had also
been in the Hejaz in the 1920s and he it was who wrote the most
entertaining volume ever of diplomatic memoirs.[6]

Bullard acted as interpreter when his boss from the Foreign Office
visited Ibn Saud, in Riyadh. Rendel, the same man who had proposed to Wahba dropping the name of 'Saudiya' was deeply pre-
occupied with the question of the effect on Anglo-Saudi relations of
the differences over the eastern frontiers of the Kingdom. He had
been reassured by the course of his discussions with the King and
had heard from the Crown Prince that 'the keystone of Saudi policy
was friendship with Britain'[7] but had come to the conclusion that the
King 'probably regarded us at the time as the least dangerous of the
foreigners with whom they had to deal.' There was clearly much still
to be done and Bullard was assiduity itself in maintaining contact
with the King.

Ibn Saud made a great impression personally on this diplomat, as
he did on so many others. Bullard's situation allowed him to make a
telling comparison between Hussain bin Ali, with whom he had had
dealings at the most critical time in the Hejaz and the new master of
the Peninsula.[8]

He had not lived in a capital as Hussain had lived in Istanbul bι his manners were equal to any situation; and in talk he coul easily have overthrown Hussain in politics and probably equallε him in theology, which occupied much of his reading and conve sation.

The diplomat had much opportunity to evaluate the King's knov ledge of affairs and concluded that

Ibn Saud's most remarkable quality was his political wisdom. had grown with the extension of his responsibilities until it wε equal to any situation. . . . He managed to be better informed c international affairs than many educated Europeans.[9]

Part of the reason for the King's stock of knowledge of the interni tional scene was that, as Bullard observed, an entire department ι the palace was occupied in monitoring and translating Europea radio news bulletins, which were then read out to the King after tl evening prayer.

Bullard had the opportunity to inspect the King's new palace, tl Murabba', which had been built to house the King's ever-growin family. The Mismak palace, which Ibn Saud had stormed in 190 had long ago became inconvenient but it was only in the late 193(that the King was able to commission a new palace. He took pa personally in designing the new residence but did not gain tl wholehearted endorsement of one observer for his skill in desigι The King, said Bullard, had been 'less successful as an architect tha as a statesman.'[10]

The King's utter simplicity Bullard found charming, as had s many others. He noted with amazement that, even at the most spleι did banquets, the King always drank camel's milk[11] from a larg violet and white enamel mug, chipped from long use and held fς him by an armed retainer.

When the King gave a farewell banquet in the western style fς Bullard there came a moment when the King could not contain hι bafflement at the great array of cutlery before him any longer. H picked up what was laid out before him in one huge hand an dropped the lot into the lap of Bullard's assistant, saying, 'I don understand these things!'

In August 1938 Bullard was again in the presence of Ibn Sau when he travelled to Riyadh for the inauguration of the Arab service of the BBC. The occasion was ruined because of the content of the first news bulletin, which recounted the death by hanging of a young Palestinian tried by the British for having arms in his possession. As Bullard relates, the next day the King had tears in his eyes.[12] 'If it had not been for the Zionist policy of the British government that Arab would be alive today.'

Bullard confesses that he did not know what to say to the King but he had every reason to be uneasy since he knew that the course of British policy in Palestine could only be a source of comfort to the enemies and potential enemies of Britain.

The British Minister again made the three-day journey from Jedda to Riyadh to visit Ibn Saud in November 1938. He stayed for two weeks and later wrote his impressions of Ibn Saud, which are worth quoting at some length since he manages to bring in the views of Philby on the position of Ibn Saud at just this crucial time. Oil had been discovered in commercial quantities, Ibn Saud had received his first substantial payment in accordance with the concession terms and work was almost completed to enable Saudi Arabia to begin shipping oil from Ras Tannura. The signs were that the country had weathered the difficulties of the world depression and that an end was in sight to the period of deprivation. None of this could Philby see.[13]

He was, Bullard reported, 'in a state of violent pessimism about Ibn Saud, who, according to him, had done nothing all the summer except build his new palace and flounder about in family affairs, was for ever doctoring himself even in public, frequently fell asleep in his own majlis and left the rule of the country, except Beduin affairs to Shaikh Abdullah Sulaiman, the Minister of Finance. . . . He now wondered whether the period of chaos which it was always expected would follow Ibn Saud's death might not now come during his lifetime.'

As a sensible diplomat Bullard pondered these remarks which, after all, came from someone who had almost unique access to Ibn Saud. He concluded that Philby's judgement was clouded for two reasons. The King had, Bullard observed, very sensibly refused to allow Philby to use him as a stick with which to beat the British Government on the subject of Palestine. (An error so serious, in Philby's view, that Ibn Saud had lost the chance of gaining the leadership of the Arab world, which had now gone to Iraq.) The second reason for Philby's not being reliable in his judgement of Ibn Saud was that he was owed some £100 000 by the Saudi Govern-

ment for Ford cars bought on credit and was getting ever deepe
into debt.

Bullard then gave his own views on the points made by Philby. He
noted that the King 'certainly looks older than 56 but he had not led
an armchair life.' He moved stiffly when walking but showed no
signs whatever of falling asleep when discussing bilateral relations
with Bullard. As to dosing himself, 'It is known that he is taking
injections but that is merely to counteract the menace of impotence.'

Overall, in Bullard's view, the King was in pretty good shape for
one who had led the dramatic life which he had and the truth of the
matter was that 'perhaps the King was finding it more difficult than
he used to to do the work of six men.' Bullard notes that Ibn Saud
had indeed begun officially to delegate even some of his most important functions as a religious leader and had, for the first time in his
life, that very year asked Saud to take his place at a huge reception
for the Eid Al-Fitr.

Elsewhere Bullard notes another way in which the King was light-
ening his own workload. In April 1938 Ibn Saud gave instructions
that petitions were no longer to be addressed to him personally
unless the petitioner had failed to find satisfaction with the relevant
government department and/or one of his Viceroys, Saud or Feisal.
This leads one to suggest that here may be a factor which accounts
for Ibn Saud's having been observed to drop off in his own *majlis*, a
feeling of boredom after such a long period of being accustomed to
being constantly on the alert to act and take all decisions, great and
small.

After describing his visit to the King, Bullard goes on to describe
the activities of the newly-appointed German representative in
Bagdad, Grobba, who was clearly making friends and influencing
people. As a result of Yusuf Yassin's contacts in Bagdad in 1937,
when he was seeking German help over Palestine, Grobba was to
pay a call on Ibn Saud in Jedda in January 1939.

Ibn Saud received Grobba on a number of occasions in January
and February 1939. The German representative reported to Berlin[14]
on what he judged to be the hatred which Ibn Saud felt in his heart
for the British. As a result of Grobba's reports a lively debate took
place in Berlin on the merits of a more interventionist policy in the
Arab world and in particular in dealings with Ibn Saud. The German
documents seem to show[15] that Ibn Saud wished to smuggle German arms to Palestine and that he hoped to replace Abdullah in
Transjordan with one of his own sons. In Berlin, however, the non-

interventionist party won out and instead an agreement was made in July 1939 for the purchase of 4000 German rifles and ammunition and for the construction of an arms factory near Riyadh.

Palestine remained the topic of the hour for Ibn Saud after his talks with Grobba, for in February and March 1939 the British held a conference in London of all Arab states to discuss with Zionist representatives the future of Palestine. The King sent Prince Feisal to represent Saudi Arabia at the conference which did not reach any conclusions other than the negative one of rejecting solutions such as Partition. It was the first of its kind when Arab delegates refused to sit down with Zionists, so that the British officials present had to engage in shuttle diplomacy.

In May of 1939 a film of historic significance was made at Ras Tannura when Ibn Saud was shown performing the ceremony of starting the loading of the first shipment of Saudi oil for export. The officials of Casoc, the new company formed to replace Socal, and the predecessor of Aramco, were able to show the King how the undeveloped site chosen by Twitchell so many years before had now become a modern oil-shipment port. When the King performed the symbolic act of opening the valve for starting loading it seemed that Saudi Arabia could look forward to a future immediately bright with wealth and material comfort.

Ibn Saud's fabled generosity[16] was evident on this occasion also. Not only did he give fifty thousand riyals to the poor of Dhahran but after making a regal procession by launch to Manama he gave away a similar amount to the poor of Bahrain.

Ibn Saud had received the £200 000 due for the commercial oil-strike of 1938 and the access to world markets seemed to indicate endless prosperity but on 1 September 1939 Hitler invaded Poland.

The war did not immediately reach the Peninsula but by 1940 it was clear that Saudi Arabia was not to benefit from its new source of wealth until the war was over. As to how the war would progress, the country was clearly going to have to remain a helpless spectator,[17] and indeed it would have to depend on subsidies to survive.

The problems facing Ibn Saud were not merely financial but problems of survival for, in 1940, the country suffered from both drought and famine. Like a number of countries in the Peninsula, Saudi Arabia had to be rescued from mass deaths by starvation. Food supplies had to be organised from abroad with the result that, for example, the explorer, Bertram Thomas, found himself employed in the Trucial States as officer in charge of food supplies and morale. In

Saudi Arabia, Ibn Saud had, as his link with the British Government, the same Colonel Gerald de Gaury who had visited him in 1935.

Abdullah Philby had sought to be given this job of British liaison and intelligence officer when he was in London, accompanying Prince Feisal in early 1939, but his record spoke against him. He returned to Riyadh at the summons of the King after the outbreak of war in September 1939, having lingered over a leisurely holiday and attempted in vain to gain a seat in Parliament as a pacifist with support from the Peace Party Union.

On Philby's return Ibn Saud found himself at loggerheads with his only British courtier, for Philby was convinced that Britain must lose the war, if only because of the shipping losses which must reduce the country to starvation. Ibn Saud was equally robust in his urging the British to strike back at the Germans. Listening day after day to the news of the war in early 1940 he would call out to Philby, 'What has happened to you English? You should strike, and strike now!'[18]

Nor was it only in relation to Philby that the King's support for the British war effort came out. Throughout the period when Britain in many theatres of operations suffered heavy defeats, till approximately the end of 1942, the mood of Ibn Saud could be observed[19] by his court and his servants to change totally according to whether the news from the fronts was good or bad.

Philby's relations with Ibn Saud in 1939–40 were of a sensational nature but in the absence of documentation are not capable of being described accurately and objectively, especially in relation to Palestine.[20]

The outlines of the story are well-known, that Philby made contact with Zionist leaders in London with a view to achieving a solution of the Palestine problem through the involvement of Ibn Saud. He began with a meeting at his London home in February 1939 which brought together the King's foreign affairs adviser, Fuad Hamza (who had discussed gun-running to Palestine with the Germans in the summer of 1938)[21] and himself and, on the Zionist side, Chaim Weizmann and David Ben-Gurion. No second meeting ever took place with a representative of Ibn Saud present. Just before Philby returned to Riyadh he had a meeting with Moshe Shertok and Chaim Weizmann, arranged through the British historian L. B. Namier, at which Philby argued that Saudi Arabia could be persuaded to give Britain its support if Ibn Saud got money and arms. He went on to outline a scheme whereby if Ibn Saud could be given £20 million

Jewish immigration could be freely organised to the western part of Palestine, whose inhabitants could be absorbed into Saudi Arabia and other Arab countries. Among the advantages to Ibn Saud would be that he would emerge as the leader of the movement to Arab unity.

Weizmann promised to promote this scheme through his contacts in the United States and Philby promised to urge the plan on Ibn Saud.

Philby discussed the idea with Ibn Saud in January 1940 and, according to Philby, the King said 'that he would give me a definite answer at the appropriate time.' Philby told his wife that 'the scheme has been accepted'[22] but that Ibn Saud had told him not to discuss the matter with anyone. It will probably surprise no one to learn that Philby then went on to discuss the subject with Yusuf Yassin.

Ibn Saud was reported to be quite favourably inclined to the proposal when Philby wrote to Weizmann in April 1940. He was 'just thinking about how it can be worked out without producing a howl of anger among certain Arab elements.'

In May 1940 the German armies overran the Low Countries and by 14 June Paris had been occupied and France was defeated. Britain now faced the possibility of invasion with no allies in Europe and with the United States in a position of neutrality. Philby was outrageously anti-British and exultant about the prospects of British defeat, to such an extent that the British representative Stonehewer Bird received an intimation from Ibn Saud himself that Philby was mentally deranged.[23] He himself took the step of forbidding Philby the Legation under any circumstances.

Ibn Saud nonetheless at this time gave Philby a house in Riyadh, possibly, as has been suggested, in order to keep an eye on him. The next step in the story of the King's relations with Philby was that Philby was arrested while preparing in Karachi to make his way to the United States where he was to carry out a tour of speaking engagements.

A successor to Stonehewer Bird, Laurence Grafftey-Smith, who was to present his credentials to Ibn Saud in 1945 puts it this way.

When Philby planned and set out on a visit to lecture in the United States a tip-off from the most exalted source advised examination of his suitcases and when this was done at Karachi he was arrested.[24]

Ibn Saud had already, he told Stonehewer Bird, given orders that Philby was to be arrested if he were heard indulging in more anti-British talk. It is characteristic of Ibn Saud, however, that he did not keep this secret from Philby, for he hated tale-bearing.[25]

The threat of war did not mean that Ibn Saud gave his undivided attention to world politics. He still carried out, as the British Legation reported in August 1939, his role as the tribal leader.[26] The Legation's report for that month describes 'the annual meeting of tribal representatives held by the King at Riyadh at the end of July . . . (which) include the following: Shammar, Harb, Mutair, 'Ateyba, Qahtan, Al Rashayda, Anaza, Nejd, Al Ajman, Al Murra, Dawasir, Sibei, Suhool, Banu Khalid, Bani Hajir, and Al Awazim.'

Following this meeting the King received plenipotentiaries from the same tribes in a meeting on 14 August which was also attended by the Ulema. On this occasion 'His Majesty delivered an oration on religious matters.'

The sequel to the contacts with Zionists took some time to work out and involved Winston Churchill, who seems genuinely to have believed that it would be possible for Ibn Saud to become, with Zionist sympathy and understanding, a 'boss of bosses' in the Middle East. His choice of vocabulary from the world of Mafia chieftains probably derived from his frequent stays in New York in the 1930s but may well be regarded as less than felicitous. Weizmann visited Churchill before making a visit to the United States and discussed the scheme at Downing Street on 11 March 1942.[27] Weizmann relates that Churchill told him, 'Keep this confidential but you might talk it over with Roosevelt . . . There's nothing he and I cannot do if we set our minds on it.'

Weizmann goes on to relate how he had discussions in Washington with the President's personal representative to be sent to discuss policy with Ibn Saud, Colonel Hoskins, and how, when he met Hoskins on his return from Riyadh he found the atmosphere had changed totally.[28] Ibn Saud, he reported, had spoken with contempt of Weizmann for attempting to bribe him with £20 million to sell Palestine to the Jews. Hoskins went on to report that Ibn Saud had sworn that Philby would never again be allowed to enter the country.

The truth of the matter can never be established. Of the participants' accounts of the affair this can be said: Philby has only scant reference to the master in some of the relevant books; Weizmann's account is inaccurate in dates since he claims to have first heard of

Philby's ideas for a deal when Philby was emerging from detention in Britain; the British and American leaders' references to the affair are fleeting and inconclusive.

Of the position of Ibn Saud there are well-documented accounts of his conveying to Hoskins his indignation at the idea of a bribe.[29] It is only in Weizmann's account that Ibn Saud is quoted as saying that he would ban Philby from ever again entering the country. In the event when the war ended and Philby became free to travel once more, Ibn Saud sent an aircraft to convey him from Cairo back to Saudi Arabia.

It is worth noting that the account given of the affair in Zirikli's book makes clear the amount of planning and foresight in the American approach made to Ibn Saud. In the President's letter to Ibn Saud he asked if the King would be willing to meet Weizmann in Washington or elsewhere to discuss a solution to the Palestine problem agreeable to Jews and Arabs. If such a meeting were not possible, would the King agree to a meeting of his representatives with Weizmann's representatives somewhere, not in Riyadh? It was also made clear by Hoskins that both Churchill and Eden were aware of the approach being made by Hopkins.

Zirikli quotes the King's reply to the effect that the Arabs' rights in the matter were as clear as daylight and that it was out of the question to have any dealings with Weizmann since 'we cannot be protected from the treachery of the Jews.' Moreover, there was a special hatred between him and Ibn Saud, since Weizmann had proposed that Ibn Saud should be 'a traitor to my religion and to my country.'

The Philby/Weizmann affair in its timing neatly covers the period when the United States began to be heavily involved in the affairs of Saudi Arabia as a matter of deliberate government policy. The question of oil supplies had come to be dominant in American thinking once the United States had become fully committed to the Second World War after the attack on Pearl Harbor.

Before the American entry into the war Ibn Saud had to exercise considerable political judgement on Arab affairs when he was approached for his support for the rising of elements of the Iraqi army against the regime and in support of Nazi Germany. Even though the military news for the British at this time was almost universally disastrous Ibn Saud refused to give his support even though it was the Hashimites who had been (temporarily) expelled. He is recorded by a British official as having told an Iraqi envoy to remove himself without delay and to have said, 'woe to us Arabs if Hitler wins!'[3] England, he said, had never shown any desire to take the Arabs lands from them.

In the beginning, however, it was agriculture that brought th Americans officially into the Kingdom.[31] Twitchell, the America engineer, whom Ibn Saud had known since 1931, when he had bee supplied *gratis* by Charles Crane to survey the country's minera resources, had been in the country again in 1940 at Ibn Saud's invi tation. This time – Philby being detained at His Majesty's pleasure i Britain – Twitchell was asked to survey the possibilities of roac construction in the Asir region. Whilst he was about it the King asked him one day to investigate the resources of Nejd in terms o water and agriculture: would it be possible to interest an America company or group of companies in such a venture?

Twitchell was unable to interest commercial companies in th project but cabled the King, asking if he would accept an officia US agricultural delegation to carry out the work. The King agree and the delegation flew from Washington on 19 March 1942. Afte delays in Cairo the party left from Bahrain on 9 May, flying on th next day to Bir Ruma where they were met by the sight of a considerable tented camp. The King, the Crown Prince and Princ Feisal and their advisers had come to meet the first American di plomats to arrive in the Kingdom, for along with the agricultura experts were the first American Minister, Alexander Kirk, come t open the Legation, and his assistant, who was to remain for years i the country, Raymond Hare. The Americans were fêted and afte lunch were shown films supplied by the British Legation, after whicl they were taken on the three-hour drive to Riyadh where a Nejd feast awaited them. The King had invited them to the Murabba Palace where, as Twitchell reports, he sat at the head of a table towering above his 32 guests.[32]

From there the agricultural specialists went to Al-Kharj wher Abdullah Sulaiman's scheme was developing whereby, with hel from the oil company, the land was able to supply most of Riyadh' vegetable needs. The Americans had chosen well in making an effor in this particular sector: as Twitchell modestly says, the King mucl appreciated it.

Next year even more serious matters were taken up. The Ameri can involvement in the total war effort on both the Pacific an Atlantic fronts meant that the US oil reserves were being depleted a a rate of about 3 per cent per year. By February 1943 it had bee brought to the attention of the President that Saudi Arabia was an essential alternative source of oil to be developed and on 18 February the President issued his finding that the security of Saudi Arabia was 'vital to the defense of the United States'[33] and the country was therefore eligible for Lend-Lease aid.

In August 1943 Ibn Saud received the President's special envoy, Colonel Hoskins, who was able to spend many hours in discussions with him on a daily basis for one week. At the same time there had been movement of British personnel, with the result that Stanley Jordan had arrived at the British Legation in Jedda. Having known Jedda in the 1920s – and been spoken highly of by Ibn Saud when he arrived in Jeddah – Jordan seemed well placed to develop good relations with Ibn Saud, but he is worthy of individual mention since it was 'on his watch' that Anglo–American relations in relation to dealings with Ibn Saud reached their nadir.

As an old hand, Jordan presumably felt qualified to speak his mind, and made no secret of his views about the financial recklessness of the Saudis, who were in receipt of both British and American aid. By the end of 1943 British aid to Saudi Arabia had reached a total of over £8 million but Whitehall was loud with complaints of the money being spent on more and more princely cars and palaces.[34] Jordan offered to the King ideas for introducing order into the country's finances and when one of the advisers, a Lebanese named Najib Salha, was removed amid accusations of embezzlement, rumour had it that the King had acted at the behest of the British Minister. As the idea of a British bank was being discussed at the same time it was perhaps understandable that certain overheated spirits should see evidence of British plans to move in to keep out American influence. The plot thickens when a new Minister arrived at the American Legation, Colonel William A. Eddy. Eddy, born in Sidon, Lebanon, spoke fluent Arabic and had recently come from being the North Africa Head of OSS, the predecessor of the CIA. He moved quickly to save the situation and an official protest was made to the British about the anti-American activities of Jordan. The British were inclined to adopt a robust attitude to such complaints but Ibn Saud himself took a position on the matter which he confided to Eddy: 'Jordan is our enemy and an enemy of the USA too. To the extent of his power he has sought to prevent our good relations and to injure my country.'[35]

The poor man seems much maligned but what was important was the way in which he was viewed and in particular by Ibn Saud. He had to go, and he was replaced by Grafftey-Smith, who was to be in the ideal position to describe Ibn Saud at the end of the Second World War, since he also had fluent Arabic and long experience in the Peninsula. He also had the priceless assets of a sense of humour and an ability to make connections not immediately obvious to everyone, as may be seen from the account of one type of his assistance to Ibn Saud's family. 'My Cairo dentist, summoned to Riyadh to pull a few royal teeth, took three weeks off from his Egyptian labours and returned with a hatful of gold.'[36]

Grafftey-Smith was to spend two years in Saudi Arabia and to write of the country and its King in affectionate manner but the occasion of his first meeting Ibn Saud could hardly have been more dramatic. Making his routine way to Saudi Arabia via Cairo in February 1945 he was startled to find that Ibn Saud was on his way to Suez on an American destroyer to meet President Roosevelt and Winston Churchill.

FAMILY LIFE

In this period Ibn Saud married three wives who bore surviving sons. These wives were all of Yemeni origin.
They were:
1. Sa'ida who bore him Hidhlul.
2. Baraka who bore him Miqrin.
3. Futaima who bore him Hamud, who was Ibn Saud's last surviving son.

Ibn Saud was also reported to have taken another wife from among the Rashidis 'and to have acquitted himself well in the sword dance which accompanied the festivities.'[37]

The wife known to have been the last wife taken by Ibn Saud is described in Lees, *The Al Saud: Ruling Family of Saudi Arabia*, 36, as 'unknown.'

Sons born to Ibn Saud in this period were:
1. Abdul-Majeed, born 1940.
2. Sattam, born 1940.
3. Ahmad, full brother to King Fahd, born in 1940.
4. Mamduh, born 1941.
5. Hidhlul, born 1941.
6. Mashhur, born 1942.

7. Abdul-Salaam, born between 1942 and 1944.
8. Miqrin, born 1943.

The grandsons born to the end of this period are as impossible to enumerate as the granddaughters.

10

Ibn Saud on the World Stage, 1945–51

I am happy to say that most of my men are from Syria.
Ibn Saud, 1946, to Syrian delegation quoted in Zirikli, p. 1237

The fault lies not with others but in myself! If it were in my power to choose I'd have Doomsday now.
Ibn Saud on morality in Riyadh 1948 to Philby, quoted in Philby, *Saudi Arabia*, p. 351

King . . . now considers USA only world power on whom he can rely. . . . He does not feel he can count . . . as he once did on Britain's ability to keep Hashimites in line.
Cable from Ambassador Childs to State Department 3 January 1950 in Ibn Al-Rashid *The Struggle between the Two Princes*

When the year 1945 began, Ibn Saud was almost 70 years of age and throughout the period to 1951 he showed signs of rapid physical deterioration. It is sad that it was in just this period that there occurred a climax in the problems facing a ruler of a vast country occupying most of the Arabian Peninsula, problems of the vulnerability of the country to external forces, problems of the adaptation to the enormous wealth which was becoming available to the monarch, problems of the creation of a system of management to confront these unprecedented situations. Externally there were violent upheavals in neighbouring countries: Yemen, Palestine, Lebanon, Jordan, Syria and Iraq while Egypt became engaged in the armed resistance to British presence which would lead to the evacuation agreement of 1954; in the Gulf region Saudi Arabia embarked on a collision course with the British because of its border claims in the eastern regions of the country, while Iran was approaching the crisis of the attempt to nationalise the oil industry. Domestically the King was not able to create the systems needed to handle the social, economic and financial problems created by oil-income, which by 1950 would exceed $50 million in one year. His lament to Philby in 1948 about the situation in Riyadh has often been quoted in illustration of the helplessness of Ibn Saud at this time.

There is a danger of regarding the King as totally unable to cope and resigning himself to 'après moi le déluge,' but we shall find much evidence of the way in which Ibn Saud was yet able to impose himself in this period in many ways. He achieved, for example, what may be his greatest victory, when he obtained from Aramco in late 1950 the agreement on 50–50 distribution of the profits of Saudi oil production.

The year 1945 began, however, not with the famous meetings with Franklin Delano Roosevelt and Winston Churchill in Egypt but with a visit of King Farouq to Saudi Arabia. The two kings met at Yenbo[1] on 25 January 1945 to discuss the progress of moves to establish what eventually became the League of Arab States, or Arab League, founded in March 1945. The two kingdoms became founder-members but there was much preliminary discussion and manoeuvring before and after the declaration of Arab Foreign Ministers at Alexandria in October 1944. The British had, to the puzzlement of not only Ibn Saud, given every encouragement to the establishment of the League, with the curious result that Anthony Eden, who launched British forces against Egypt in 1956 became in 1945 the only British Prime Minister ever to have his head commemorated on Egyptian postage stamps.

Relations between Egypt and Saudi Arabia had been restored in 1936 when the young Farouq succeeded his father, who had presided over the long breach in relations following the *mahmal* incident of 1926. They were to become ever closer as Saudi oil-wealth increased: there was to be much Saudi tourism and investment in Egypt while Egypt had much to offer Saudi Arabia in terms of an educated work-force for the growing needs of development. The question of the British presence in Egypt was often discussed: in particular, when guerrilla fighting began around 1950. Clearly the possibility of Saudi assistance to Egyptian resistance to the British was one which had constantly to be borne in mind, in particular when Saudi Arabia also found itself at loggerheads with Britain over the Buraimi dispute.

Farouq had suffered the ultimate humiliation in his view when the British Ambassador had in February 1942 presented his ultimatum on the choice of Prime Minister for Egypt with the support of tanks ringing the King's palace in Cairo. There was much to discuss be-tween Ibn Saud and the young King, but the course of their talks was not always untroubled.

In their meeting of January 1945 the King's understanding of Ibn Saud's breathy, Bedu colloquialisms finally broke down and Ibn Saud, realising what had happened, turned to the Egyptian who was to become the first Secretary-General of the Arab League and said, 'Tarjim, yaa Azzam!' ('Translate for us, Azzam!')

If a native Arabic speaker such as the King of Egypt could not understand Ibn Saud the many foreign diplomats and visitors with a knowledge of Arabic who confessed to missing large extracts of his speech may also be forgiven. Grafftey-Smith in 1945 was not the first or the last to confess to language difficulties.

His Arabic was not easy for me to understand, being a mixture of the classical (which I could follow) and tribal and beduin locutions (which I could not). His voice too, had no timbre, and much was said in a hoarse whisper, confusing to the ear.[2]

It is not difficult to imagine the problems facing an interpreter between the King and a visitor and it is perhaps because of such problems that Ibn Saud had robust views on the necessary evil of the existence of interpreters. In March 1926 when closeted alone with the Dutchman van der Meulen he confided, 'Now we can be alone without those interpreters, the most dangerous and harmful people in the world.'[3]

Ibn Saud had an approach to language which was as simple and direct as was his attitude to so many other things, whether Gertrude Bell, western cutlery, British foreign policy, or Palestine. Reader Bullard, while praising Ibn Saud's wide knowledge of international affairs, has reservations on Ibn Saud's care for the fine detail of foreign names: Mussolini would become 'Miss O'Looney' while Czechoslovakia would produce 'a sort of hiss and a helpless wave of the hand.'[4] Even Arabic words, if he found them a problem, would lead to his taking short cuts: his close adviser, Khalid Gargani (from Tripolitania) was always called Abu Waleed by Ibn Saud since he found his real name something of a mouthful.[5]

Language was clearly going to be a matter of importance for Ibn Saud's meetings with Roosevelt and Churchill and it is a sign of the maturity of the King's system of management that by 1945 he was able to have his own Saudi interpreter,[6] a graduate of the American

University of Beirut, Abdullah Abal-Kheir. He was to play a major role in the talks with Churchill, while the main interpreter for the talks with Roosevelt was Colonel Eddy.

Eddy had become privy to the plans for a meeting with Ibn Saud[7] in October 1944 and had approached Yusuf Yassin on the subject. The King agreed readily to the idea and plans were laid in the greatest secrecy. Security for the King and the President could be guaranteed only on the basis of total secrecy and the absolute minimum number of people knowing of the trip.

In early February 1945 the King's motorcade made its way from Riyadh to the Hejaz with all but Yusuf Yassin believing that their destination was to be Mecca. On 12 February the party left its last overnight encampment in the early hours, to be told at the last minute that part of the group was to make, not for Mecca, but for Jedda pier. The King had given instructions for an accompanying party of 48 people which was just twice the number expected by Eddy, though he had been told by Washington to ensure that the absolute maximum should be 12 persons.

The plan provided for an American destroyer, the USS *Murphy*, to bring the King and party to the Great Bitter Lake in the Gulf of Suez where the American President would receive the King abroad the USS *Quincy*. Eddy related some years later the first documented contact between modern military technology and Bedu culture as represented by Ibn Saud. The King had given orders for a flock of sheep to be made ready for the two-day voyage from Jedda, as was only fitting if he were to fulfil his duty to feed those travelling with him.

The negotiations on the dockside need not long detain us by which Colonel Eddy, interpreting between Abdullah Sulaiman and the captain of the destroyer, saved the lives of 93 sheep and saw only seven swung aboard, to be duly slaughtered, thus providing *halal* meat for the Muslims.

The King had been assigned a cabin fitting to his status but joined the members of his party in sleeping on deck. It was on deck also that Ibn Saud led his men in praying towards Mecca.

Meanwhile, back on land, the King's son, Feisal, had had the greatest difficulty in calming the breasts of the populace and especially those of the womenfolk of the household who had accompanied the motorcade, only to see the King disappear over the horizon out to sea. Jedda was loud with the bewailing of the kidnapping of Ibn Saud by the Americans but, eventually, calm was restored.

The King's party had as principal members his brother Prince Abdullah bin Abdul-Rahman, his sons Mansour and Muhammad, and close advisers Yusuf Yassin, Hafez Wahba, Rashad Pharaon, Bashir Saadawi, Abdul-Rahman Tobaishi and one described by Zirikli as 'one of the retinue of the King'[8] but among whose functions was confirming to the King that the navigation officer's indication of the direction of Mecca for prayer five times daily was correct.

Ibn Saud showed the same lively curiosity in this, his first, encounter with American armed might as he had shown in 1916 when the British showed him his first aircraft and X-rayed his hand. He was given demonstrations of target practice by the anti-aircraft guns and of the technique of using depth-charges, to all of which he responded with appreciation and dignity.

The Americans took every possible step to show the King consideration and hospitality, including specially-prepared cookies for breakfast. When these were served to him by a black steward the King, a notoriously light eater, declined but Yusuf Yassin who was at hand, reached out to help himself, encouraged by the King who said,

'You are fat and need more food!'

The steward withdrew his tray smartly and told Yusuf Yassin,

'No! These were made specially for the King and no one else.'[9]

The King was also shown an American documentary on the deck of the destroyer which related the adventures of an American aircraft-carrier in the Pacific, which may well have been the first film he had ever seen. His reaction was one of reserve for himself but he was perfectly clear that his people should not be exposed to such things as they would serve only to distract them from their religious duties.[10]

When the King disembarked he had distributed among the crew suitable going-away presents: $40 each for all members of the crew, with gold daggers and swords for senior officers. The Captain returned the compliment by presenting Ibn Saud with binoculars and machine-guns.

The King had to be hoisted aboard the *Quincy* since he was by now almost crippled with arthritis. He had a first meeting with the President of an hour-and-a-half, with Eddy interpreting, after which the President invited the King and party to lunch. The meetings between the two men lasted five hours, all told, including lunch.

The subjects of their conversation have often been described and in particular the question of Palestine.[11] Ibn Saud was rightly described by Roosevelt as more informative in five minutes on the subject than all the memoranda and presentations he had received on the matter. The President three times made a distinct effort to persuade Ibn Saud to be more forthcoming on allowing freer Jewish immigration to Palestine, in view of the appalling sufferings of the European Jewish community during the Second World War, now inevitably coming to an end in defeat for Germany. The King's reply was,

'Give the Jews and their descendants the choicest lands and homes of the Germans who have oppressed them.'

When the President countered by saying that the Jewish refugees would prefer to go to Palestine the King replied by saying that it was the criminal who should make amends, not the innocent bystander.

Ibn Saud resisted firmly all the President's arguments on behalf of freer immigration to Palestine by Jewish refugees and eventually was rewarded with promises in writing from Roosevelt that he would never undertake any action hostile to the Arabs and that there would be no action from the American side affecting the interests of Jews and Arabs without prior consultation with them.

Palestine was not the only question discussed in the meetings between Roosevelt and Ibn Saud. The question of Saudi participation in the war effort was raised and the King made a curious commitment not to attack the Allies, which eventually became a declaration of war on Germany and Japan in March 1945.

The use of bases in Saudi Arabia was discussed for the first time, but eventually the King gave a delaying answer in relation to the development of Dhahran as a military base.

Oil could not, of course, be far from the minds of the participants[12] and agreement was reached so as to give both sides something: the Casoc concession area was extended and the royalty per barrel was increased, from 18 to 21 cents. The possibility of building a pipeline for the oil from Hasa to the Mediterranean had been raised as early as 1943 and in discussion with Roosevelt Ibn Saud made perfectly clear his preference for the involvement of a private company.

Before parting that day, the President made the King a present of a wheelchair identical to his own to aid the King in his arthritic condition, which the King was hereafter to call cheerfully his *hisan* – his charger. Roosevelt also made the gesture of presenting Ibn Saud

with a DC-3 aircraft, which eventually became the means of estab
lishing Saudi Arabia Airlines, with the assistance of the America
airline, Trans World Airlines.

The President's warship was due to leave its mooring later tha
afternoon in order to make rendezvous with its convoy to make th
journey back across the Atlantic, so that Ibn Saud was not able t
repay the President's hospitality with a banquet of his own. H
insisted, however, on having Arabic coffee brewed on deck for th
President as some small token of Arabic hospitality.

After the President's departure, as Zirikli relates, occurred th
incident of the medicine chest. The King had already reached hi
next stop, to meet Winston Churchill, when Zirikli was sent-for i
the middle of the night to attend on the King. Some fool of a servan
said Ibn Saud,[13] had managed to leave his medicine chest on th
American destroyer and Zirikli must get it back. Zirikli realised tha
this was a matter for the resources of the American armed forces an
so he wakened Eddy, who arranged for an American aircraft t
pursue the disappearing *Quincy* to its next port of call and to delive
the medicine chest to its rightful owner.

The question of a meeting with Churchill had only arisen in th
British mind when Roosevelt mentioned to the British Prime Minis
ter on 11 February, the night before leaving Yalta, that he was plan
ning to meet Ibn Saud. In his 1954 version of events, Eddy portray
Churchill moving heaven and earth to ensure parity of treatment fo
himself, to which Grafftey-Smith replies that 'the King informed ou
Jedda Legislation that he would only travel to Egypt if he could mee
the British Prime Minister as well as the American President.' Th
King may have observed a curious form of deference[14] to his host o
the *Quincy* by asking the President if he had any objection to hi
meeting with Churchill.

Ibn Saud's meeting with Churchill took place at a slightly *louch*
hotel in the Fayyum oasis. The Hotel du Lac had been evacuated c
all its usual guests and it was there that Churchill gave a ceremonia
lunch for Ibn Saud and his party. Grafftey-Smith, who did some c
the interpreting on this occasion, describes the lunch party as a grea
success but his view does not correspond with that of the Ara
participants.[15] Possibly Grafftey-Smith was unduly relieved that th
Prime Minister had not made any effort to persuade the King t
relent towards Jewish immigration and that he had not advanced a
argument which he discussed with Grafftey-Smith before the mee
ing, namely that the British had done a great deal for the Hashimite

Abdullah in Jordan and Feisal in Iraq and that it was surely time for 'the Arabs' to do something in return. Another source of relief for the anxious British diplomat was that Churchill appeared to have got away with the device of having alcohol served in opaque glasses so as to disguise its identity.

The King offered the Prime Minister a sample of his favourite water from a well near Mecca which Churchill in his War Memoris describes as 'the most delicious that I had ever tasted.' The King bestowed lavish presents on his hosts: 'We were all given jewelled swords, diamond-hilted, and other splendid gifts,' while Sarah, the Prime Minister's daughter, discovered in the portmanteau which she received not only beautiful Arab robes but perfumes and a diamond with the valuation of £1200 attached. Churchill relates his embarrassment at having made so poor a showing himself as he had sent his detective to Cairo to buy £100 worth of perfume to present to the King, but he said to Ibn Saud, 'What we bring are but tokens. His Majesty's Government have decided to present you with the finest motor-car in the world, with every comfort for peace and every security against hostile action.'

Grafftey-Smith was later that year charged with supervising the delivery of a silver-grey Rolls-Royce on whose equipment he had given advice, bearing in mind security guards and the needs of hunting. He duly sent Cyril Ousman across the desert with the precious vehicle which was presented to the King in the courtyard of the Murabba' Palace. The King expressed his admiration for the present from the Prime Minister, but Ousman, before he left, heard the King say to his brother Abdullah that he could have it: the King had noted the right-hand drive which would have meant that he would have to sit at the left hand of his driver, since he habitually sat in the front of his cars. This was not fitting, as the place of honour is on the right. As Grafftey-Smith says sadly, 'The finest motor-car in the world was unusable.'[16]

Ibn Saud did not linger in Egypt, after the meeting with Churchill. The King resisted the idea of a sightseeing tour of Cairo and its environs so that he could return swiftly to Jedda and reassure his people. Cars were summoned after the morning of 19 February and the motorcade swept towards Cairo, creating totally unfounded stories of the King having strewn the road from the Pyramids to the centre of town with his abundant largesse.[17] On passing the Pyramids and having the story of their construction explained to him he delivered his judgement: 'israf!' ('A terrible waste of money!')

Embarkation on to a British warship for the King had to be by means of a crane, with his newly-acquired wheelchair accompanying the party. When the King disembarked in Jedda there was unparalleled rejoicing that he had returned from the dangers of the outside world, which was still at war.

A curiosity of the meeting with Churchill is that the British official interpreter for Churchill gives a different account of the course of political discussion from the Saudis, the Americans and Churchill himself. Grafftey-Smith in his book is clear that he managed to keep Churchill off the subject of Palestine. The Prime Minister in his own report of the meeting, however, confirms having discussed Palestine with Ibn Saud. Eddy reports the King as having told him of his indignation at Churchill's having the effrontery to suggest that British subsidies over so long a period should entitle Churchill to ask for moderation on Ibn Saud's part and a realistic approach to some form of compromise with Zionism.

Possibly the King, in recounting his discussions with Churchill, was reading back into the encounter his knowledge of Churchill's long involvement with the Palestine problem. He had, after all, been the Secretary of State for the Colonies who had called the 1921 Cairo Conference which had installed Feisal in Iraq and Abdullah in Transjordan and was viewed by many Arabs as being overly sympathetic to Zionism.

Whatever the case, Ibn Saud had come away from his meetings under a profound delusion, for the promises of Roosevelt were to mean nothing, firstly because by mid-April he was dead and secondly the new President, Truman, was won with comparative ease to the view that American domestic political considerations must be paramount in deciding on whether to give or withhold support for Zionism. It may be also that, had he lived, President Roosevelt would have had recourse to another approach to Ibn Saud since he was quoted by his intimates as saying that with a few million dollars he could do anything he wanted with Ibn Saud.[18]

In March 1945 Ibn Saud was able to claim a place for Saudi Arabia in the meeting halls of the new world organisation, the United Nations, at whose meetings his son Feisal represented his country. The San Francisco meetings had one long-term effect in that they opened wide the eyes of generations of Saudis to the delights of California

The King received in June 1945 one of the first of the many foreign visitors who were to make detours for the opportunity to know this man who was now becoming internationally famous as a patriarchal figure, newly-emerged from years of campaigning and poverty and yet the possessor of fabulous wealth. The last but one Viceroy of India, Field-Marshal Wavell, a soldier and a poet and a former Commander-in-Chief of British forces in the Middle East, was due to fly back to India in midsummer and was proposed for a visit to Ibn Saud by Grafftey-Smith. The King accepted the idea with pleasure and after landing at Jedda the Viceroy was ushered into the King's presence in Riyadh in June 1945.[19] Grafftey-Smith describes the scene, typical of so many times when he visited the King.

> The reed-like voices of five blind devotees, chanting the Koran, blended with the droning concert of distant water-wheels behind the bravery of brocades and gold of Ibn Saud's fantastic body-guard.

He goes on to describe one banquet, typical of so many. 'Ibn Saud was not a great eater and preferred to our succession of viands a great bowl of warm camel's milk, slightly curdled.'

The King, as was his wont, overwhelmed his visitors with farewell gifts but on this occasion was himself delighted with the presentation made to him. The Viceroy presented Ibn Saud with a beautiful illuminated Koran. It could not have escaped the notice of Ibn Saud that he was being courted by the direct successor of the Viceroy who had ignored his father's attempt in 1902 to establish treaty relationships between Britain and the Al Saud.

In July 1945 he had another visitor from England when Philby was able to make his way, a free man, from England to Cairo. The King sent his private plane to fetch him from Cairo to Riyadh and Philby was able to resume a life in which he paid no taxes, had free accommodation and air travel, did not need to register his car, and ate from the King's kitchen, not to mention his being the recipient of nubile young ladies from time to time.[20]

Ibn Saud seems genuinely to have believed, as he told many people, that Philby had given up a career with the British Government in order to serve him. Zirikli comments, 'This is how many people explain the King's continuing to look kindly on Philby.'

The King was not, however, blind to Philby's faults and not unaware of the need to observe due caution. Zirikli mentions how the King would often, on catching sight of Philby entering the *majlis*, abruptly change the subject.[21]

New experiences were not beyond Ibn Saud in spite of his

advanced years. In October 1945 he made his first journey by aircraf
and after this late and tentative start became every afterwards enthu
siastic about flying. He did, however, dislike flying at great heights
It is worth noting that despite the possibility of air travel Ibn Sauc
did not seize all opportunities to travel the length and breadth of th
country. He does not appear, for instance, ever to have visited Asir

In the same month as that in which he boarded an aircraft for th
first time, Ibn Saud was faced with a most delicate question, involv
ing Arab hospitality, relations with the British and relations with th
Iraqi monarchy. He was greeted one day at the mosque in Riyadh b
one who had made his entry to the country as one of a group o
Syrian journalists[22] but revealed himself to be a fugitive from Iraq
justice, Rashid Ali Gailani, one of the leaders of the rising against th
monarchy in Bagdad in 1941. The revolt had been suppressed wit
British military assistance and the Regent and Nuri Said had bee
able to return to the country. Gailani had in turn made his escape t
Europe and at war's end had escaped from France and with a forge
passport made his way via Beirut and Damascus to Riyadh. It woul
have been possible for Ibn Saud to adopt the position that his en
emy's enemy was his friend but the King exercised caution. Grafftey
Smith relates how the King consulted him as to what action h
should take and how he advised him to extend due Arab hospitality
but then to put him over the border.[23] Grafftey-Smith goes on to sa
that he deliberately did not suggest extradition to Iraq, as that woul
have been too shameful an act for the King, but hoped that extradi
tion to, say, Kuwait, would lead to the British getting their hands o
him some time. Ibn Saud took the position, however, that if he wer
responsible for the capture of Gailani, his womenfolk would spit i
his face.

The King also consulted King Farouq about the possibility o
Farouq mediating with the Iraqis but the Egyptian monarch, in
meeting with Zirikli on the Red Sea, advised that the Iraqis would b
controlled by the British so there was no hope of a pardon fo
Gailani. Ibn Saud therefore concluded that to hand him over woul
mean that he would be hanged and that that would be an eterna
shame on Saudi Arabia[24] and on the King personally.

Relations with King Farouq became closer with the beginning o
the New Year, for on 6 January the King arrived in Egypt in respons
to Farouq's invitation to make a State Visit. This was the first an
only State Visit made by Ibn Saud outside the Gulf or Peninsula are

and the first official international function which he performed following the end of the Second World War.

The Egyptians sent three ships to Jedda to convey the Saudi party and Ibn Saud embarked on the *Mahrousa*, Farouq's yacht and, indeed, the vessel on which he was to depart Egypt after the Revolution of 1952. The King was awaiting the arrival of Ibn Saud at Port Tewfik and the Saudi party made its way to Cairo by royal train from Suez. There was a triumphal arrival in Rameses Railway Station and a ceremonial procession to the Abdin Palace greeted by enthusiastic crowds. The Saudi party stayed as guests of the King at the Abdin Palace initially and then moved by train once more to the Ras El Tin Palace at Alexandria.

Ibn Saud had included Philby among his party but he was not included in the official guests of the Egyptian Government. The presence of an Englishman in the entourage of the most famous Arab leader to visit Egypt until that time was probably a genuine puzzle to them. The British themselves quite naturally took a particular interest in the visit of Ibn Saud and a delicate gesture was performed to compensate even more for the poverty of Churchill's gift to Ibn Saud of the previous year. Bearing in mind the King's poor sight and his need to have spectacles available in many places the Embassy arranged to have presented to the King no less than 365 pairs of spectacles.[25]

The King's 15-day visit to Egypt had several long-term consequences. Agreements were made for the supply of Egyptian technical and educational assistance to Saudi Arabia, King Farouq received an annual subsidy paid in gold, and Saudi Arabia acquired a railway.

The King had been enormously impressed by the rail journeys which he made during his visit and immediately on his return gave instructions for the necessary technical studies to be made which resulted in 1951 in his performing the opening ceremony for the Riyadh–Dammam railway. The choice of this mode of transport resulted from the King's very direct and realistic approach to problems. Knowing full well that the Kingdom would need to make enormous imports for construction and development Ibn Saud could see perfectly well that road construction and the use of motor transport could be brought about much more quickly than a railway line could be fully operational. However, he took into account a factor which the present writer knows, from a transport manager, in an

oil-rich Gulf country, is still important – that the Bedu habit o
calling in to see friends is guaranteed to throw out of joint the mos
careful logistics schedules.

Ibn Saud received a Syrian delegation in 1946, following up preliminary meetings which he had had in Egypt early in 1945. The
Syrian struggle for independence had at last managed to remove
French forces from Damascus and the Syrian visit of 1946 represented the first step in a process which was to make Syrian–Saudi
relations some of the most tortuous over the next 40 years. At this
stage Ibn Saud was content to utter praise for the Syrians in genera
and for those who were his advisers in particular. To the members of
the delegation he was at his most eloquent in reminiscing about his
own period of heroic effort, in order to give them encouragement
He displayed his wounds and graphically described how at times
during the 25 years of combat he had an occasion had to go ten days
without food.[26]

The question of Syria was even then intimately bound up with
that of Palestine, and it was Palestine which was to occupy the
thoughts of Ibn Saud constantly, and in particular in the period
leading up to the proclamation of the state of Israel on 15 May 1948

There can be no doubt of the depth of Ibn Saud's feeling over
Palestine, as was made clear when he was visited by the Anglo-
American commission in March 1946. In their international inquiries
the commission can probably never have heard such fearsome, ever
unwise, denunciation of the Jews in general.

> The Jews are our enemy everywhere. To every spot on earth to
> which they come they spread corruption and work against our
> interests.

The King spoke to the commission as representatives of the countries which he had loyally helped during the recent war. He recalled
his assistance to the British in ensuring the loyalty of British Muslim
troops from India and the promises which he had received from the
British for the support which he gave them. He recalled also how, he
said, the British Minister in Jedda had come to him after the war to
get him to keep the Arabs calm as the Zionist terrorist activities were
showing up the Zionists in their true light. 'I did everything possible
in this regard until we reached the situation we are now in.'

He then elaborated for the members of the commission the humiliation which he felt.

I am now in a very difficult situation with my people and my community, with the Arabs and with the Muslims. If the United Kingdom now wishes to turn away from what is the clear right and wishes its promises to be utterly worthless then I have no choice but to say to the Muslims: 'Kill me. Depose me. Because that is what I deserve. I have done you wrong and I have frustrated your determination.'[27]

To the unspoken question about the option open to him of doing something about the situation he replied that his country could not fight the Jews because that would be tantamount to fighting against Britain.

He referred again to friendship with Britain, saying that he did not wish to hurt the feelings of the British members of the commission but he was being frank out of friendship.

The Jews are coming to the countries of the Arabs and taking their possessions and expelling them, and doing them harm. So what reason or religion or policy could persuade the Arabs to accept such a situation?

And so saying, he told the members of the commission that his advisers would prepare a memorandum of his views. This they did and Philby stayed up all night translating it and typing it, to the members' entire satisfaction.[28]

The oil-wealth to which Ibn Saud was now gaining access in ever-increasing quantities, as the world entered the postwar reconstruction phase, was the major reason for the King's prominence in the Palestine question as in other Arab-world and international questions. In the first full year after resumption of exports Saudi Arabia received over $10 million but had only the most primitive means of accounting for the wealth. Royalties were paid into a New York account operated by Abdullah Sulaiman[29] which also contained his personal wealth. The Finance Minister would have been very pressed to handle questions of income and expenditure had he been at the peak of his form but years of stress and penny-pinching had reduced him to drunken incompetence and a severely limited working day. He was described by Grafftey-Smith at this time as 'the only Finance Minister I ever met who drank methylated spirit.'[30]

The King was not informed of the true state of the finances of the country, which had reached a point where the gap between income and expenditure meant that one dollar in four spent had to be borrowed. There was as yet no sensible way of allocating funds to house and feed the enormous extended family which Ibn Saud had created and to meet their exorbitant demands for luxuries, let alone to provide funds for development purposes, such as the needs of the population for schooling, medicine, housing and roads. It was this process of runaway expenditure on useless luxuries, with its resultant corruption, which Philby denounced even in the lifetime of Ibn Saud, whom he loved and revered. 'The bounty of the King began to pass beyond the bounds of wisdom and bred corruption in its path.'[31]

Philby also quotes an example of the way in which the King's will had to be obeyed in all matters and especially in the allocation of financial resources.

In the immediate postwar period the United States had offered Saudi Arabia $25 million worth of aid in kind, in the form of foodstuffs and silver. Abdullah Sulaiman had rejected this offer in favour of $10 million in cash to be spent on the lighting of Riyadh streets, on hospitals for Riyadh and Taif and on Jedda harbour. These heads of expenditure in turn were rejected by Ibn Saud,[32] so that absolute priority could be given to the construction of the Riyadh–Dammam railway.

Philby describes the King at this stage in his life in regretful tones: having had the benefit of five years' enforced absence from the King's company Philby was in an excellent position to note the contrast in Ibn Saud's conduct, attitudes and physical appearance. He also had the benefit of the fact that Ibn Saud was remarkably frank to him on the most intimate matters of his own sexual preferences and development.

The King is quoted by Philby as saying that he felt constrained at this point in his life to limit to once per night the performance of his marital duties.[33] Philby deduces, which may or not be correct, that Ibn Saud's inability to produce another son after the birth of Hamud in 1947 weighed heavily on his mind. What is certain is that Ibn Saud recognised the effect of the passing of time by ceasing to lead the *Hajj* cavalcade each year. His son Mit'ab was now assigned the honour of leading the Nejdi pilgrims while his father continued to perform the role of Custodian of the Two Holy Mosques by performing the *Hajj* himself and leading the senior princes in performing the traditional ceremonies.

Philby regrets also the way in which the King had become the prisoner of his medicine chest: 'He encouraged his physicians to ply him with drugs and medicines for his slightest ailments.'[34]

This may explain a curious feature of Ibn Saud's last years, that there was a very sudden and marked trend towards senility within a short period of his being given a clean bill of health by qualified foreign physicians.

An American doctor from the US Legation who examined him in 1947 gave his opinion that Ibn Saud's condition was 'one of excellent health for a man of his age'[35] with all teeth intact and in excellent condition and with no undue harm caused by a soft and rather obese abdomen and a small umbilical hernia which had been present throughout his life. Yet by April 1950 American doctors were reporting that Ibn Saud was now increasingly senile and confined permanently to his wheelchair.

Even in 1947 when he was visited by a British journalist, George Bilainkin, the King **dozed** off during his reception of Philby and the journalist.[36] 'The King **dozed** off for a few moments, woke and looked with surprise at the gathering of guests and guards around him.'

The King was, however, able to show Bilainkin his undiminished mental vigour when his visitor raised the subject of Palestine.

Staring at me long and pitifully Ibn Saud went on, 'I am ashamed for the British, because the Jews are making the policy of Britain. The road is quite clear. The country is Arab. We like peace in Palestine, we want independence for Palestine. The Jews are invaders and of course the Arabs demand freedom from the invaders'.[37]

The Palestine question was the most immediate but not the only ground for the King's feeling deep pessimism about the world political situation. He still followed very closely the course of international politics and until 1951 read for himself the reports of his diplomatic missions as well as having summaries of the day's world news read to him. By late 1946 he was expressing to Philby his despair over the spread of Communism[38] and the prospects for world peace. He even made a bet with Philby that there would be world war by spring 1947.

Philby was at this time continuing to play the role which Ibn Saud had jocularly attributed to him, that of constituting the opposition. He was particularly ready to disagree with the King on the subject of Palestine since, whereas Ibn Saud was ready to see some good in the

British Mandate, Philby was adamant that the continued existence of the Mandate could only lead to the spread of Bolshevism in the Arab world. On one famous occasion in 1947 Philby's indulging in his freedom to disagree with the King in open court led to 'a tornado of royal rage'[39] and the creation of a very suspicious attitude towards Philby on the part of those entitled to attend Ibn Saud's *majlis*.

This atmosphere may also have been present on the second occasion when Kim Philby entered our story. The son of Abdullah Philby having become a member of the British overseas intelligence service during the Second World War, whilst acting covertly on behalf of the Soviet Union, had been given a post in Turkey and now in February 1947 visited his father in Jedda. The father duly presented his son proudly at Court to Ibn Saud but the meeting was not a success: the King, for whatever reason, chose to be uncommunicative.

The King may also have been killing two birds with one stone in relation to Abdullah Philby when he sent him to India to make arrangements for the purchase of large quantities of tents to be used to house the pilgrims. While this was a fascinating opportunity for Philby to visit the country for the first time since 1915 where he had begun his official career it is difficult to imagine that Ibn Saud could not have found some other person to perform a comparatively undemanding task. The King may have wished to be free of his presence for a time and it is also not inconceivable that he wished to get a first-hand account of developments in India now that it was clear that Mountbatten, the Viceroy, had been commissioned to bring the British Empire in India to an end. Philby was well-qualified to report since he had *entrée* at the highest level throughout the country and indeed was received by Mountbatten.

When the King made his bet with Philby on the likelihood of a world war there were no clear signs that there would be a replacement for the British as a world power able to exercise influence in the Middle East. The Truman doctrine was announced only in March 1947, by which the USA committed itself to defending Greece and Turkey against Soviet expansion. (The USSR had already threatened Ibn Saud's neighbour Iran, until Soviet forces were forced to withdraw from Azerbaijan.) Ibn Saud lost that particular bet but he continued to be doubtful about the resolution of the United States: it remained a puzzle for him as a military strategist of some experience why the Americans did not exploit the fact that they had at this time indeed until 1949, a monopoly on atomic weapons.

Nor was the American attitude on Palestine of any comfort to Ibn Saud. The King sent his son Feisal to New York to argue at the UN against any such solution as partition of Palestine but had to endure not only the failure of Arab efforts to prevent the UN resolution of November in favour of partition but Feisal's exposure to insults. The King's son was booed and spat upon in New York by Jewish demonstrators,[40] which caused Feisal to tell the US Minister in Jedda that, had it been in his power, he would have there and then taken the decision to break off diplomatic relations with the United States.

The King's attitude to taking such a step and to making use of what came to be called the Arab oil weapon has been frequently discussed and indeed the case was argued to him at the time in his *majlis* and by outsiders. The irony of his position was not lost on him, that his country was entirely dependent for its one source of revenue – apart from the *Hajj* – on close relations with the one country which was doing the most – in Ibn Saud's view – to damage the interests of the Arabs by handing over Palestine to the Jews. Zirikli describes the way in which frustration built up in the King when, in front of his advisers, he burst into tears.[41] He explained to them, 'I was thinking about the state my community and nation has been reduced to, and what is to be its fate.'

Ibn Saud, on this occasion, as on so many others took the long view and frequently told people who urged him to cut off the oil, that it was better to build up wealth to become a strong force than to try to fight with feeble resources. He could, however, have no illusions in 1947 and 1948 about how the Saudi position would be regarded widely as that of a stooge of the Americans helping to finance the establishment of Israel. For the sake of guaranteeing the continuance of the flow of oil revenue Ibn Saud felt he had no alternative to concluding the negotiations for the building of the oil pipeline from Hasa to the Mediterranean (Tapline). The Tapline agreement was signed in the summer of 1947.

Ibn Saud faced problems nearer home than Palestine, for in January 1948 his agents brought him news of the failed coup in the Yemen where an attempt was made to assassinate the Imam Yahya. The actual assassination took place in a further attempt in February 1948, of which Ibn Saud also received very timely and detailed information. That he was not totally enfeebled was shown when he received the delegation of the perpetrators of the coup. He denounced them openly in his *majlis* as murderers.

In May 1948 Ibn Saud received in Jedda the son of the former King of the Hejaz, Abdullah bin Hussain, now King of Transjordan. Abdullah, the most embittered and articulate enemy of the Al Saud, had steeled himself to make this journey to the heart of his lost patrimony in order to win the blessing of Ibn Saud for his plans in relation to Palestine. Looking to the phase of territorial adjustments which would be needed following armed conflict in Palestine, Abdullah wished to incorporate the West Bank area into his Kingdom of Transjordan. Ibn Saud refused to give his blessing to these proposals.

The year 1948 could well be regarded as the blackest in the life of Ibn Saud, with the loss of Palestine, the coup in the Yemen, the threat to world peace in the Berlin Blockade and the increasing evidence of the vice and corruption invading his country. There had already in 1947 been public scandals such as a notorious drinks party given by his son Prince Nasir when seven people had died as a result of drinking wood-alcohol, one of them being a descendant of Ibn Rashid. It was with sincere feeling that Ibn Saud would say to Philby that he wished Doomsday would come now.

Perhaps an indication of light at the end of the tunnel might be seen in the agreement made at the end of 1948 by which a major oil producer, Venezuela, managed to negotiate a 50–50 agreement for the division of profits. From this time on Saudi Arabia moved forward actively, some would say aggressively, to maximise its returns from oil. The King was by no means an idle spectator in all this.

A young Saudi, trained in the oil industry at home and in Texas, was to be a token of the new approach. Abdullah Tariqi was assigned from this time to work in the careful monitoring of production in the concession area of Aramco which had come into existence in March 1947. Aramco was in varying ways given notice that the halcyon days could not last for ever. A new concessionnaire was allowed into the Saudi part of the Kuwait Neutral Zone, in the form of Pacific-Western, the vehicle of J. P. Getty. Abdullah Sulaiman ensured that Tariqi and his colleagues treated their responsibilities with due conscientiousness and pressure was put more and more on Aramco to be more forthcoming with advances of royalties.

In pursuit of a more active development of oil resources Aramco began exploration activities towards the Qatar frontier but the most significant measure which Ibn Saud authorised in this period was to put forward in October 1949 a new frontier claim in the entire eastern part of the country. As we have seen the matter had been left in beyance since discussions with Rendel representing the Foreign Office in 1937. Prince Feisal, who was to remain the moving figure in he oil negotiations until his father's death, had made it clear that the status quo was unsatisfactory but the proposals put forward now were breathtaking in their sweep.

The Saudi claim in the eastern regions now for the first time specifically included Buraimi, which had not so much as been mentioned in the various coloured lines proposed from 1913 to 1949. The frontier claimed represented a demand for 80 per cent of the sheikhdom of Abu Dhabi, including the Liwa oasis, the ancestral home of he rulers of Abu Dhabi, the Al Nahayan, which was an area specifically included in Abu Dhabi in the Saudi claim of 1935.

The British Government was now bound to take very careful note of Ibn Saud's proposals and prepare a careful response, but the story of the period from the initial claim of 1949 until Ibn Saud's death is one of continuous lack of understanding on both sides. Philby, for all his *parti-pris* in the matter, was probably correct to say that the matter of the dispute with Britain over Buraimi was one which caused deep upset to Ibn Saud. At the same time it is almost certain that the sweeping claims put forward were made in the belief that Britain, engaged in the process of withdrawal from obligations of Empire under a Labour government, would probably not have the stomach for confrontation with Saudi Arabia in defence of the sheikhdoms which were bound to Britain by exclusive treaty arrangements.

Ibn Saud was also committed to a forward policy in relation to Syria. The newly-independent republic had a dual significance for Ibn Saud as a partner in the confrontation with Israel and as a partner in opposition to the Hashimites in both Iraq and Transjordan (from 2 June 1949 called 'The Hashimite Kingdom of Jordan'). From the summer of 1949 began an imbroglio with the Syrian Government whereby a loan of $6 million was to be made to Syria by Saudi Arabia, the sum to be provided by Aramco as an advance of royalties. Oil and international politics became intermingled through this one transaction in a most illuminating manner.

Because of the Saudi Government's improvidence in budgeting, Aramco through 1949 and 1950 began agitating for repayment of the $6 million advance, only to be told by an Egyptian lawyer acting for the Saudi Ministry of Finance that the Saudi Government, in exercise of its sovereignty, was not bound by the terms of the original concession agreement.[42] This move, taken together with the exclusion of

Aramco from the Neutral Zone, was an indication of ominous developments in the future for the oil consortium.

The British also were feeling the draught of the King's displeasure at this time, through their Military Mission in particular. The Mission, which had had training responsibilities, had arrived in the country as early as 1947 but as the atmosphere became cooler between Saudi Arabia and Britain over Palestine and the eastern frontiers the Mission felt less and less welcome, so that by 1950 it was clear that their departure was only a matter of time.

Efforts were made to preserve some cordiality in the relationship, however. In January 1950 the consort of the Queen of England, the Duke of Edinburgh, who was still a serving officer in the Royal Navy, visited Jedda on board HMS *Chequers* and was received by the King and many princes with the greatest friendliness.[43] The effect of the visit was probably countered by the news that a Persian Gulf Frontier Force was to be formed, the forerunner of the Trucial Oman Scouts. This force, which was to have soldiers from Oman and Trucial Oman with British officers, was to have a specific and decisive role in the unfolding of the Buraimi crisis.

The year 1950 marked the passage of 50 years in the Islamic calendar since Ibn Saud's recapture of Riyadh and elaborate preparations were made to mark the event with festivities in the major centres of population. Ibn Saud was obliged to cancel the celebrations at the very last minute because of objections by the Ulema. In this respect there were limitations on the King's authority.

Nonetheless, in spite of rumours of Ibn Saud's increasing senility, he was still the seat of all power in matters large and small. When Wilfred Thesiger arrived at Sulayyil in 1948 without authorisation from the King, the local governor had no option but to consult Riyadh, from where he received Ibn Saud's blunt instruction to put Thesiger in jail. It was only the personal intervention of Philby which allowed the release of the explorer.

Similarly, it should be borne in mind that no plane could land or take off without the King's authorisation, in particular in Riyadh. Furthermore the King's role as military commander of the tribes was not now a factor to be ignored. The British Ambassador in Jedda had to make plain to the Saudi Government the unease of the British Government over tribal raids into the Aden Protectorate by tribes owing allegiance to Ibn Saud. In the same way tribal raids and counter-raids were still embittering relations between Iraq and Saudi Arabia as late as 1950–51.

The King experienced great sadness in the summer of 1950 when his beloved sister Nura died. They had always been extremely close, even before the recapture of Riyadh, and he had derived considerable comfort from her at many difficult periods of his campaigns. Following the end of his campaigns, when Riyadh was able to enjoy the benefits of telephone contact, the first line after Ibn Saud's was run to the home of his sister, Nura.[44]

The outbreak of the Korean War in June 1950 was an event which caused Ibn Saud great concern, as is recorded by American diplomats who discussed the world situation with him at length. To the State Department via his Ambassador in Washington he confided that he was lining up with the US with respect to Korea. 'I am with you and I want you to know it,'[45] but he preferred to delay making a formal announcement until he could get clarification of the Arab states' position on the subject.

Relations with the Arab states represented a minefield with so many conflicting interests and differences of regime but at this time relations with the Hashimites were the issue of the hour.

In January of 1950 Childs reported to Washington that Ibn Saud was genuinely concerned at what he saw as his vulnerability with respect to the Hashimites and, in particular, Jordan. Whereas five years ago he felt that he could rely on the British to rein in the Hashimites' ambitions he no longer had that confidence and felt that it was only the US that could guarantee his security. But he had no firm assurance, Childs reported, that the US Government was prepared to protect him from a Hashimite move to reoccupy the Hejaz.

Ibn Saud occupied a great deal of the attention of the State Department at this time since American diplomacy had been involved in continuous discussions with American oilmen about the implications of worldwide oil developments such as the Venezuelan 50–50 profit-sharing agreement. The result was that a similar 50–50 agreement between Aramco and Saudi Arabia was signed in Riyadh on 30 December 1950.

'Ibn Saud had won a notable victory perhaps his greatest off the battlefield.'[46]

FAMILY LIFE

Ibn Saud married in this period the following wives who had children who survived.

1. In 1946 Futaima, who the following year bore him his last surviving son, Hamud.

2. A wife unknown, who bore him three daughters.

11

The End, 1951–53

Assuredly there will be no hoarded treasure at the death of Abdul-Aziz to be passed on to his family.

K. Williams, *Ibn Saud*, p. 256

Do heroes make good rulers? Not this one.

D. van der Meulen, 1952, after farewell visit to Ibn Saud, in *Wells of Ibn Saud*, p. 257

He certainly died with the feeling that his British friends had never shown any disposition to redress the one personal grievance which he had of them (the Buraimi dispute).

Philby on Ibn Saud's death, in *Forty Years in the Wilderness*, p. 214

In 1951 *The Statesman's Year Book* could describe Ibn Saud as follows:

The King has over 30 sons of whom the following are the most prominent:- Saud, born 1905, the heir apparent; Faisal, born 1907 the Minister for Foreign Affairs and Viceroy in the Hejaz; Mansour, born 1921, the Minister of Defence; Mohammed, born 1913, the Amir of Medina.[1]

Having misstated the number of his sons – which was then over 40 – and the birth-dates of the most prominent of them, the reference book then goes on to find nothing to report under the usual heading for all countries, namely education.

A picture is sometimes painted of Ibn Saud reaching the end of his days and coming to the appalled conclusion[2] that he had done nothing to prepare his country to face the problems of adjustment to the modern world and the development of human resources.

Muhammad Asad writes that:

some of the best among the people of the Nejd now speak in bitter terms of what they consider a betrayal of their trust. . . . When I saw him last in the Autumn of 1951 . . . it seemed to me that he had at last become aware of the tragic waste of his life . . . when he spoke of himself he seemed to be speaking of something that was already dead and buried beyond recall.

It is possible, however, to view matters in a different light. Ibn Saud was, at all stages of his career, conscious of the limitations on his freedom to act and in relation to education and the introduction of modern technology and means of communication it was always crystal-clear to him that, in view of the entrenched conservatism of the Ulema, he would have to proceed with great caution in the matter of the education of the young.

Ibn Saud tackled the problem of educating the princes of the royal family in spite of the resistance of Philby.[3] When the topic came up in the King's *majlis* Ibn Saud summed up the position of the man whom he was happy to describe as the equivalent of the Opposition to his rule. 'Philby does not want me to educate my sons!'

He made arrangements for a private school to be run in the Palace, known as 'The Princes' School' not out of a wish to make education the exclusive privilege of the royal family but so as to avoid problems with the Ulema.

Education in Saudi Arabia then as now had always to take into account the wishes of the religious establishment and up till the last days of his life Ibn Saud had to make allowances for the position which insisted that all education must be religious, with exclusive emphasis on teaching the Koran and the Sunna, Hadith and Islamic Jurisprudence.

Ibn Saud chose the path of least resistance by opting for private education for the royal family and by putting no obstacles in the way of other projects for private education, both in the country and abroad. Egypt, Lebanon and Syria were the favoured centres for education above the primary level in the King's lifetime. Egypt in 1950 attracted Saudi young men in their hundreds: there were 206 at the two modern Cairo universities, 30 at Al-Azhar and 11 at Victoria College. It was Victoria College in particular which accounted for the comparatively large numbers of Saudis with excellent English in key positions in the 1960s, such as Adnan Khashoggi, Hisham Nazir and members of Hejazi trading families, for the College was run on the lines of English public schools. English was the medium of instruction, with penalties for anyone daring to revert to Arabic, and even cricket became part of the cultural equipment of young Saudis. Lebanon provided not only university education, with over 100 studying at the American University of Beirut between 1949 and 1952, but also secondary education, as individual families began to experiment with education for their sons at, for example, the Quaker school at Brummana. Aramco also sent young men to receive higher education at Aleppo College.[4]

Within Saudi Arabia a modest start had been made with the introduction of primary education, with assistance from Egyptian teachers and inspectors. By 1950 some degree of specialisation had been reached, since there were in that year primary schools, rural primary schools, secondary schools and evening schools. How modest the start was can be gauged from the total number of students: for 1950 the number of boys in day-time education for the entire country hardly reached 20 000. There was, of course, no question of arranging public education for girls.

The King's interest in medical matters has been well-documented but he has often been portrayed as having a blind spot for matters of public health.[5] Even in the 1920s he had taken measures to prevent epidemics on the *Hajj* which were in complete contrast with the irresponsible neglect of public health measures by Hussain bin Ali. By the time that oil revenues became substantial in the late 1940s Ibn Saud moved as soon as it was possible to mobilise resources in money, American assistance and available manpower to put in the beginnings of a health-care system.[6] Before his death there were hospitals in Riyadh, in the Eastern Province and at Mecca, Jedda and Taif and for the year before the King's death the health budget was increased from $2 million to $7 million with a further $8 million allotted to buildings and equipment. There were plans in that year for setting up 38 clinics to cover the country with mobile clinics planned for the Bedu areas. By 1951, with American assistance, malaria had been eradicated at Jabrin oasis which had had to be abandoned for years. Similar action was taken in the Khaibar region north of Medina, where water-logged lands had been reclaimed, thus eliminating the scourge of mosquitoes. Ibn Saud had welcomed the locust and anti-malarial researchers in the 1940s with a view to the long-term elimination of malaria.

The area of defence of the realm was, as we saw from Ibn Saud's discussions with the US Ambassador, a matter of deep concern for the King, knowing as he did how little his small regular forces could do against even a modest army providing that it was professionally led and trained. Such forces he could see in Jordan and it was as much with the threat from Jordan in mind that Ibn Saud moved the bulk of the army to the Hejaz in his last year, as from fear of secession by the Hejazis. The King had also moved in the late 1940s to bring about better training of the regular army by use of both British and American military training missions but only modest progress had been achieved. An air arm was an aspiration for the future but little had been achieved to replace the training done before the war of Saudi pilots by the Italians. Some pilot-training had been begun by the Americans with whom Ibn Saud had at last in June 1951 signed an agreement for five years for the use by the Americans of Dhahran air base, which they had constructed in 1946. A navy simply did not exist, with the result that the protection of the coastal waters was a matter of relying on the continued existence of good relations with neighbouring countries and with protecting powers.

To coordinate what defence activities there were and to institute some sort of forward planning Ibn Saud had created the fourth ministry of his reign, that of Defence, in 1946 and had nominated his son Mansour, then aged 25, to be the Kingdom's first Minister of Defence.

The other ministries were Foreign Affairs, Interior and Finance, where Abdullah Suleiman was still the Minister. Although he was by now, as a British official called him, 'a worn-out old toper' he held the threads of not only the Finance Ministry but also of an embryo Ministry of National Economy and of numerous directorates dealing with health, education and transport and communications. Since the Minister's day was by 1951 limited by the effects of alcohol to an average of an hour and a half the country was sinking rapidly into total disorganisation. As the American Ambassador commented to Washington on 11 June 1951 succinctly, and with feeling: 'Organisation means little to this government.'[7]

Although it is possible to speak of separate ministries it was Ibn Saud who, almost until the moment of his death, controlled the activities of all aspects of government and it must be Ibn Saud who should be held responsible for the primitive state of the administration of the finances and destiny of the Kingdom which he had created.

It must also be said that the King bears responsibility for the rejection of reforming ideas, especially in the handling of the country's wealth. By 1951 the same Najib Salha who had been removed for embezzlement in 1943 had returned with a brief to bring the administration of the government's financial affairs into the modern era, so that there might at least be some means of identifying expenditure. His modest proposals did not win the endorsement of the King who referred them to Saud, who rejected them entirely. Salha persevered and even managed to introduce income-tax proposals but these were of negligible effect since, from the start, the royal family in its entirety and the Ulema were exempt, and, after violent protests the merchants were also made exempt. Financial management was so reckless[8] that in the budget for 1950–51 some two-thirds of the entire expenditure was earmarked for 'State Palaces, Princes and Royal Establishments.' By 1952–3 this figure had been reduced to a quarter of national expenditure but no less than one-sixth of expenditure was for debt-servicing. By the time of the King's death Najib Salha was to estimate the Kingdom's indebtedness at 150 to 200 million dollars, while oil income for the boom year of 1951 was approximately $110 million. There was, however, if not salvation in sight, at least movement to rationalising the use of the oil income, with the establishment of the Saudi Arabia Monetary Agency, in effect the country's central bank. The King had approved the setting-up of the Agency in May 1952 on the recommendation of visiting American experts and by the time of his death, royalties were no longer paid into Abdullah Sulaiman's New York account but into SAMA.

The King had made a further important decision in relation to oil operations by having Aramco move its operational headquarters from New York to Dhahran. This had the effect of concentrating the attention of company executives on the local environment and the development of the local workforce and creation of local business. There were many instances of Saudi employees of Aramco being set up in business, servicing the company with transport, food supplies and the like, and building on these modest beginnings, becoming very wealthy. Sheikh Sulaiman Oleyan began as a truck driver for Aramco at 300 riyals a month and became a dollar-billionaire.

Such stories represent the happy ending of Aramco's presence in the country but this felicitous outcome was achieved only after some bitter experiences. Before Ibn Saud died, the oil operations were almost totally closed down, for in October 1953, 17 000 of the 19 000 work force went on strike for better pay and working conditions.

The strike had come about after a petition had been presented in May 1953 by Saudi and other non-American employees, asking for better housing, higher wages and more privileges. Too great a disparity had grown up between the comfort provided for the American expatriates living in their models of 1950s American towns at Dhahran and the bachelor dormitory accommodation and working conditions of the rest of the labour force, drawn from Saudis, Palestinians and other Arabs. Since Aramco was not authorised to deal with trade unions, it could deal with the petitioners only on an informal basis during the summer until the Saudi government moved to take a role in the dispute. The petitioners, however, refused to answer the questions of the Saudi government officials and were gaoled for their pains. The next day there was an eruption of apparently spontaneous anger with attacks on a police station and on company vehicles. Thousands of troops were drafted in for fear of sabotage of the oil-installations but a confrontation was avoided and gradually there was a return to work, shortly before the King died.

The King's last two years were undoubtedly times of great personal unhappiness and physical pain. Not only did he cease to be able to produce children but a favourite son, Mansour, died after an operation in Paris in May 1951. Another son, Mishari, had caused distress of a different kind since he had, under the influence of drink, shot dead a British engineer who had lived for many years in the country. The most severe bodily complaint from which the King suffered was the accumulated effect of an injury to his knees which made him almost totally immobilised. As a result he had a very noticeable gain in weight which accentuated the pain he felt in his knees. He performed his last *Hajj* in 1951 in great heat, having missed the 1950 *Hajj* when Saud had deputised for him. He also missed the 1952 pilgrimage and by 1953 a journey to Mecca in the heat of summer was out of the question. Instead the King was flown to the coolness of Taif after performing his last act as King, the signing of the decree establishing a Council of Ministers, which the US Embassy believed might do something 'to bring order to the present chaotic state of the administration.'[9]

On 8 August 1953 Ibn Saud was flown to the airfield near Taif in the DC-3 presented to him by the American President. When he was transferred to his car to be driven to his summer palace he was seen by Zirikli[10] who records that his gaze was frozen and that he recognised no one around him. His relatives assembled quickly and Feisal and Saud in particular were always in attendance on him. Zirikli recalls that the King never ceased to urge the two brothers to work together after his death but it is perhaps symbolic that Saud had left temporarily for Jedda at the moment when on 9 November 1953 Ibn Saud died in the arms of his second son Feisal.

Following the ceremony of giving allegiance to Saud the body was flown immediately back to Riyadh. It was buried in an unmarked grave 'and today one must ask of the desert winds and of the cold Arabian stars to find his resting-place.'[11]

The clothes of Ibn Saud were sold in the market place: had he not said to Philby in almost his last conversation with him,

A man's possessions and his children are his worst enemies.[12]

FAMILY LIFE

A son was reported to have been born to Ibn Saud in June 1952 and was described in the press as the King's 64th child.[13] He died in infancy.

12

Envoi

Feisal, Saud is your brother.
Saud, Feisal is your brother.

There is no power and no strength save in God.
The last words of King Abdul-Aziz bin Abdul-Rahman Al Saud

The visitor to Riyadh today who goes in search of information about Ibn Saud may find the way to the Darat al-malik Abdul-Aziz, or The King Abdul-Aziz Research Centre. This lies just near the beginning of the road to Dar'iya and immediately before the palace of the late King Feisal.

From the mosque, to the left immediately after entering, the call to prayer marks intervals in the visitor's enquiries and researches. An enquiry at reception will produce an offer to open the museum where the visitor can see examples of the swords with which Ibn Saud fought, the 1940s American cars in which he rode, the books which he read and the chairs in which he sat. If the visitor moves upstairs the first things to catch the attention will be oil-paintings representing the King's meetings with both Roosevelt and Churchill beyond which lie the research facilities for the study of the life of the founder of the Kingdom of Saudi Arabia.

Much remains to be done in investigating the life of this complex man who for more than fifty years was the source of all decisions and power, whose name occurs for almost fifty years in the records of the power most concerned with the Peninsula, Britain. Many episodes in his career are capable of as many interpretations as there are accounts by him of the capture of Riyadh in 1902. His personality was as complex as the photographs of him are various: one of the curiosities of the many photographs of Ibn Saud which exist is that they often do not seem to be of the same man, even within a quite short time-span. The stories of his utter ruthlessness with opposition and his ordering the killing of prisoners are hard to reconcile with the stories of his gentleness and vulnerability to tears of profound emotion. Accounts of his violent rages and beatings of servants are as common as those of his charm and gentleness. His delight in playing with his young children contrasts with apparent indifference to their development as young adults.

Can it be true, as Muhammad Asad wrote, in the year of Ibn Saud's death, that 'his failure lies rather in his having failed to be as great as the people had thought him to be . . . He . . . simply remained a benevolent tribal chieftain on an immensely enlarged scale'?[1]

To answer this question it may be useful to examine the story of Ibn Saud's life and achievements under the headings which are suggested in Chapter 6, dealing with Ibn Saud at fifty.

It is to some extent misleading to parcel up the subject in this way since many of the headings overlap: for example Ibn Saud's crucial decision in 1933 to nominate his son Saud as Crown Prince could be viewed under the headings of Ibn Saud's roles as head of the family, monarch, tribal leader and even, possibly, as religious leader, given that Ibn Saud, as a good Muslim, would have been well aware that one of the greatest causes of division in the Islamic community resulted from the Prophet's not having nominated a successor.

Nonetheless a reasonable basis for discussion in evaluating Ibn Saud may be to highlight certain features of his character and conduct under the ten headings suggested.

It is as monarch above all, that Ibn Saud suggests himself as an outstanding figure. At his death he was the world's longest-established head of state who not only reigned but ruled. By 1953 Ibn Saud had been for, at the very least, 25 years the all-in-all as the motive force in the running of a vast country which, at the beginning of his reign as King of Saudi Arabia, had negligible resources and which at his death had income from one resource, oil, which could be measured in hundreds of millions of dollars. No decisions in the running of the country could be taken without reference to him even in his last two years. Moreover Ibn Saud showed great awareness of how to avoid a situation where, for example, the concerns and complaints of ordinary people could be kept from him through his being involved with matters of world affairs and high finance. He gave specific instructions that all petitions addressed to him must reach him without delay and without amendment.

His concern for carrying out his role as leader of all his people could not be questioned, but the greater issue is whether Ibn Saud could have done more to ensure good government and proper administrative procedures to handle the country's problems. Saudi Arabia from 1945 faced problems of adjustment to a role in world politics but in the period of eight years till Ibn Saud's death apparently very little was done in a systematic way to prepare for a smooth process of adaptation. It was only in the last year of his reign, and indeed one month before his death, that a formal approach was made to having a system of council of ministers with defined responsibilities. It was almost too late, since the ministers were helpless to stop the collapse into chaos which occurred in the reign of his son Saud. Ibn Saud must bear responsibility for this lack of preparation of the country as a whole, and possibly the greatest contributing factors to the lack of preparation were his concentrating all executive power and power of decision in his own hands for so long and his choice of his son Saud as his successor.

The choice of Saud may be related to the second of Ibn Saud's roles, that of tribal leader. Saud's mother was of the bani Khalid, not of the families related to the Al Saud such as the Sudairis and the Al-Sheikh, into which they were accustomed to marry. Throughout his adult life Saud had close relations with the tribes, was popular with them and loved to travel amongst them. Following his nomination as Crown Prince, Saud was annually to receive the fealty of his brothers and of the tribal leaders: the implication was clearly that of the renewal of the tribal fealty.

Ibn Saud saw with great clarity the need always to preserve the loyalty of the tribal leaders and used with great skill the traditional ways of maintaining contact with them, through marriage and hunting expeditions. His realism made him in no doubt of the need always to ensure that the loyalty of the tribes was bought and paid for. That the country did not disintegrate at his death was in large measure due to his skill in maintaining the loyalty of the tribes to the Al Saud.

As a military commander Ibn Saud was a highly gifted amateur. He had no formal training in military affairs but learned through hard-won experience how to conduct military operations. The scale of his operations would be viewed by most professional military men as amounting to little more than skirmishes, commando raids and siege operations conducted with less than total respect for the principles of, say, a Vauban. They were, however, 'the only game in town' and were decisive in establishing the defeat of his domestic rivals, the expulsion of the Turks and recognition by the dominant foreign power, Britain. In the period after the Second World War,

Ibn Saud had to adjust to the use of the air weapon and the existence of the atomic bomb, which he did with considerable success. He saw clearly the need to take account of the need for foreign protection and had little doubt that this meant the United States: the only problem was how to reconcile this with Saudi independence and the need to respect growing nationalism in other Arab countries. Furthermore Ibn Saud ensured that foreign military expertise was brought to bear on the needs of Saudi armed forces especially after 1945, which eventually came to mean US military training since relations with Britain deteriorated because of the Buraimi dispute. What was achieved before his death was little enough but the foundations were laid for the development of professional armed forces.

It may be regarded as an impertinence for any parent to pronounce on the capacity of another as a head of family but the question must be dealt with since Ibn Saud's sons have, to date, provided all the monarchs of Saudi Arabia since 1953 and seem likely to continue to do so. It is a temptation for outsiders to concentrate on undoubted scandals which have occurred amongst his sons (there is no information on his daughters) and in some to blame the father for the errors of his offspring. As Ibn Saud produced sons over a period of more than fifty years the way is clearly open for venture into a sort of numbers game with the object of establishing points for and against. The present writer begs leave not to embark on such a process but would argue that it is a very striking achievement for one man to have produced so many able, educated and energetic sons as have emerged, most of whom were born at a time when the dominant feature of Saudi Arabia was dire poverty, with an accompanying lack of educational resources. A feature of Ibn Saud's outlook noted throughout this biography has been his concern for the education of his sons and, as resources allowed, for the education of the youth in the country. It deserves to be pointed out that the first young men to study abroad were dispatched soon after the taking of the Hejaz, in 1927.

Ibn Saud always had the view of himself as a teacher, primarily because of his position as Imam. It is this which explains his readiness to indulge himself in homilies which Amin Rihani commented on with some scepticism. He regarded it as crucial to the continued existence of the Saudi state to maintain the closest links with the religious establishment of the country and the foremost consideration at all times was that all change must be with the consent of the Ulema, whether it was the introduction of cars, or education, or broadcasting, or the telephone or of the press. It is this which explains the painful slowness of change at many points in the history of the third Saudi state, during the time of Ibn Saud and after, but it was the insight of Ibn Saud that slow change without disabling disputes was better than speed of change with great disruption.

As a world statesman Ibn Saud had a uniquely long period of apprenticeship and practice. From the time when he began to attend the *majlis* of Sheikh Mubarak of Kuwait in the 1890s Ibn Saud learned the ways of the world at the level of dealings between states and, in particular, was able to observe the ways of the great powers with small, weak states and protectorates. Within ten years of recapturing Riyadh he had almost completed the process of ending the Turkish presence in his future domains and from that time on he was intimately involved in relationships with Britain. It was only in 1945 that it became clear that the United States would play a greater role in the future of Saudi Arabia than Britain. Sir Percy Cox would undoubtedly, had he lived, have revised his view that he had never known Ibn Saud put a foot wrong, but his views would have been somewhat United-Kingdom-centred. From the point of view of Saudi interests it could be argued that Ibn Saud was distinguished by his ability over a period of fifty years to discern clearly where the long-term benefit to his country lay.

The role of Ibn Saud as welfare state is one which was clearly to be seen when his realms were confined to Nejd and he could playfully refer to himself as the *jasur*, the animal prepared for the slaughter, from which all could take their cut. He provided, and was seen conspicuously to provide, food, hospitality and presents for many thousands of individuals. When he became the beneficiary of great wealth the same mentality prevailed. There seems to have never been any question of the wealth from oil being other than the personal wealth of the ruling family, to be dispensed to the population at the monarch's sole discretion.

A similar continuity of view is evident in Ibn Saud's playing the roles of foreign minister and finance minister. We have seen how he personally conducted foreign relations from the time when he was in exile in Kuwait and how personal and active a role he took in handling the financial resources available to him. Even at the end, Ibn Saud read or had read to him all his ambassadors' reports and only in the last year of his life did he finally agree to the establishment of the Saudi Arabian Monetary Agency. Although this step was almost too late, since the Agency could do little to staunch the waste of money in the days of King Saud, it is at least evidence of Ibn Saud's slow conversion to agreeing to the introduction of foreign expertise into the country's management.

It is tempting, when examining the life of Ibn Saud, to say not only as was said at the beginning, 'Si monumentum requiris, circumspice . . .' but also 'Si la jeunesse savait, si la vieillesse pouvait. . .'.

The sad feature is that it was only when Ibn Saud was in his seventies that the country that he established came to have the resources which would have enabled him to introduce those systems and procedures which might have softened the shocks to the country's being which it was to suffer. Saudi Arabia, under the leaderhsip of King Saud, had to face a concentrated eleven-year period of not only the appearance of wealth beyond the dreams of avarice but a period in the history of the Arab world which was unique for its concentration of the impact of the Cold War, the Arab Cold War, the rise of Arab nationalism and republicanism, the end of Empire, and the diffusion of new ideas through the mass media and the spread of education. Even a long-established regime would have had the gravest difficulty in maintaining stability in the 1950s and 1960s. That Saudi Arabia was able to come through the ordeal is in large measure due to the manner in which elements of continuity were introduced and maintained by Ibn Saud.

Appendix A
Chronology of the Life of Ibn Saud

(The most significant dates before 1921 are marked*)

Year	Event	Remarks
1876*	Probable date of birth of Ibn Saud in Riyadh	Father: Abdul-Rahman Mother: Sara Sudairi (See Note to Introduction)
1877 1878	Russo-Turkish War Congress of Berlin	Beginning of final phase of dismemberment of Turkey in Europe. Britain takes over Cyprus.
1881	French take Tunisia	At expense of Turkey
1882	British forces land in Egypt	Evacuation treaty: 1954
1885	Death of Gordon in Khartoum. End of Saudi rule in Riyadh	Final British victory: 1898 Philby notes that this coincides with his own birth-date.
1889	Britain makes 'exclusive' treaties with Bahrain, Trucial Coast and Muscat	Qatar: Ottoman Turkish rule Kuwait: Treaty with Britain only in 1899
1890	Bismarck dismissed as Chancellor: Kaiser Wilhelm II pursues more adventurous foreign policy	Kaiser in Syria and Palestine 1898

Year	Event	Remarks
1891*	Defeat of Al Saud and departure from Nejd Rashidis dominant in Nejd, Qassim	Two years wandering before settling in Kuwait
1892(?)	Ibn Saud takes first wife	She dies after 6 months
1895	Visit of Russian surveyor to Gulf of Hormuz	Challenge to British role in Gulf
1896	Ibn Saud takes second wife. Mubarak of Kuwait kills half-brother and takes over	Umm Turki, the mother of Turki
1897	Zionist Congress, Basle Death of Muhammad bin Rashid, ruler of Hail	Following the Dreyfus Affair
1899*	Britain makes exclusive treaty with Kuwait	Ibn Saud takes note
1901	Saudi forces raid Nejd	Defeat at Sarif
1902*	Ibn Saud recaptures Riyadh Al Saud return to Nejd	Son, Saud, born same day (?)
1903	Lord Curzon tours Gulf	Insists on British dominance
1904	Battle of Bukairiya: defeat of Turks and Rashidis by Ibn Saud	Ibn Saud accepts nominal Turkish suzerainty
1905	Ibn Saud visits Trucial Coast	British alarmed
1906*	Abdul-Aziz bin Rashid killed in battle against Ibn Saud	Ibn Saud wounded
1907	Britain and Russia divide up Persia	Spheres of influence

Year	Event	Remarks
1908	First Middle East oil-strike	Persia
	Hussain bin Ali becomes Amir of Mecca	Later: King of the Hejaz
1909	Deposition of Sultan Abdul-Hamid	'Young Turks' in power
1910*	Ibn Saud first meets Captain Shakespear	First known photos of Ibn Saud
1911	Turkey at war with Italy	Tripolitania lost to Italy
1912*	First major Ikhwan settlement	Artawiya
1913*	Ibn Saud expels Turks from Hasa	Today 'The Eastern Province' of the Kingdom
1914*	First World War begins	British–Turkish treaty aborted
	Secret treaty Ibn Saud/Turkey	Denied by Saudis and Philby
1915*	Ibn Saud in battles with Ajman and dissident Al Saud	Ibn Saud wounded. Brother Saad killed
	Ibn Saud treaty with Britain*	Subsidy paid to Ibn Saud
1916*	'Arab Revolt': Hussain bin Ali declares himself 'King of the Arabs'	Ibn Saud takes no part
	Ibn Saud sees British armed might	Basra
1917	Balfour Declaration	
	Bolshevik Revolution	
	Philby arrives Riyadh	As British representative
1918	Fall of Damascus and defeat of Turks	
	Philby leaves Riyadh	Ibn Saud: 'Who will trust you now?'

Year	Event	Remarks
1919*	Versailles Peace Conference	
	Feisal, son of Ibn Saud, visits London and Versailles	Meets Curzon and King George V
	Three sons and wife of Ibn Saud die.	Influenza epidemic
	Ikhwan defeat Hashimite forces	Battle of Turaba
1920	Saudi forces attack Kuwait, Asir	
1921*	Final defeat of Rashidis by Ibn Saud	Capture of Hail. Clemency shown.
	Ibn Saud: Sultan of Nejd	
	Feisal bin Hussain: King of Iraq	
1922	Ibn Saud confers with British at Ujair	Borders with Kuwait and Iraq drawn
1923	Ibn Saud grants first oil concession	To 'Eastern & General'
	Britain announces end of subsidy for 1924	
1924	Subsidy ends	
	Ibn Saud invades the Hejaz	Mecca falls, October 1924
1925	British begin negotiations with Ibn Saud	
1925	Medina and Jedda fall to Ibn Saud	December
1926	Ibn Saud proclaimed King of the Hejaz	8 January
1927	Britain recognises Ibn Saud as King of the Hejaz and Nejd	20 May

Year	Event	Remarks
1928	Death of Ibn Saud's father Ikhwan Conference at Riyadh	November. Rebel chiefs absent
1929	Defeat of Ikhwan rebels, Sibilla Revolt flares again	March Hasa
1930	Final surrender of Ikhwan rebels	Kuwait. January
1931	World financial crisis	*Hajj* income almost disappears
1932	US oil company engages Philby. Kingdom of Saudi Arabia proclaimed.	September
1933	Hitler comes to power. Oil concession signed with Americans. Saud becomes Crown Prince	King 1953
1934	Brief war with Yemen	Saudis win
1935	Assassination attempt on Ibn Saud	Yemeni assailants
1936	Saudi/Egyptian relations restored Treaty with Iraq	Broken 1926
1937	Peel Plan for Palestine	Rejected by Ibn Saud
1938	Well 7 at Dhahran: oil in commercial quantities	
1939	First shipment of oil from Ras Tannura Palestine Round Table Conference Outbreak of Second World War	Ibn Saud on film London. Saudis attend

Year	Event	Remarks
1940	Philby arrested by British at Karachi	Returns Saudi Arabia in 1945
1941	USA and Japan enter war	US Legation, Jedda, 1942
1942	Churchill to Weizmann: Ibn Saud to be 'boss of bosses' in Middle East	('provided he settles with you')
1943	US Lend-Lease for Saudi Arabia	
1944	Saudi Arabia founder-member Arab League	League proclaimed 1945
1945	Ibn Saud meets FDR and Churchill Saudi Arabia declares war on Germany	Egypt
1946	Ibn Saud's State Visit to Egypt	Decides to have railway in Eastern Province
1947	Aramco founded. Ibn Saud's last son born.	
1948	Establishment of State of Israel Coup in Yemen King Abdullah visits Ibn Saud	
1949	Paul Getty gets concession. Beginnings of Buraimi dispute.	Saudi Neutral Zone
1950	Outbreak of Korean War. 50/50 agreement with Aramco.	
1951	Saudi/US agreement on Dhahran Base Ibn Saud opens Dammam Railway Ibn Saud's last *Hajj*	

Year	Event	Remarks
1952	Revolution in Egypt	
	Saudi force sent to Buraimi	Forceful British response (1955)
1953	Council of Ministers formed	For succession phase
	Ibn Saud dies	9 November, Taif
	Ibn Saud buried in Riyadh	Grave unmarked

Appendix B
Chronology of the Al Saud before AD 1900

(*) = ruler of Saudi state

Year	Ruler/Personality	Remarks
1446	Mani' Al-Muraidi settles near Riyadh	First recorded ancestor of Al Saud
1638	Sultan Murad of Turkey	Occupies Bagdad
1667	Sultan Muhammad bin Ibrahim bin Ahmad of Turkey	Occupies Basra
1703	Saad bin Zaid (Hashimite): Sherif of Mecca	Abdicates
1703	**Muhammad bin Abdul-Wahhab, of the Unitarian movement ('the Wahhabis')	Born Ayaina, Nejd
1725–65	Muhammad bin Saud*	Ruler of Dar'iya
1744	Agreement between Muhammad bin Saud and Muhammad bin Abdul-Wahhab for Saudi protection of Wahhabis	
1745–1818	**THE FIRST SAUDI STATE**	
1765–1803	Abdul-Aziz bin Muhammad*	38 years of rule, extends Saudi power to the Hejaz and Iraq. Assassinated Dar'iya 1803.

Year	Ruler/Personality	Remarks
1811	Muhammad Ali, Viceroy of Egypt	Sends expedition against Saudi state
1819	Ibrahim, son of Muhammad Ali	Destroys Saudi state and Dar'iya
1803–14	Saud bin Abdul-Aziz*	Succeeds Abdul-Aziz
1814–18	Abdullah bin Saud*	Succeeds Saud. Captured and executed in Constantinople.
1824–91	**THE SECOND SAUDI STATE**	
1824–34	Turki bin Abdullah bin Muhammad*	
1834–8	Feisal bin Turki*	
1834–91	Rivalry between members of Al Saud	Great instability
1843–65	Feisal bin Turki*	Return from exile to rule again
1834	Abdullah bin Ali *bin Rashid*	Rewarded by Feisal bin Turki with governor-ship of Hail for help against dissident Al Saud. Beginning of Al Rashid dominance of Northern Nejd.
1838–42	Khalid bin Saud*	
1842–3	Abdullah bin Thunayan*	
1866–70 and		
1875–89	Abdullah bin Feisal*	
1870–5	Saud bin Feisal*	

Year	Ruler/Personality	Remarks
1876	Birth of 'Ibn Saud'	Abdul-Aziz bin Abdul-Rahman*
1889–91	Abdul-Rahman*	Father of 'Ibn Saud'
1889	Arranged massacre of Rashidis on Eid Al-Adha: pre-emptive strike.	Ibn Saud present
1891	Abdul-Rahman flees Riyadh with family, after defeat of Saudi allies by Al Rashid	
1897	Death of Muhammad bin Rashid	Greatest of Rashidi rulers. Reigned 25 years

Appendix C
Simplified Family Tree of Al Saud and Related Families

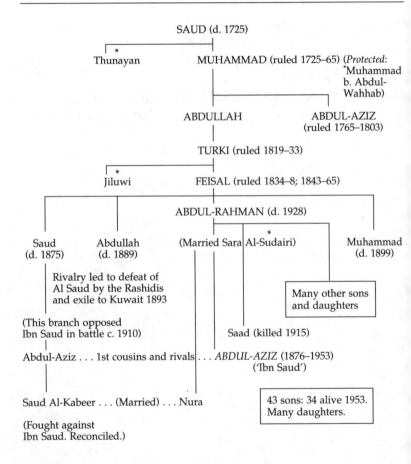

SAUD (d. 1725)

*Thunayan

MUHAMMAD (ruled 1725–65) (*Protected*: *Muhammad b. Abdul-Wahhab)

ABDULLAH

ABDUL-AZIZ (ruled 1765–1803)

TURKI (ruled 1819–33)

*Jiluwi

FEISAL (ruled 1834–8; 1843–65)

ABDUL-RAHMAN (d. 1928)

Saud (d. 1875)

Abdullah (d. 1889)

(Married Sara Al-Sudairi)

Muhammad (d. 1899)

Rivalry led to defeat of Al Saud by the Rashidis and exile to Kuwait 1893

Many other sons and daughters

(This branch opposed Ibn Saud in battle c. 1910)

Saad (killed 1915)

Abdul-Aziz . . . 1st cousins and rivals . . . *ABDUL-AZIZ* (1876–1953) ('Ibn Saud')

Saud Al-Kabeer . . . (Married) . . . Nura

43 sons: 34 alive 1953. Many daughters.

(Fought against Ibn Saud. Reconciled.)

Notes. Much remains totally unknown about Al Saud, especially in relation to female members of the family.* Indicates families into which Al Saud traditionally marry.
See also: B. Lees *A Handbook of The Al Saud*, London, 1980.

Appendix D
The Main Tribes of the Arabian Peninsula

Tribes: 'local, mutual-protection self-administrative units . . . conceived of in real or fictitious 'kin' terms.

E. Gellner, *International Affairs*, London, Vol. 67, no. 1, January 1991

Ibn Saud said to Amin Rihani in 1922,
These Arabs fear the sword only . . . sheathe the sword and they will only ask for more pay.

Ibn Saoud, p. 75

The tribes numbered 1 to 8 are *asil*, that is of the most esteemed pedigree.

A.   THE MAIN BEDU TRIBES WHICH REBELLED AGAINST IBN SAUD IN THE PERIOD UP TO 1930.

1   **Ajman** Related to Al Saud by marriage, but to the branch which opposed Ibn Saud's claim to rule.
   Area of presence: the north-east of the Peninsula.
   Leader in 1930: Dhidan bin Hithlain.
2   **Utaiba** Distrusted by Ibn Saud after their alleged involvement in the capture of his full brother, Saad, by the Hashimite forces in 1910.
   Broke word after surrender in 1929 following battle of Sibilla. Ibn Saud then ordered the complete destruction of their famous settlement of Ghot Ghot near Riyadh.
   Area of presence: straddling the area between Nejd and the Hejaz.
   Leader in 1930: Sultan bin Bijad.
3   **Mutair** Famous for their herd of black camels, the *shuruf*, driven before them in battle.
   First Ikhwan settlement established in their tribal area of Artawiya, between Riyadh and Kuwait.

The element which opposed Ibn Saud held out the longest to 1930
Area of presence: between Riyadh and Kuwait.
Leader in 1930: Feisal Duwish.

The above three leaders all stayed away from Ibn Saud's Riyadh
conference of November 1928, called for discussion with the Ikhwan
It should be emphasised that not all elements of the above tribes
opposed Ibn Saud.

B.   OTHER MAJOR TRIBES, ALL OF WHICH ESTABLISHED IKHWAN SETTLEMENTS.

4   **Harb** The name was known in the time of the Prophet. A traditional saying attributed to Muhammad is that 'the worst of the
names are *Harb* ('war') and *Murr* ('bitter').
5   **Al-Murra** Famous as legendary trackers and so employed by Ibn
Saud in cases of tribal crimes.
Ibn Saud grew up with them in the period before the Al Saud settled
in Kuwait, and spoke their dialect to the end of his days.
6   **Shammar** Possibly the most famous of the tribes which divided
for and against Ibn Saud, this tribe provided the main support for
the Rashidis of Hail.
Many dissidents left for Transjordan and Kuwait.
7   **Anaiza** The tribe to which Al Saud belong.
8   **Al-Dawasir** From the area around Sulayyil.
Curiously, many were seasonal pearl-fishers off Bahrain until the
industry collapsed in the 1930s.

C.   LESSER TRIBES BUT OF GREAT IMPORTANCE IN THE LIFE OF IBN SAUD

9   **Al-Awazem** One of the tribes which took tribute from lesser
tribes such as the Hutaim, but which might have to render tribute to
the *asil* tribes.
10   **Ruwalla** Roamed the north-west of the Peninsula and into Syria
Frequently opposed to Ibn Saud.
Still call the current Saudi ruler 'Ibn Saud'.

11   **Qahtan** The name refers to one of the eponymous ancestors of all Arabs of the Peninsula, the other being Adnan, from whom the Al Saud claim descent.

12   **bani Khalid** One of the tribes into which the Al Saud traditionally married. Ibn Saud and his father both had sons of wives from this tribe.

Nonetheless they frequently opposed Ibn Saud and he had to resettle elements of them.

13   **Suluba** Looked down on by all other tribes. Tinkers and craftsmen. Unrivalled huntsmen. In Philby's day had a monopoly of white asses.

Racially questionable in Bedu eyes: said to be of Christian origin.

14   **Muntafiq** Shepherds, straddling the Nejd–Iraq border. Frequently attacked by the Ikhwan in the 1920s. Glubb Pasha spent years among them.

15   **bani Hajir** Tribal area opposite Bahrain.

Much valuable information on the tribes is scattered throughout the works of Philby.

For a more condensed study in one work: C. M. Helms, op. cit., is of value.

D.   NUMBERS OF TRIBESMEN

Throughout the life of Ibn Saud statistics were lacking but comparisons of taxes and numbers of worshippers in mosques suggest figures approximating:

1926:	Fully-mobilised Ikhwan	150 000, including:
	Mutair	40 000
	Ajman	15 000
	Harb	30 000
	Al-Murra	10 000
1920s:	Total Bedu in Nejd and the Hejaz	375 000
	Bedu in Nejd population	50 per cent

(Based on Habib, op. cit., p. 138 and Helms, op. cit., p. 33.)

Appendix E
The Islamic and Christian Calendars

AH (*Anno Hegirae*) refers to the *hijra*, or departure of the Prophet Muhammad from his birthplace, Mecca, to Medina, where he was eventually buried ten years later.

AH	AD
1	622
458	1066
898	1492
1203	1789
1318	1900
1328	1910
1339	1920
1349	1930
1359	1940
1370	1950
1373	1953

The above are approximations since the two calendars have years of different lengths. The Islamic calendar is lunar and has normally 354 days while the Christian calendar is solar and has 365 or 366 days.

Appendix F
Glossary of Arabic Words

Abu 'Father of'. A man is frequently called by the name of his eldest son. Ibn Saud was frequently called by the Bedu 'Abu Turki'. A man with no children will frequently have a son attributed to him. Thus Yasser Arafat became 'Abu Ammar'.

Abdul 'Slave of'. The name is incomplete without one of the ninety-nine 'Most Beautiful Names of God'. Abdul-Aziz means 'The Slave of Him Who is Mighty'. (See The Koran, Chapter VII, verse 179)

Araif A word not in 'Lissan Al-Arab' but said to mean 'camels lost in a raid but found again in a counter-raid'. Applied to those of Al Saud who fought against Ibn Saud, some of whom were indeed captured in battle.

Bedu Those who live in the *badia* or desert, that is, true nomads.

Caliph A corruption of *khalifa* or successor to Muhammad as leader of the Islamic community. The first four Caliphs are called The Rightly-Guided Caliphs and are accepted by Sunni Muslims. Those who believe that Ali should have been the immediate successor to Muhammad are called the Shia (that is, 'partisans') of Ali.

Eed Feast day; religious feast. Many strict Muslims recognise only two: Eed Al-Fitr, to mark the ending of the fast of Ramadhan; Eed Al-Adha to mark the Sacrifice during the rites of Pilgrimage. (See **Hajj** below.)

Emir or **Amir** Usually translated as 'Prince' but literally means 'he who commands'. Even today can mean 'Governor' of town or region.

Hazz The gift of good fortune. Ibn Saud was said to possess *Hazz*.

Hadar Those living in settled communities as opposed to the Bedu.

Hadith   Saying traditionally attributed to the Prophet Muhammad

Hajj   The pilgrimage to Mecca in the Pilgrimage season. This is one of the five 'Pillars of Islam', the others being:

– *shahada*: the testifying that 'There is no god but God and Muhammad is the Messenger of God';

– *Salat*: praying to God five times daily in the prescribed fashion;

– *Sawm*: observing strictly the fast of Ramadhan;

– *zakat*: giving alms to the poor according to quotas laid down in the Sharia, or Islamic law.

hijra   'Departure, new beginning with something better'. It is thus applied to the Prophet's 'Flight' from Mecca to Medina (AH 1) and to the settlements established for the Bedu who became Ikhwan.

Ikhwan   The Brethren. The name adopted by those Bedu who settled in *hijras*, or colonies devoted to agriculture and religion and who, in effect, became the shock troops of Ibn Saud's armed forces before 1930, available for mobilisation on call.

imam   The title given to Ibn Saud and his father, and their forebears as 'the one who leads the community in prayer'. A title particularly used of Ibn Saud by the Ikhwan.

jihad   'Heroic endeavour in the cause of God', not merely 'Holy War'. The year of the Saudis' attack on the Hejaz, 1924, was called by the Bedu who went with Philby in 1933 to the Empty Quarter 'the year of *jihad*'.

Kaaba   Cube; a cube-shaped structure containing the Black Stone symbolising the sacrifice of Abraham. It is at the heart of the Great Mosque in Mecca and is richly draped in black and gold hangings, renewed annually. The focus of prayer for all Muslims. A focus for the rites of *Hajj*.

Until 1926 the coverings were brought from Egypt in procession, on the *mahmal*. In that year shooting broke out involving the Egyptians and the Ikhwan, who disapproved of the playing of the accompanying band.

In 1935 an attempt was made to assassinate Ibn Saud at the Kaaba.

Koran 'Recitation'. The Word of God, in Muslim belief, revealed through Muhammad, and existing from all eternity.

majlis Place of sitting. A hall for receiving guests.

Muslim One who has submitted; that is, who has accepted Islam, which the Koran says is 'the religion with God'.

Ramadhan The month of fasting. The first verses of the Koran were revealed in Ramadhan.

Salaam Peace, as in *'al-salaam 'alaykum!'* ('Peace be upon you!') The Ikhwan would normally give and acknowledge the greeting only among themselves.

Sharia The body of Islamic law which regulates the entire life of the community, spiritual and material.

Sharif As in Al-Sharif Hussain bin Ali, the great-grandfather of King Hussain of Jordan, descended from Hashim, the great-grandfather of the Prophet. A title given to those claiming direct descent from the Prophet. From Hashim comes the term 'Hashimite'.

Sheikh Literally, 'an elder'. Often a title of respect, earned not inherited. In Saudi Arabia the Al Al-Sheikh are the descendants of *the* Sheikh, that is, Muhammad bin Abdul-Wahhab, who preached a return to the original purity of Islam. His agreement with the Amir Muhammad bin Saud about AD 1744 became the basis of the political and religious entity sometimes called the *First Saudi State*. The Al Al-Sheikh are one of the leading families of Saudi Arabia and intermarry with the Al Saud.

The plural of *sheikh* is *shuyookh*, which was one of the titles given to Ibn Saud.

Shia See under **Caliph**.

Sunna Literally, the 'path' (of Muhammad). The precepts embodied in what the Prophet said and did and approved silently.

Ulema The plural of *aalim* or religious scholar. The ruler of Saudi Arabia normally receives the *Ulema* once a week, even today.

Umm Mother. Wives are frequently referred to by the name of the eldest son. In Saudi Arabia there is no 'Queen' but royal consorts might be referred to as *Umm Muhammad* or *Umm Mansour*, etc.

Wadi Valley or watercourse.

Wahhabi In the Arabian context one who strictly follows the religious code of Muhammad Abdul-Wahhab. The term is used by outsiders, since the believers themselves use the term *Al-Muwahhidun*; that is, 'Those who say "There is no god but God"'.

It should be noted that the Ikhwan were Wahhabis but not all Wahhabis were Ikhwan.

Zakat Alms-giving. (See also **Hajj**.)

Notes

INTRODUCTION

1. *1867*: Musil, A., *Zur Zeitgesch. v. Arabien*, Vienna, 1918; *Enciclop. Italiana*, Vol. 18, Milan, 1933, p. 683.

    1876: Lacey, R. *The Kingdom*, London, 1981, p. 561 (hereafter *Lacey*); Prince Talal bin Abdul-Aziz, *Ash-Sharq Al-Awsat*, London 1 December 1988.

    1879: Philby, H.St. J.B. *Royal Central Asian Journal*, London, 1950.

    1880: *Grande Diz. Encic.*, Vol. 10, Turin, 1988, p. 568; Rihani, A., *Taarikh Nejd*, Beirut, 1928, p. 107; Philby, H.St. J.B., *Saudi Arabia*, London, 1955, p. 239 (hereafter *Philby/S.A.*).

    1887: *Larousse du XXe Siècle*, Vol. 4.1, Paris, 1931, p. 4.

2. Almana, M. *Arabia Unified*, London, 1980, p. 273 (hereafter *Almana*).

3. Troeller, G., *The Birth of Saudi Arabia* London, 1976, p. 282 (hereafter *Troeller*) puts the proclamation of Saudi Arabia in 1934.

    Helms, C.M., *The Cohesion of Saudi Arabia*, London, 1981 (hereafter *Helms*) mistranslates the Ikhwan slogan hilariously, p. 60;

    Gives the wrong date for the end of the British subsidy to Ibn Saud, p. 215.

    Lacey dates the decisive battle of Kinzan in both 1915 and 1916, pp. 123 and 212 resp.

4. Curiously the index does not pick up its own reference to Saudi Arabia as a founder member of the UN and a participant in the London Round Table Conference on Palestine, 1939.

    Stranger, perhaps than the above omission are omissions and errors in many reference books:

    SOAS, *Handbook of Oriental History*, London, 1951 mentions the Hashimites but not Al Saud. Freeman-Grenville, G.S.P., *Chronology of World History*, London, 1975 places the proclamation of the Kingdom of Saudi Arabia in 1926. *Encyclopedia Britannia*, 15th edn, Vol. 10, p. 474: 'The British . . . had held Saudi lands as a protectorate since 1915'; Vol. 13, p. 896: Ibn Saud was 'from 1906 the undisputed master of Arabia'; Rihani, A., *Ibn Saud*, London, 1928, p. xiv, gives the area of Nejd as 900 million square miles and the population as 3000.

    King Saud University Press, *Riyadh – The City of the Future*, 2nd edn, n.d., p. 23 gives the wrong century for the first Saudi state; Lipsky, G.A., *Saudi Arabia*, New Haven, 1957, p. 8 refers to Ibn Saud's 'final conquests in the period after World War II'.

5. There are many examples of hagiography and glowing tributes to Ibn Saud to be found in: Al-'Inani,S., *Al-Mamlaka Al-'Arabiyya Al-Su'udiyya: dirasa biblyojrafiyya* Riyadh, 1982. Among the better and more accessible Arabic works on Ibn Saud is Khair Al-Din Zirikli, *Shibh Al-Jazira fee 'Ahd Al-Malik Abdul-Aziz*, 4 vols, Beirut, 1970 (hereafter *Zirikli*). The

work contains a great deal of information but must be treated with caution not only because the author was a Foreign Ministry official but because his sources are frequently less than original such as the Mecca newspaper *Umm Al-Qura* and even the *Edgbaston Gazette.*

6. Specialists on Stalin will point out that notwithstanding the 16 volumes of the works of Stalin in Russian there is still no definitive biography.

7. Ben Pimlott, *The Sunday Times*, 2 March 1989.

8. See Philby's map of Riyadh in his *The Heart of Arabia.*

9. Figures based on Philby/S.A. p. 333.

10. Philby, *The Heart of Arabia*, p. 93.

11. Other approaches to the subject may be found in Lacey, pp. 90–2 and 294–5 etc.; Holden, *The House of Saud* (hereafter Holden), pp. 14, 101, etc.; *Oriente Moderno* 7/22 quoted by the US Consul Aden 15 August 1922: this quotes a Hejazi as saying that by then Ibn Saud had 184 wives and 93 cars, two of which were Rolls-Royces.

12. J.C. Rylaarsdam, in *Encyclopedia Britannica*, 15th edn, Vol. 3, p. 907.

13. A notable example of the ambivalence of the relationship was in the 1986 London exhibition staged by the Saudi Government and opened by a son of Ibn Saud, Prince Salman: 'Riyadh – yesterday and today'. The section given to photos and text in English was markedly warm in tone while in another section a video in Arabic emphasised the difficulties in relationships.

14. The degree of quite genuine devotion which Ibn Saud attracted is striking. Philby frequently described him as the greatest Arab since the Prophet Muhammad. See especially his *Saudi Arabia*, p. xiv.

1 THE SETTING

1. Palgrave, W.G., *Narrative of a Year's Journey Through Central and Eastern Arabia*, 2 vols, London, 1863. Later writers, especially Philby, were very sceptical about his descriptions and some doubted that he had made the trip at all.

2. Blunt, W.S. and Lady Anne, *A Pilgrimage to Nejd*, 2 vols, London, 1881.

3. The classic wry description of Jedda in the early twentieth century is Reader Bullard, *The Camels Must Go*, London, 1961.

4. The Asir and other regions of Saudi Arabia have been memorably caught on film by McKinnon Films, 1990.

5. 'Hasa' is more correctly 'Al-Ahsa' which means 'sandy ground with water close to the surface'.

    The names of the main regions of the Kingdom are expressive:
    Nejd: 'elevated stony table-land';
    The Hejaz: 'the obstacle/barrier';
    Asir: 'very difficult';
    Nefud: the Arabic root implies an exhausted well;
    Dahna: the word has to do not only with 'desert' but also with 'a she-camel giving a little milk'.

6.   Fisher, W.B. *The Middle East* p. 471 gives the area as 400 000 square miles.
7.   Philby eventually became the second person to cross the Empty Quarter and write about it, following Bertram Thomas. See their respective books *The Empty Quarter*, London, 1933, and *Arabia Felix*, London, 1932.
8.   Thesiger, W., *Arabian Sands*, London, 1959, especially Chapter 7.
9.   It was this desert which Doughty wandered and described so memorably in his *Travels in Arabia Deserta*, London, 1926.
10.   See Philby, *Saudi Arabia*, pp. 39–40.
11.   See Thesiger, *Arabian Sands*, passim, for the stubborn persistence of non-Islamic customs, and Ibn Saud's attitude to this phenomenon.
12.   See Lacey, p. 91. His childhood friends in Kuwait, reminiscing in 1936, recalled things differently: see *Political Diary of the Gulf*, Vol. 12, Archive Editions, 1990, pp. 13 ff.
13.   See Zirikli, p. 58, where he states that Ibn Saud's brother, Prince Abdullah bin Abdul-Rahman, confirmed 1876 as the true date of birth.

2   THE CHALLENGE: ARABIA IN THE LATE 1890s

1.   Zirikli, p. 57 ff.
2.   See Dickson, V., *Forty Years in Kuwait*, London, 1971.
3.   *Zirikli*, pp. 953–9.
4.   See Lewis, B., *The Emergence of Modern Turkey*, 2nd edn, London, 1968, p. 82.
5.   See Goldberg, J., *The Foreign Policy of Saudi Arabia: the formative years 1902–18*, Harvard, 1986, p. 33.
6.   See *Historical Atlas of the Saudi State*, King Abdul-Aziz Research Centre, Vol. 11, 1979. (Arabic) (hereafter: *Historical Atlas (Saudi)*).
7.   See Amin Rihani, *Ibn Saud*, London, 1928, p. 71. There is contradiction in the record here. Almost certainly Ibn Saud's first wife died within six months of marriage. See Zirikli, p. 953.
8.   See Philby, *The Heart of Arabia*, London, 1922, pp. 100–1.
9.   *Almana*, Appendix 5.
10.   See Lacey, pp. 41–52 and notes, for the difficulty of establishing the facts on the capture of Riyadh in 1902.

3   RETURN TO NEJD, 1902–13

1.   See Lorimer, J.G., *Gazeteer of the Persian Gulf*, pp. 1592–3.
2.   See Lacey, p. 68.
3.   See Philby, *Saudi Arabia*, p. 240.
4.   Glubb has a memorable comparison to describe the usual 'form' in tribal raids: they were a combination of medieval jousting and Test

cricket.

5. Philby, *Saudi Arabia*, pp. 240 ff.
6. See Philby, *Arabia of the Wahhabis*, London, 1928, p. 31.
7. Quoted in Lacey, p. 72.
8. Ibid.
9. See Philby, *The Heart of Arabia*, passim.
10. See Winstone, H.V.F., *O.C. Desert*, London, 1982, p. 130, on the taking and retaking of Kusaiba and Kuwara.
11. The 1865 visit had resulted in an understanding that the Saudis would not attack Abu Dhabi.
12. See Goldberg, op. cit., p. 51.
13. Quoted in Philby, *Saudi Arabia*, p. 247.
14. See *Russian Ships in the Arabian Gulf 1899–1903*, Moscow, p. 26. (Arabic, trans. from the Russian.)
15. Of Curzon, his fellow-undergraduates said in the late 1870s:
    > My name is George Nathaniel Curzon
    > I am a most superior person.

    A later addition to this couplet was:
    > My face is pink, my hair is sleek
    > I dine at Blenheim once a week.

    See *The Oxford Dictionary of Quotations*, London, 1975, p. 8.
16. See Busch, B.C., *Britain and the Persian Gulf 1894–1914*, Cambridge University Press, 1968, p. 225.
17. Troeller, op. cit., p. 11.
18. See *Lacey*, pp. 79 and 569.
19. See Rihani, op. cit., p. 64.
20. See Philby, *Saudi Arabia*, p. 254.
21. F.O. to Sir N. O'Conor, 11 December 1905, quoted in Bourne and Watt, *British Documents on Foreign Affairs*, Vol. 17.
22. 15th edn, Vol. 13, p. 896.
23. As Barclay Raunkaier, said, writing in 1912 in his *Through Wahhabiland on Camelback*, London, 1969, p. 147 ff. 'The East Arabian nomads may be reckoned as the Imam's people subject to such reservations as they make for themselves.'
24. A quite different version of this famous incident is found in *Jedda Diaries* for 1910.
25. Quoted in Philby *Arabian Jubilee*, London 1952, p. 32.
26. See Rihani, op. cit., pp. 182 ff. for an account of Ibn Saud at home with the Bedu of Nejd.
27. See Almana, op. cit., p. 163. On the other hand Zirikli, op. cit., p. 1060, quotes Ibn Saud's brother, Prince Abdullah bin Abdul-Rahman, as saying that Ibn Saud was no poet.
28. See 'Donkan, R. *Die Auferstehung Arabiens*, Leipzig, 1935, pp. 94–5.
29. See Philby, *Saudi Arabia*, p. 259.
30. See Philby, *The Heart of Arabia*, p. 303.
31. See Muhammad Asad, *The Road to Mecca*, London, 1954, p. 176.
32. An important side effect of Ibn Saud's capturing Hasa was that the American medical missionaries could now reach Nejd easily from Bahrain. See *Neglected Arabia*, no. 182, p. 17.

33. Quoted in Howarth, D. *The Desert King*, London 1964, p. 70.
34. See Helms, op. cit., p. 289. See also Winstone, H.V.F. *The Illicit Adventure*, London, 1982, pp. 103 and 123 for the thesis that the Arab officers in the Ottoman forces, operating through secret societies, planned specifically that Ibn Saud should be the leader of the new political entity to emerge from a planned Arab Revolt.

The evidence does not appear to go beyond suggesting that, if anyone were in mind to lead a revolt against the Turks, it should be the one Arab leader who had, in May 1913, succeeded in capturing an entire province from them, after expelling the Turks from Central Arabia some years before.

35. Cf. *Burke's Royal Families of the World*, Vol. II, p. 207, for a variant account, including a second wife, Ibn Saud's cousin, Sara, the daughter of his paternal uncle, Abdullah, said to have died without issue.
36. Lees, B., *A Handbook of the Al Saud*, London, 1980, p. 36.

4 EXPANDING HORIZONS, 1913–24

1.   See Donkan, op. cit., pp. 78 and 94.
2.   A nice irony is that at just this time the American medical missionaries based in Bahrain were hopeful of penetrating the Nejd. 'We pray that another doctor may be sent that one of us may ... finally take the Bible into Nejd'. See the *Arabian Mission*, no. 42 April–June 1902, in *Neglected Arabia*, Archives edition, 1986. The volumes of their reports present many interesting sidelights on the history of Ibn Saud before the Second World War.
3.   See Philby/S.A. passim, esp. p. 333.
4.   See Armstrong, H.C. *Lord of Arabia*, Penguin, London, 1938, p. 118.
5.   Minute by A. Hirtzel of the India Office, 2 April 1914, quoted in *Troeller*, p. 7, n. 97.
6.   The treaty is omitted from *Historical Atlas (Saudi)*, for example.
7.   Text in both Troeller and Goldberg, op. cit.
8.   Text in both Troeller and Golberg, op. cit.
9.   See Winstone, H.V.F. *Gertrude Bell*, London, 1980 p. 152. Shakespear to G. Bell: 'Bin Saud is as pleased as possible. He is making preparations for a big raid on Ibn Rashid ...'
10. Quoted in Troeller, op. cit., p. 87.
11. See Winstone, op. cit., p. 181.
12. See *Arabian Personalities of the Early 20th Century*, Cambridge, 1986, p. 85.
13. See *Letters of G. Bell*, Vol. 2, Pelican Edition, London, 1939, p. 497.
14. Winstone, op. cit., p. 188.
15. Winstone, op. cit., p. 189.
16. For Saudi–Hashimite relations at this period, see Troeller, op. cit., pp. 94–8.
17. At just this time the British representative in Jedda, Grafftey-Smith, was hearing from Hussain bin Ali himself just how irreconcilable

were the Al Saud and the Hashimites. See Grafftey-Smith, L., *Bright Levant*, London, 1970, p. 157.

18. See Bray, N.N.E., *Shifting Sands*, London, 1934, for a vivid account of events in London and Paris and for a scathing view of T.E. Lawrence.
19. Quoted in Lacey, op. cit., p. 159.
20. Bray, op. cit., p. 297.
21. The remoteness of events in the Pensinula at this time can be judged from the London *Times* of this period. The fall of Hail is indexed under 'Fighting in Yemen' and the headline is: 'Hail captured by Emir Abdul-Aziz *from son of the late Emir Ibn Saud*.' (Furthermore, the news item was nearly four weeks out of date.)
22. Curiously a British official, Gerald de Gaury, says of the Rashidis: 'All of their family, except women and infants, were put to the sword when Hail was taken.' De Gaury, G. *Arabian Journey*, London, 1950, p. 26n.
23. Rihani, op. cit., p. 37.
24. During which Ibn Saud was warned by Abdullah Gosaibi not to put his head into the British noose. . . . See Gosaibi's account to Philby in 1940 in Monroe, E., *Philby of Arabia*, London, 1973, p. 228.
25. For detail see Troeller, op. cit., pp. 181–2.
26. See Troeller, ibid.
27. Rihani, op. cit., p. 49.
28. See *Neglected Arabia*, no. 208, p. 10.

5   THE IMAM IN MECCA, 1924–28

1. See Rihani, op. cit., p. 171.
2. Rihani, op. cit., p. 73.
3. Rihani, op. cit., p. 131.
4. Rihani, op. cit., p. 134. Compare the impression Riyadh made on the American missionaries. 'No one would speak to us, except indeed the King (in) his castle.' Doctor Paul Harrison, *Neglected Arabia*, Vol. 182, p. 19.
5. Rihani, op. cit., p. 134.
6. The same care for security is to be noted in the film of Ibn Saud's visit to Ras Tannura in 1939.
7. Rihani, op. cit., p. 182.
8. Rihani, op. cit., pp. 138–9.
9. Rihani, op. cit., p. 171.
10. Rihani, op. cit., p. 178.
11. See Monroe, op. cit., p. 123.
12. Rihani, op. cit., p. 214.
13. Cheesman, R.E., *In Unknown Arabia*, London, 1926, p. 169.
14. Cheesman, op. cit., p. 173.
15. Cheesman, op. cit., p. 177.
16. Lawrence, T.E. *Seven Pillars of Wisdom*, London, 1935, p. 76: 'a pleasant gentleman, conscientious, without great force of character, nervous and rather tired.'

17. Hirtzel, of the India Office, quoted in Lacey, op. cit., p. 184.
18. Zirikli, op. cit., pp. 335 ff.
19. See Goldberg, op. cit., pp. 177 ff.
20. For discussion of Ibn Saud's ambivalence see Lacey, op. cit., p. 192.
21. Quoted in Philby, *Arabian Jubilee*, London, 1952, p. 126.
22. The British representative rather unkindly wrote of him to London: 'He lacks the resolution even to run away', 15 July 1925, in *The Jedda Diaries*, Vol. 2, p. 311.
23. See *The Jedda Diaries*, Vol. 2, for British accounts of Ibn Saud's secret contacts with the Hashimites.
24. They did manage, however, to bomb Mecca and destroyed the house of Saqqaf, where Ibn Saud often stayed. *The Jedda Diaries*, Vol. 2, pp. 357–8.
25. See Clayton, Sir Gilbert, *An Arabian Diary*, Berkeley, CA, 1969, pp. 119–20 for the emotional nature of Ibn Saud's stand. Clayton quotes as saying, 'He would prefer to have his throat cut with a sword rather than have anyone infringe upon his rights in his own dominions.'
26. See Lunt, J., *Glubb Pasha*, London, 1984, p. 40–2.
27. See Lunt, op. cit., pp. 49–50.
28. See Helms, op. cit., p. 230.
29. See Philby/S.A. p. 304.
30. Zirikli, op. cit., p. 484.
31. See Philby, *The Heart of Arabia*, pp. 196–7.

6   IBN SAUD AT FIFTY

1. Quoted in Armstrong, op. cit., p. 118.
2. Rihani, op. cit., p. 52.
3. Philby, *Heart of Arabia*, p. 225.
4. Zirikli, op. cit., p. 1426.
5. See Hughes, T.P., *Dictionary of Islam*, reprint, Lahore, 1964, p. 142, where the categories are regrettably transposed.
6. See Lacey, op. cit., for some legendary examples of Bin Jiluwi's style.
7. Rihani, op. cit., p. 214.
8. *Neglected Arabia*, no. 167, pp. 12–13.
9. Almana, op. cit., p. 241.
10. Rihani, op. cit., p. 62.
11. Ibid., p. 119.
12. Almana, op. cit., p. 238.
13. See Zirikli, op. cit., pp. 581 ff.
14. See Zirikli, loc. cit., and *Jedda Diaries*, Vol. 2, pp. 357–8.
15. See Almana, op. cit., p. 239, where no details are given. If Ibn Saud did not say this, *e molto ben trovato*.
16. See Zirikli, op. cit., p. 629.
17. See Philby *Heart of Arabia*, p. 350.
18. The eye condition worsened after the 1922 Ujair Conference and seems to have been erysipelas. See van der Meulen, D., op. cit., p. 89.

For a different picture of Ibn Saud's condition at this time, with echoes of Gertrude Bell, See Lacey, op. cit., p. 207.

19. Quoted in Lunt, J.D., *Glubb Pasha*, London, 1984, p. 49.

7 THE KINGDOM ESTABLISHED, 1928–32

1. Asad, op. cit., p. 225.
2. Almana, op. cit., passim.
3. Almana, op. cit., p. 96.
4. Almana, op. cit., p. 101.
5. Almana, op. cit., p. 103.
6. See Lunt, op. cit., p. 54.
7. Almana, op. cit., p. 124.
8. See Asad, op. cit., p. 224.
9. See Helms, op. cit., pp. 239–41.
10. Asad, op. cit., pp. 228 ff.
11. Author's italics.
12. See Lacey, op. cit., p. 219 and n.
13. Ryan, A., *The Last of the Dragomans*, London, 1951, p. 278.
14. J. Loader Park. For the US Consul's dispatches, see al-Rashid, I. *Documents on the History of Saudi Arabia*, Vol. III, Salisbury, NC 1976.
15. See Zirikli, op. cit., pp. 335–6.
16. See Zirikli, op. cit., p. 627.
17. Almana, op. cit., p. 194.
18. Quoted in Rihani, op. cit., p. 164.
19. Philby, *Arabian Jubilee*, p. 99.
20. Philby, ibid., p. 109.
21. Philby, ibid., p. 132.
22. Philby, *Saudi Arabia*, p. 333.
23. See, for much detail on the King's plight, *The Jedda Diaries* for 1930–33, passim.
24. See Monroe, op. cit., p. 173.
25. See *Neglected Arabia*, no. 163 for May 1932, pp. 10–11.
26. Ibid., p. 11.
27. *Political Diaries of the Persian Gulf*, Vol. 10, Archive Editions, London, 1990, p. 304 (hereafter PD/PG).
28. Zirikli, p. 560.
29. Rendel, G., *The Sword and the Olive*, London, 1957, p. 60.
30. Zirikli, p. 360.

8 THE LOCUST YEARS, 1932–38

1. An appendix to the book dealing with 'Walking stones' is headed 'Swalking tones'.
2. See Monroe, op. cit., pp. 175–7.

3. Philby *Empty Quarter* p. xxiii.
4. Gulbenkian was the adviser on this question of boundaries and indeed himself drew the famous Red Line. See Sampson, A., The Seven Sisters, London 1980, p. 84.
5. See Lacey, op. cit., p. 236 and n.
6. There is a dispute on the date as between Almana, op. cit., and Lacey, op. cit. (29 and 9 May respectively).
7. For samples see PD/PG, Vol. 10.
8. See PD/PG, Vol. 10, p. 221.
9. Philby, *Arabia*, London 1930, pp. 363–4.
10. See Dickson in PD/PG, Vol. 10, p. 221.
11. See Zirikli, p. 338.
12. See de Gaury, G. *Arabian Journey*, London, 1950, pp. 16–17.
13. A charming touch in diplomacy was that the telegraphic address for Saudi diplomatic missions was 'NEJDIA'.
14. Rendel, G., quoted in Kelly, J.B. *Eastern Arabian Frontiers* London 1964, p. 129.
15. See Zirikli, pp. 622–4.
16. De Gaury, *Arabia Phoenix*, London, 1946, p. 100.
17. Ibid., p. 64.
18. Ibid., p. 66.
19. Ryan, op. cit., p. 273.
20. Ibid., p. 297.
21. Quoted in Niblock, T., *State Society and Economy in Saudi Arabia*, London, 1981, p. 42.
22. Philby, *Arabian Highlands* Cornell 1952, pp. 75 ff.
23. Philby, *Saudi Arabia*, p. 335.
24. Zirikli, op. cit., pp. 1071 ff.
25. See Zirikli, op. cit., pp. 1092–1103.
26. See Zirikli, op. cit., p. 991, and Ryan, op. cit., p. 272.
27. See Zirikli, op. cit., p. 1100.
28. See *J.D.*, Vol. 4, p. 187.
29. See *Neglected Arabia*, no. 180, pp. 6 ff.
30. See Lacey, op. cit., p. 254.
31. See PD/PG, Vol. 12, p. 580.
32. See Zirikli, op. cit., p. 1244.
33. See *J.D.*, Vol. 4, p. 307. See aslo above, 'Family life', at end of Chapter IV.
34. See *J.D.*, Vol. 4, p. 407.
35. Ibid.

9 THE CUP DASHED FROM THE LIPS, 1938–45

1. For discussion of Ibn Saud's overall position at this time, see Niblock, op. cit., pp. 42 ff.
2. For an unofficial view of secret comings and goings at this time, see Ladislas Farago, *The Riddle of Arabia*, London, 1939, p. 38. Farago took

the trouble to get himself to the Hodeida area and reported on German arms salesmen, mysterious submarines, etc. He also alleged that the British bribed Ibn Saud to withdraw from the Yemen in 1934 with a sum in excess of their total subsidies to him up to 1924 (pp. 203–4).

3. See Bullock, A., *Hitler: A Study in Tyranny*, London, 1973, pp. 367 ff.
4. See Kelly, op. cit., p. 67.
5. Bullard, R.W., *The Camels Must Go*, London, 1951.
6. Grafftey-Smith, L. *Bright Levant*, London, 1970. Grafftey-Smith's memory was at fault, however, as we shall see for events in 1945.
7. Rendel, op. cit., p. 112.
8. Bullard, op. cit., p. 137.
9. Ibid., p. 197.
10. Ibid., p. 202.
11. Ibid., p. 202.
12. Ibid., p. 205.
13. See *J.D.*, Vol. 4, p. 367. (In this meeting Ibn Saud confided to Bullard that he was aged 58. Cf. Note 1 of Introduction above.)
14. The author has been unable to consult the original German documents but prefers this view of Ibn Saud's view of the British.

    Lacey, op. cit., p. 257, quotes Hirszowicz to endorse his remark that Ibn Saud told Grobba that 'at heart he hated the English' but Hirszowicz, quoting from the documents, says only that Grobba reported that 'the King, *in his opinion*, hated the English . . ., Hirszowicz, L., *The Third Reich and the Arab East*, London, 1966.
15. See Nicosia, P., *The Third Reich and Palestine*, London, 1985.
16. See Zirikli, op. cit., p. 687.
17. Ibn Saud was careful to let the British Legation know in May 1940 'Saudi Arabia is neutral but my sympathies are with the Allies for whose victory I hope . . .', *J.D.*, Vol. 4, p. 536.
18. See Zirikli, op. cit., p. 963.
19. Private information.
20. See *J.D.*, Vol. 4, p. 461, for an example of Ibn Saud's secret contacts with the British Legation in September 1939 on Palestine.
21. See Hirszowicz, op. cit., p. 48. Hirszowicz has much detail on the high level of Saudi–German contacts in 1938–9. Another of the King's advisers, Khalid Gargani, was received by Hitler himself at the Obersalzberg on 17 June 1939 (pp. 54 ff).
22. See Monroe, op. cit., p. 222.
23. Ibid., p. 228.
24. Grafftey-Smith, op. cit., pp. 262–3.
25. The mixture of rage and amusement in Ibn Saud's attitude to Philby is well caught in Bullard's account of a conversation he had with the King about Philby's contrary attitudes. He told the story of the proud mother who pointed to a group of soldiers marching and said, 'They're all out of step except our Jack.' The King would later retell the story to his courtiers in illustration of Philby's attitude to life. See Bullard, op. cit., p. 198.
26. See *J.D.*, Vol. 4, p. 450.

27. Weizmann, C. *Trial and Error* London 1949, pp. 525–6.
28. Ibid., pp. 531–2.
29. See Zirikli, op. cit., pp. 1134 ff. Philby remained convinced that Ibn Saud had been seriously interested in the Weizmann 'deal' since one of the conditions was that in return for the surrender of some land all the Arab countries in Asia would get full independence. Moreover, Ibn Saud's indignation to Hoskins was in his view merely a show put on, as he gradually realised, during Hoskins' visit, that FDR's envoy was not authorised to make a deal with him.

    See Philby to de Gaury 17 November 1943 in The de Gaury Papers, The Royal Geographical Society, London (Black Tin Box, Notebook, 6/2).
30. See *PD/PG*, Vol. 14, p. 542.
31. See Twitchell, K.S., *Saudi Arabia*, Princeton, 1947, pp. 165 et seq.
32. Twitchell, op. cit., p. 169.
33. Ibn Saud maintained a degree of closeness with the British, however. He sent his son Mansour, who was later to be the Kingdom's first Defence Minister, to the Alamein area before Montgomery's battle of October–November 1942. The Prince seems to have established a good rapport with the Indian Muslim forces who were part of Montgomery's army.
34. See Rubin, B. *The Great Powers in the Middle East 1941–7*, 1980, p. 48.
35. Ibid., p. 61.
36. Grafftey-Smith, op. cit., p. 261.
37. See *J.D.*, Vol. 4, p. 353.

10 IBN SAUD ON THE WORLD STAGE, 1945–51

1. See Zirikli, op. cit., p. 1151.
2. Grafftey-Smith, op. cit., p. 265.
3. See van der Meulen, D., *The Wells of Ibn Saud*, London, 1957, p. 99.
4. See Bullard, op. cit., p. 197. Bullard goes on in his usual waspish manner to note that Ibn Saud 'was a good talker: his conversation was interesting and apposite. It is true that he often said that the subject could be divided under three headings and proceeded to divide it under many more but that did not affect the good sense of his conclusions.' Ibid.
5. See Zirikli, op. cit., p. 399.
6. See Bilainkin, G. *Cairo to Riyadh Diary*, London, 1950, p. 135.
7. Zirikli, op. cit., p. 1168 dates the first discussion of the meeting in February 1944 but this seems unlikely.
8. Zirikli, op. cit., p. 1168.
9. Zirikli, op. cit., p. 1176.
10. Ibid.
11. See Holden, op. cit., pp. 137 ff, Lacey, op. cit., pp. 271 ff and Howarth, op. cit., pp. 191 ff.
12. See Benoist-Mechin, *Ibn Seoud: le Loup et le Leopard*, Paris, 1955,

pp. 352–3. The author reaches the satisfied conclusion on Ibn Saud's attitude to the British that 'in a single afternoon Ibn Saud had taken his revenge for 20 years of insults'.

13. See Zirikli, op. cit., p. 1186.
14. See Grafftey-Smith, op. cit., p. 251.
15. Private information. Zirikli, in a one-volume summary of his four-volume work, gives four lines to Ibn Saud's meeting with Churchill. Zirikli *Al Wajiz*, 4th edn, Beirut, 1984. The Ibn Saud–Churchill meeting is described with varying degrees of accuracy in Zirikli, loc. cit.; Howarth, pp. 207–8; Lacey, pp. 272–4, etc.

    Pace several writers, Churchill did report to the War Cabinet on political discussions with Ibn Saud: see Gilbert, M. (and Churchill, R.) *Churchill*, Vol. VII, p. 1225.
16. Grafftey-Smith, op. cit., p. 272.
17. See Zirikli, op. cit., p. 1186.
18. See Lacey, op. cit., p. 289 and n.
19. See Grafftey-Smith, op. cit., pp. 269–70.
20. See Zirikli, op. cit., p. 1361.
21. See Zirikli, op. cit., p. 1358.
22. See Zirikli, op. cit., p. 1213.
23. See Grafftey-Smith, op. cit., pp. 274–6.
24. See Zirikli, op. cit., p. 1217.
25. Private information.
26. See Zirikli, op. cit., p. 1237.
27. See Zirikli, op. cit., pp. 1251 ff.
28. Private information.
29. See Holden, op. cit., p. 151.
30. See Grafftey-Smith, op. cit., p. 267.
31. See Philby, *Forty Years in the Wilderness*, London, 1957, p. 189.
32. Ibid., p. 202.
33. Ibid., p. 190.
34. Philby, *Arabian Jubilee*, p. 125 and elsewhere.
35. See Lacey, op. cit., p. 295 and notes.
36. Bilainkin, op. cit., p. 129.
37. Ibid., p. 106.
38. Philby, *Forty Years*, p. 205.
39. See Monroe, op. cit., p. 238.
40. See Holden, op. cit., p. 144 and n.
41. Zirikli, op. cit., p. 915.
42. See Holden, op. cit., p. 153.
43. Private information.
44. See Lacey, op. cit., p. 91.
45. Quoted in al-Rashid, I., *The Struggle between the Princes*, Chapel Hill, NC, 1985 (12 July 1950), p. 17.
46. See Holden, op. cit., p. 154.

11 THE END, 1951–53

1. Page 1367.
2. See, for example, M. Asad, op. cit., p. 181.
3. See Zirikli, op. cit., p. 926.
4. See *The Middle East*, Oxford, 2nd edn, p. 99.
5. See Lacey, op. cit., p. 280.
6. See *The Middle East*, Oxford, 2nd edn, p. 98. A side-effect of this may be noted, that Ibn Saud seems to have lost his interest in the contribution of the American medical missionaries from Bahrain. See *Neglected Arabia* for this period.
7. Ambassador Hare to State Department, 14 November 1951, quoted in Ibrahim Al-Rashid, *The Struggle between the Two Princes*, Chapel Hill, NC, 1985, p. 36.
8. See Holden, op. cit., pp. 161 ff.
9. Quoted in Ibrahim Al-Rashid, op. cit., p. 129., for 12 October 1953.
10. Zirikli, op. cit., p. 1433.
11. These moving words are Grafftey-Smith's, op. cit., p. 287.
12. Quoted in Monroe, op. cit., p. 274.
    The death of Ibn Saud seems to have gone unmarked in the journal of the American missionaries who had known him since 1915. See *Neglected Arabia* for this period.
13. See Burke's *Royal Families of the World*, Vol. II, London, 1980, p. 210.

12 ENVOI

1. M. Asad, op. cit., p. 181.

Bibliography

A. GENERAL BIBLIOGRAPHIES

The reader may get an idea of works consulted by modern writers on Ibn Saud in the bibliographies found in the following:

1. Lacey, R., *The Kingdom*, London, 1981.
2. Holden, D. & Johns, R., *The House of Saud*, London, 1981.
3. Besson, Y., *Ibn Seoud, roi bedouin*, Lausanne, 1980.
4. Habib, John S., *Ibn Saud's Warriors of Islam*, Leiden, 1978.
5. Howarth, D., *The Desert King*, London, 1964.
6. Troeller, G., *The Birth of Saudi Arabia*, London, 1976.
7. Helms, C.M., *The Cohesion of Saudi Arabia*, London, 1980.
8. Armstrong, H.C., *Lord of Arabia, Ibn Saud*, Beirut, 1966 (reprint).
9. Goldberg, J., *The Foreign Policy of Saudi Arabia: the formative years 1902–18*, Harvard, 1986.

B. GUIDED READING

For the general reader in English the following is suggested as a course of reading using the above titles:

1. Armstrong, op. cit. A slightly breathless account, sympathetic and readable, taking the story only to 1934 in the 1938 edition, from which the 1966 reprint is taken.
2. Howarth, op. cit. The work of a well-informed journalist and generalist writer. Very readable but vague on chronology.
3. Lacey, op. cit. A highly readable work, going beyond the life of Ibn Saud, but presenting a lively account of his personal life and political problems which he faced. Has a number of internal inconsistencies in addition to conveying inaccurately a number of anecdotes, Philby's and others.
4. Holden and Johns, op. cit. Similar to, and directly competing with Lacey's book on publication but with fewer personal anecdotes. A useful complement but with many inaccuracies. Ends with the judgement that the Kingdom had only another five years of life from 1980.
5. Troeller, op. cit. A more scholarly and detailed work covering the period to 1925. Has some inconsistencies and inaccuracies.
6. Holms, op. cit. A thematic treatment, closely argued, whose thesis is that Ibn Saud has been overrated and that he was to a large extent only the beneficiary of historical trends working in his favour.
7. Habib, op. cit. A painstaking treatment of the Ikhwan movement up to 1930. Of great interest but spoiled by extraordinary printing errors.
8. Goldberg, op. cit. An original and readable scholarly work on the foreign relations of Ibn Saud which shows clearly the link between personal life and political factors.

C. PHILBY

Philby wrote more than anyone on Ibn Saud and Saudi Arabia but he is best approached when the reader has digested some or all of the above. His books are all too long and prone to error and carelessness but they reward careful and selective reading at the right time.

His own life should be read first:
1. Monroe, E., *Philby of Arabia*, London, 1974.
   This will help the reader through:
2. Philby, H. St. J.B., *The Heart of Arabia*, 2 vols, London, 1922.
3. Idem, *Arabia of the Wahhabis*, London, 1928.
4. Idem, *Arabian Days*, London, 1948.
5. Idem, *Arabian Jubilee*, London, 1952.
6. Idem, *Saudi Arabia*, London, 1955.

D. THE PHYSICAL SETTING

Essential reading:
1. Twitchell, K.S., *Saudi Arabia*, Princeton, 1947. He was the American engineer sent by the American philanthropist Chas. R. Crane to survey Saudi Arabia's mineral resources in 1931. His book is a delightful laconic account of the hard physical conditions of the 1930s.
2. Fisher, W.B., *The Middle East*, 4th edn, London, 1961. A geographer, he was active in the area in the Second World War.
3. Longrigg, S.R., *The Middle East* London, 1963. He was one of the negotiating team competing with the Americans for the Saudi oil concession in 1933.
4. Thesiger, W., *Arabian Sands*, London, 1959. The best travel book ever written about the Arabian peninsula, describing the explorer's journeys in the late 1940s.

E. DETAILED BIBLIOGRAPHIES

A useful introduction to the whole field is:
1. Clements, Frank A., *Saudi Arabia*, Oxford, 1988
   This must be supplemented by the observations in:
2. Frankl, P.J., *Brismes Bulletin* 17/1, 1990, 102–7 (a review of Clements, op. cit.).
3. Philipp, Hans-Jurgen, *Saudi Arabia: Bibliography on Society, Politics, Economics*, Munich, 1984. This should be read in the light of the review in:
4. Auchterlonie, P., *Brismes Bulletin* 17/1, 1990, 107–8.

The above four references will lead to the principal works in English, French, German, Russian, Arabic and Italian.

Index